James Greenwood

Unsentimental Journeys

Byways of the Modern Babylon

James Greenwood

Unsentimental Journeys
Byways of the Modern Babylon

ISBN/EAN: 9783744762373

Printed in Europe, USA, Canada, Australia, Japan

Cover: Foto ©Andreas Hilbeck / pixelio.de

More available books at **www.hansebooks.com**

UNSENTIMENTAL JOURNEYS.

FARRINGDON MARKET.

UNSENTIMENTAL JOURNEYS:

OR,

Byways of the Modern Babylon.

BY JAMES GREENWOOD,

AUTHOR OF "A NIGHT IN A WORKHOUSE;" "THE TRUE HISTORY
OF A LITTLE RAGAMUFFIN;" ETC., ETC.

LONDON:
WARD, LOCK, & TYLER, WARWICK HOUSE,
PATERNOSTER-ROW.
1867.

CONTENTS.

		Page
I.	The Hospital Gate	1
II.	Squalors' Market	8
III.	Newgate Market	17
IV.	A Dog Show	25
V.	The Night Coffee-Booth and its Customers	32
VI.	Concerning Muffins	39
VII.	The Horse Repository	45
VIII.	The Boat of All-Work	51
IX.	The Bones of London	58
X.	Mr. Dodd's Dust-Yard	64
XI.	The County Court	72
XII.	Christmas Eve in Brick Lane	78
XIII.	The Highway Pastor	87
XIV.	Eight A.M.—The Morning Post	93
XV.	The Leather Market	100
XVI.	The London Horse Market	108
XVII.	Watercresses	116
XVIII.	The Song-Bird Market	125

Contents.

	Page
XIX. A Londoner's Christmas	135
XX. The Gleaners of the Thames Bank	148
XXI. The Halfpenny Barfer	155
XXII. The Houndsditch Jewellery Market	163
XXIII. With a Set of Teaspoons	169
XXIV. A Journey to Epsom	179
XXV. The Coster's Carnival	194
XXVI. On Saturday Night—I. The "Navvy"	201
XXVII. ,, ,, II. Poor Mother!	210
XXVIII. Two P.M.—On Board Citizen B	218
XXIX. Ten P.M.—The Dancing Saloon	223
XXX. Reflections on Battered Breeches—A Newspaper Boy	229

PREFACE.

CROPPING up in the book-field, modest and unpretending as any sprig of sorrel or chickweed that ever sprouted, this book at least claims an advantage over other books in the matter of Preface.

Commonly, a Preface is like a finger-post set up in a toll-road, on which you first pay for the privilege of travelling, and then are allowed to judge for yourself whether the way indicated will suit you, or whether it will be more profitable to turn back, forfeiting the money you paid at the gate, and striking into another path in search of "pastures new." The advantage alluded to as attaching to this book, consists in the fact that its preface is fully contained in the title imprinted on the back of it. There is no more to be said about it. It is simply a collection of personal observation of experience yielded in the course of two-score or so of as unsentimental journeys as ever were undertaken by the most ordinary tramp. The collection is the result, not of a labour of love purely—although, of course, a liking for the subject was the prime inducement for entering on its investigation,—but of down-right, jog-trot journey-work.

The reader who regards elegance of style in an author as the first essential is respectfully warned that herein it is wanting—so completely, in fact, that it is scarcely worth while to mention it; it would have been discovered as quickly. If, however, the indulgent reader will deign to accept scrupulous honesty and plain, outspoken truth in lieu of varnish and elaboration, he may depend on fair dealing at the hands of his obedient servant,

THE AUTHOR.

J

I.

THE HOSPITAL-GATE.

THE notice-board at the gate notifies to all who may have come into that inheritance to which we have Shakspeare's authority for declaring all flesh has title, that the proper time to attend to be mulct as far as may be of the said inheritance is between the hours of eleven and one o'clock daily. Therefore, as the hospital clock chimed the former time, I struck out of Giltspur Street, and approached the sombre building; not, my lucky stars be thanked, as one needing aid of surgeon or apothecary, but to see one of the most melancholy and instructive pictures to be met in London's length and breadth. Being an intruder, and not disposed to flaunt my healthfulness to the dull and sorrowing gaze of those who clustered at the portal, I took my station in the shadowy lee of a fragrant hay waggon, and, sitting down on the deserted shaft of it, secured a fair view of up the street and down the street, and across the road.

I experienced little difficulty in distinguishing from among the pedestrians who thronged the pavement they who had business with Saint Bartholomew; for the notice-board, among other things, particularly stipulated that "patients must provide themselves with gallipots and bottles;" and, as a rule, the pale ones, and the lame ones, and they who were led because they could not see, were so provided. Gracious me! what a leveller of pride is Death's lieutenant, Sickness! Here comes Jones, worthy man, meekly bearing his gallipot, wrapped in paper, it is true, but palpably a gallipot, whereas, if he were unafflicted and free to perform as usual the diurnal journey out and home from Islington to the City, he would go dinnerless rather than be the bearer of his own mutton chop. Likewise comes estimable Mr. Robinson, who, before his system was shocked beyond the pomps and vanities of this wicked world, disdained to carry so vulgar an article as a gingham umbrella (perhaps that is how he caught his rheumatism, poor man), now exhibits, peeping from the tail-pocket of his coat, the throat of the quart bottle that is to contain his "mixture."

The respectable Browns or Joneses, however, are scarcely fair samples of the patrons of Saint Bartholomew: if their ailments are not very severe, their "regular" doctor will set them right for a pound or so, and they can afford to pay it. Neither is the wan army recruited specially from the squalid, loud-mouthed poverty of the City; it is the latter that obstructs the doorway and invades the narrow limits of the "parish" surgery, for the most cogent reason that bread and meat may be included in the parochial M.D.'s prescriptions, and lazy father's bad foot, or sister Polly's asthma be thus made a source of income rather than of impoverishment to the entire family. It is chiefly those whom no amount of hunger would induce to beg a loaf that demand hospital relief; who would go empty and thinly clad, and no more dream of applying at a workhouse for alms than they would dream of assuaging their distress by a larcenous onslaught on their neighbours' goods. The horny-handed ones are these, and the horny-handed ones' wives, who while they can work will, and at whose door, while health holds good, "the wolf," or its shadow even, is unknown. It is sickness alone that gives the grim beast ingress; and there he is allowed to stay, roaming about the house, and ravaging it, plucking the treasured silk gown from its sacred hiding, the hard-earned watch from the fob, the Sunday suit from the clothes-chest, the well-worn wedding-ring even from the lean finger; and, the number of the house where the wolf is sojourning being 31, neither 30 nor 32 have the least suspicion of the fact. Nobody is aware of it; least of all any gentleman in the neighbourhood whose business it is to vend advice and healing drugs at a profit. Not a penny of the wolf's plunderings goes to *him*. Why should it? The healing skill to be found at the hospital is of a higher order than can be bought for a little money, and there is no taint of pauperism in partaking of the advantage. The hospital is public property—as proper a place for a man to visit for relief for his malady as the British Museum or the National Gallery for amusement and instruction, or the common to play cricket on. So argue the honest endurers of the wolf at number 31, and, without doubt, they are perfectly correct.

Whilst, however, I sit philosophising on the waggon-shaft the human cluster at the gate has grown thicker. Along the broad steps sit mothers cuddling to their bosoms sick infants, varying in age from the tiny creature ignorant of a want beyond to the languid little fellow of four or five whom affliction has once more reduced to babyhood. Why the mothers sit here I do not know. Perhaps the gentleman appointed to the sick-baby department has not yet arrived, or, having arrived, is so besieged with mothers that these considerate ones prefer sitting in the sun with their darlings till the press has abated and they can take them in without disturbance. Perhaps, again, having so nearly reached the terrible place where for their health's sake the poor little sufferers must be put to pain, mother's tender heart fails her, and she is obliged to sit thus on the threshold to consider her little one's long-suffering, and to contemplate its wasting face, to screw her courage for the final effort.

No wonder if it is so, since from my post of observation I can see grown men and women, and tall young men and maidens, guilty of the same weakness. I am quite convinced that the pulling of teeth is not the most painful operation to which a hospital patient may be subjected; and yet, of all who "hang on and off," as the nautical phrase is, loitering among the deserted cattle-pens, and looking wistfully and alternately at the grim building and at the road that tends homeward, the ones with bandaged jaws numbered most. Of course their case is very hard (having had in my time two grinders extracted whose decay in no way shook their attachment to me; I know *how* hard their case is); but what amount of pity could be spared for them in presence of the terrible things that everywhere met the eye? The pains as well as the pleasures of the world can only be measured by comparison. By the side of a shattered limb toothache becomes a mere trifle; and, compared with many of the appalling spectacles to be met within a circuit of a hundred yards of Old Bartholomew any day between the hours of eleven and two, it becomes less than a trifle—a joke, and a thing to be laughed at.

Why, within the limit mentioned, I can see a dozen men who, if the transfer were possible, would accept the most villainous tooth that ever a mouth was troubled with in exchange for their ailment, and throw in as a bonus a good year of their lives, chancing how long they would live without it. Not the worst-looking cases either, some of these. Take, for example, that elderly man with his arm slung to his neck, and accompanied by his two sons, as pale and as anxious as himself. How wretchedly cheerful the trio are! How the eldest of the old fellow's boys, winking sternly at the younger to be sure and countenance the dreadful fib he is about to relate, launches into the particulars of a " case "—a terrible case, compared with which father's is the merest cat-scratch—in which, thanks to the blessed application of chloroform, the limb was shorn, the patient dreaming the pleasantest dreams the while! And the good old boy, to comfort the young ones, affects the most perfect belief in the story, and even essays a ghastly little joke on the subject, while all the time his heart is at freezing-point through thinking that if the amputation of those blessed fingers should cost him his life, what a woful thing it will be for Polly (his wife) and the three little ones. But there is no help for it; he will surely die unless he submits to the terrible ordeal; so, just a tiny nip of brandy to keep his courage up, and in he goes, the boys looking after him almost as people look when the undertaker's man, twiddling his screwdriver, observes, with professional melancholy, "Would any other member of the family like," &c.

"Room there, you about the gate! Ring the bell, boy, will you?" Not the least occasion. The liveried porter, hearing the hasty wheels, has just peeped out to see a cab, with a policeman descending from the driving-seat, and the next moment makes his appearance with a companion, the two carrying a "stretcher." "Slater off a roof!" exclaims the policeman, shortly; and, gently handled by a dozen willing hands, as though he were a baby, the pallid man, with his great, dirty, labouring hands, and the slating-nails dropping from his jacket-pocket and tinkling on the pavement, is borne through the gate to have his shattered bones set and be brought to life again, if the ripest skill in the kingdom can accomplish the doubtful business.

One thing is certain. The shattered slater will not pine to death in his ward from lack of company. No trade is better represented in the accident ward than that of house-building. If I was in the life-assurance line I think I would almost as soon lease the life of a soldier as of a house-painter, a bricklayers' labourer, or a slater. I think I would *quite* as soon do it, and I do not believe I should be out of pocket by it. In his battle for bread the latter risks his life equally with the former, who fights his country's battles. Where is the difference? One man in the ranks with his comrades may catch a bullet in his carcass; the other, sprawling on a slippery slant, with a clear descent of forty feet to the street stones, is at the mercy of a rotten rope or a sudden wind. The soldier, sword in hand, pitted against another soldier, fights for his life; the house-painter, a-top of a fifty-round ladder, may at any minute of his working days be seized with a vertigo, or the first drunken booby that comes up the street may stumble against the ladder's foot, and the poor painter in an instant make a swift descent to certain death. In one respect the soldier has the advantage; for whereas at least half his life is spent in consuming his rations, pipeclaying his leathers, and washing his shirts, the poor slater begins his battles with his apprenticeship, and continues them till he becomes too old and decrepit to mount a ladder.

It is wonderful how one grows used to horrors. Shortly after the commotion (very slight it was) consequent on the slater's arrival had subsided, there came in succession two "run-overs" and an Irish person severely wounded on the head with a drinking-vessel. I was enabled, however, to regard the ugly scene with perfect equanimity, and even cast about me for something more interesting. I didn't look in vain. At some distance from the casual gate there is another, and about this was a group expectant, evidently, from the way in which, every few seconds, they peered up the archway in which a beadle kept sentry. I was too far off to hear what they said, but presently one, who happened to be watching at a moment when no one else was, made a sudden observation, and then the whole party eagerly turned and looked too, and it was easy enough to see, by the way in which all the lips moved, that "Here he comes!" was uttered by them all.

Who was "he"? A tall young fellow, with lanky legs, very thin, and with a delicate, newly-made-looking face. These were his most remarkable points, as far as I could judge; but the watchers at the gate saw more than this plainly, or they would never have made such a fuss with him. He didn't come out alone. There was with him a little elderly woman, who held his hand in hers, as though afraid of losing him the moment they reached the corner of the street; while, at the same time, one was made aware, by the little woman's bright, brimming eyes, that a more cruel thing could scarcely happen. No sooner, however, did the odd pair approach the group than a man with grey hair and spectacles, and a little taller than the little woman, seized the lank young man by the disengaged hand, and for a moment seemed inclined to wrestle with the old lady for possession of the prize. This, however, the old lady appeared to object to, not unkindly, however, for she first shook hands with the old fellow in a queer sort of way, and then, turning broadside on to the slender young man, clutched at his neck, and, pulling his face down to hers (he seemed very supple, poor fellow!) kissed him, till he with the spectacles exclaimed in an ashamed voice, and quite loud enough for me to hear, "Come, mother, that'll do—in the street, you know!"

If it had not have happened that the way of the curious party lay in the direction of my hay-waggon, I might have been puzzled till my dying day to know what it all meant. I was, however, spared that infliction, for just as they were trooping past I heard the little grey-haired man say,—

"I'm bothered if it isn't, mother! A year and two months come the 23rd, and he has grown a foot if a single inch!"

The year and two months must have been the time the young fellow had lain at Old Bartholomew's.

II.

SQUALORS' MARKET.

EXACTLY opposite each other stands a church and a gin-palace. The former is dedicated to St. Luke, the latter to his head merely, and stands sentinel at the corner of Squalors' Market. Just as it was growing dusk, and the potman pertaining to the palace was kindling the gorgeous outside lamps, I passed under his tall ladder and into the narrow and sinuous thoroughfare.

The business of the evening was yet young. The naphtha man's white horse, harnessed in the evil-smelling cart, was still in the highway, and the naphtha man, carrying his big can and clinking his measures, had still a goodish many stall-keepers to serve; the secondhand shoeseller was busily arranging along the kerb, and in single file, his dissipated regiment of "wellingtons" and "bluchers," administering a little more blacking to this one to make its patches seem less patchy, and solicitously patting and caressing that whose constitution was so fatally undermined that, for all its blooming appearance, it would succumb before a day's wear, and part body and sole; the Hebrew who sold cloth caps and slippers was idly chatting with the Hebrew who, having nicely arranged his brummagem jewellery, had nothing else (but customers) to do; the "unfortunate miner" was, with his afflicted wife, partaking of a final whet of rum at the "Black Boy" before taking their stand, their five sleekly-combed but starving children for the present larking in the gutter, while from out the horrible courts and alleys—head-quarters of fever and pestilence—came pouring great stores of cabbages and turnips, and fruit and shell-fish—the latter looking none the more refreshed for their night's repose beneath the truckle bedstead, and the former yet tearful from their long soaking in grimy tubs in the cellar. Besides these, there likewise streamed out from the courts and alleys "trotters" and hot penny puddings, and "ham sandwiches," for the delight of the most dainty of the thousand, who would presently crowd every inch of road and footway.

Of the two hundred and twenty houses of which Squalors' Market is composed, *one in every thirteen* is devoted to the sale of intoxicating liquors; and it must be borne in mind that in this calculation are not included several public houses that, skulking in crooked chinks and under dark archways, although deprived of the manifest advantages enjoyed by their seventeen brethren in the open highway, yet by means of a beckoning claw in shape of a signboard, affixed at the mouth of the court or alley, "To the George and Dragon," "Back way to the Chip in Porridge," &c., manage to trap many drinkers of the sly and sneaking sort.

That bread even is less in demand in Squalors' Market than gin and beer is demonstrated by the fact that but *ten* bakers' shops can there find support. The catsmeat interest is liberally represented, no less than five establishments of that character flourishing in the market. How is this? Do the squalid court and alley dwellers, with their proverbial extravagance, each keep a cat? or—— No; the supposition is too dreadful. Besides, it should be fairly stated that the five horse-flesh dealers vend sheep's heads, split and baked, and the livers of bullocks, and other offal.

The butchers of Squalors' Market number two less than the gin and beer sellers, and are, dear reader, by no means quiet, well-behaved creatures, such as you are acquainted with. *Your* butcher wears a hat, generally a genteel hat, and a blue coat, and a respectable apron; perhaps, even snowy sleeves and shiny boots, and a nice bit of linen collar above his neckerchief. You give your orders and he receives them decorously, and wishes you good morning as you quit his neatly-arranged and sawdusted shop. Contrasted with him the butcher of Squalors' Market is a madman—a raving lunatic. He unscrews the burners of his gaspipes, and creates great spouts of flame that roar and waver in the wind in front of his shamble-like premises, endangering the hats of short pedestrians and the whiskers of tall ones; far out from his shop, and attached to roasting-jacks, revolve monstrous pigs' heads and big joints of yellow veal, spiked all over like a porcupine with figure-bearing tickets, that announce the few pence per pound for which the meat may be bought. He wears on his head a cap made of the hairy hide of the bison or some other savage beast; his red arms are bare to the elbows, and he roars continuously, "Hi-hi! weigh away—weigh away! the rosy meat at three-and-half! Hi-hi!"—clashing his broad knife against his steel to keep time. How is it that my butcher is charging me $9d.$ per lb. for leg of mutton, while Mr. Blolam, here, is charging only $4\frac{1}{2}d.$? Is my butcher a rogue, or is Mr. Blolam going headlong to the debtors' prison at the end of his street? I know my butcher to be an honest fellow, and to judge from appearances, Mr. B. is not the man to bring his sleek, redhanded wife and his glossy children to grief, either by reckless trading or excessive charity. This being the case, let the court and alley dwellers thereabout, rather than regret, rejoice and thank their lucky stars that they have no money wherewith to trade with Mr. Blolam.

The business of the market grows with the night. First come the decent folk—men and their wives, with the chief olive-branch to carry the big basket. Shrewd people are these early birds with an eye to plump worms. It is not, however, till it has grown quite dark, and the gas is lit, and great tongues of naphtha flame start from crazy lamps, and scorch and lap up the living air greedily, that the buyers come shoaling in. Then the fruit and vegetable mongers give tongue, and roar the quality and price of their various wares with a bullying air, and the brummagem Hebrew jabbers of his rings and brooches;

and the secondhand shoeman, having beguiled a gentleman to take off his boot and "try something on," keeps him standing on one leg in the mud (and so he will be kept till he consents to buy a pair of shoes); and the miner and his family, ranged in a row, chant their necessities.

Strolling through the market out of market hours the dearth of fishmongers at once struck you. True, there are fishshops, five or six of them, but the dealings of the proprietors are almost entirely confined to vending the article in a dried or fried state, one or two of them dabbling in shrimps and periwinkles. Where, however, is the fresh fish—the plaice, the soles, the cod—of which, according to Billingsgate statistics, at least one half of all that comes to market is consumed by the very poorest of the London population? Now, however, when the business of the market is in full blast, the question no longer exists. Here is the fresh fish, in broad flat wicker baskets, slung round the neck, in solitary "pads," standing in the mud, on little boards or trestles, lit up by a feeble candle, and on great boards, eight or ten feet feet long and six broad, standing on substantial legs, and lit by a great flaring naphtha lamp. The owners of these broad boards are no mean fish-pedlars, standing dumbly behind their wares till a customer happens to call. They are wholesale dealers, fish auctioneers. As many people stand round the board as would fill the largest fishmonger's shop in the metropolis. Yet, excepting a heap of copper money—half a peck of it, probably—the board is quite clear. Surrounding the auctioneer, however (who is dressed in corduroy trousers and blue guernsey shirt, the sleeves of which are rolled above the elbows of his great hairy arms), is a large number of "pads" of plaice, and, just behind him, is a big tub full of water. One of his attendants (he generally has two) presently plunges his arms into one of the "pads," brings out a couple of fish, souses them into the water-tub, and then hands them to his master. Without paying the least attention to the lookers-on the man coolly proceeds to disembowel the fish, to chop through the backbone, to make them handy for the frying-pan, and to thread them on a willow twig. All this while, and unsolicited, the people round are bidding "Threeha'pence!" "tuppence!" "two-un-arf!" "Yours, mum," observes the laconic fishman, handing the fish to the "two-un-arf," and proceeding to disembowel and thread two more. It was curious to observe the various countenances of the bidders and buyers; the eagerness with which some women scrambled over the heads and shoulders of their neighbours to get at their bargains, and with a look that plainly said "the price of these will astonish my Jack, I'll be bound;" while others parted with their halfpence regretfully, and as though conscious of having been a *little* too hasty in their bidding. Worst of all, however, were the gaunt women with their mites of shawls and ample aprons, and with husband out of work and any number of children, looking out of their anxious eyes as they watch the cutting up of the fish, and whether it be thick or thin. That seems a likely lot! Shall they bid? Better not, perhaps; wait and see the next lot. So they wait till ashamed to wait any longer, and take the "next lot" and chance it.

It is, however, a great consolation to know that these poor mothers may at the worst depend on ample value for their precious halfpence. Soles and plaice were the fish chiefly dealt in by the auctioneers, and the prices they realised were absolutely ridiculous. Soles, for a pair of which Mr. Greves would charge half-a-crown, were disposed of, after a by no means spirited bidding, for threepence-halfpenny. Touching the cheapness of plaice, I can't do better than quote an instance to which I was an eyewitness. A monstrous fellow, broad and thick as a turbot, was fished out of a "pad," cleaned, gutted, and made ready for the pan, and, after all, the price it brought was *fourpence*. "If you aint got him at a 'apenny a pound it's furny to me," observed the auctioneer, and a friendly potato salesman's stall adjoining his, he put the fish in his scales. The potato-man had no weights of less than a pound, but the fourpenny plaice asserted its superiority to the seven-pound weight, and only consented to a balance when a large potato was added and brought to bear against him.

It is a curious fact—and one more proof of the extravagance of poverty—that in nine cases out of ten the fish purchased was intended for the frying-pan, and not for the pot. It was easy to ascertain this, as whenever a bidder wanted a fish to boil, she signified the same at the time she made her bid. "Thrippence—for bilin!" some one would exclaim; whereon the auctioneer would arrest the descent of his big chopping-knife, and deliver the fish entire. Among the squalid poor the same prejudice exists as regards mutton. Fish fried, and mutton baked or roast, if you please; but as to boiling either, except when ordered by the doctor, the practice is regarded as "namby-pamby," and French.

This universal fish-frying is the key to another mystery common to the neighbourhood. In every "general shop," in every rag and bone shop, in the high street, and in the hundred courts and filthy alleys that worm in and out of it, may be seen solid slabs of a tallowy-looking substance, and marked with a figure 6, 7, or 8, denoting that for as many pence a pound weight of the suspicious-looking slab may be obtained. It is bought in considerable quantities by the fish-eaters for frying purposes, and is by them supposed to be simply and purely the fat dripping of roast and baked meats, supplied to these shops by cooks, whose perquisite it is. This, however, is a delusion. The villainous compound is *manufactured*. There is a "dripping-maker" near Seabright Street, Bethnal Green, and another in Backchurch Lane, Whitechapel, both flourishing men, and the owners of many carts and sleek cattle. Mutton suet and boiled rice are the chief ingredients used in the manufacture of the slabs, the gravy of bullocks' kidneys being stirred into the mess when it is half cold, giving to the whole a mottled and natural appearance.

"Mine uncle" of Squalors' Market—at least, judging from the only specimen there to be seen—is a totally different character from that generally represented. The pawnbroker elsewhere found is a highly respectable person, smug and decorous of mien and subdued of voice. His shop is the shop of an ordinary dealer in jewellery and other articles of value, and he only insinuates his real business in the most delicate way by means of a neat plate on his doorpost inscribed with an intimation that he advances money on plate, jewels, &c., and that he has a fireproof room for the safe keeping of your property. The pawnbroker before me, however, is a tall, muscular man, with great brown hands, dressed in a shaggy pilot coat with big bone buttons, and wearing his battered hat well off his expressive countenance. He has none of the modesty peculiar to the craft about him, neither is his shop a modest one, or unobtrusive, but a broad-awake and gas-lit place, as open as any potato-warehouse in the market. Over the shop-front, in great yellow letters, is inscribed the word "Pawnbroker," and the proprietor stands in front of it—off the pavement, indeed, and in the road—surrounded by an eager mob, and selling from a basket old odds and ends of wearing apparel, old canvas for towelling, any rag of any sort or shape that will fetch even so low a sum as a penny among the squalid bidders. "Here ye are," says he, with the voice of a Channel pilot, as he dangles by the strings something made of flannel; "here's a perricot! How much for the flannel perricot? 'Tant a new un, and 'tant so far gone but the sides may be turned in the middle, and kiver a body comfortable. Who ses sixpence? Tuppence, eh? Thanky; s'pose you buy taters with your money—it'll fetch more for 'ouse flannels. Goin' for fippence!—fourpence! Sold agin, and got the money."

Where had I before seen this muscular pawnbroker? At the dog-show? In the shell-fish department at Billingsgate? On board a bumboat at Portsmouth? No; men very like him at each of the places mentioned, but not he. Now I have it! That "sold again and got the money," settled the point at once. It is a year ago, and he wore a blue apron about his waist, and stood outside a sausage and cheap meat shop in this very market, but the above words were the very ones he uttered as he tossed a pickled pig's head to the young man behind the counter. Now that this circumstance recurred to my memory I no longer wondered to find my friend a pawnbroker! He had a hankering for it at the pig's head period, and kept, besides the sausage-shop, a "leaving-shop," in Brick-lane, St. Luke's.

Does the good reader know the nature of the "leaving" business? It requires no shop; any back room, cellar, or hovel will suffice for it, and any rascal possessed of a few shillings can start in it. It is a business that can flourish and grow fat in the midst of the most appalling poverty—that *does* exist, and flourish, and fatten in a thousand alleys and "slums" within the great city of London. It is a simple matter. Being too lazy to work, and having somehow obtained a pound, I take an apartment in a poverty-stricken locality, hang a few odds and ends in my window or against my door-post and put up a ticket announcing that I deal in "ladies and gentlemen's left-off wearing apparel." Presently some "lady" from one of the swarming alleys, hard up for bread or gin, brings me an article of her apparel, or perhaps a pair of still warm and muddy little boots, and requests me to become a purchaser. But no, I am too humane for anything of the kind. "Oh, don't sell the little boots, ma'am," say I; "take them to the pawnbroker's and pledge them for a trifle." "Shure it's no thrifle at all I can get on 'em at the parn-office," says my customer, "because the heels are throd down so." "Well, look here," says I; "*I'll lend* you a shilling on the boots, and what's more, I'll keep 'em for a month, and you can have them back any time between this and then by paying fourteen pence for them!" The news spreads like fever, and the existence of the new "leaving-shop" is thoroughly known within a week. Within a month of setting up I am doing a roaring trade. Everything too insignificant for the licensed pawnbroker's round the corner is brought to me, and I take the goods in pledge, the depositors well understanding that unless redeemed in a month they are forfeited. As *twopence on the shilling* is the long-established rate of interest demanded at the surrounding "leaving-shops," of course I can't exact more; however, I do as they do—make up for it on smaller sums. If I lend sixpence on a jacket, sevenpence halfpenny must be paid me before it can be ransomed; and if I lend threepence on the Sunday knives and forks or the Sunday baking-dish, nothing less than fourpence halfpenny redeems it, though I may have held it but a few days or even hours. On the whole I do a very snug business; and, what is more, I can defy all the Queen's orders and all the Queen's men, for how can the law step between a man and his simple buyings and sellings?

III.

NEWGATE MARKET.

HEN we will put that down as settled," said my friend the carcass-butcher; "you will be at the corner of St. Sepulchre's at five o'clock to-morrow morning, and I will meet you."

"Very good," replied I, and so left him.

But I thought it anything but "very good." Had May or June been the time of year I might not have entertained any very serious objections to a view of the rising sun, but the prospect of witnessing the birth of a mid-November day was quite another thing. However, my friend talked of five o'clock with a familiarity that bespoke so intimate an acquaintance with it, that I was ashamed to demur or to explain that the hour in question and myself knew so little of each other that a meeting might possibly be embarrassing—at least to one of us.

Punctually, however, I arrived at the appointed spot, at the same moment my friend suddenly emerged from the darkness and confronted me with a newly-cut pencil behind his ear, and the brightness of his blue apron already sullied and smeared with red and white. "Come along," said he; "we shall have time to walk round before the bustle begins."

Crossing the road to the prison corner, we made for the market, passing on the way a row of butchers' carts, backed to the kerb, and with the tailboards down. West-end carts they were chiefly, as the golden legends on the panels attested: the butchering interest of Bethnal Green and Whitecross Street seemed to be unrepresented. My guide, however, explained this by shrugging his shoulders significantly and observing, "That sort don't need to get here early; they can buy at any time." I observed that the vehicles in question were mostly furnished with portable cushions, and that the horses were generally clothed with valuable cloths or leather loin-covers. All alone on the dark highway stood this property, abandoned to the tender mercies of "lurchers" and "market-snatchers." At least so I imagined, and signified to my guide that I thought it a very stupid, not to say culpable system, affording as it did such opportunity for theft. My guide, however, by a mere gesture, set me right on this head; he pointed to a figure lurking in the shadow of the prison wall, holding in one hand a sheaf of cart whips, and who, holding his other hand level with the peak of his cap, kept a lynx-eye on the property entrusted to his charge.

We turned into Warwick Lane. Although the market traffic had not yet commenced, there was considerable noise and confusion. Railway vans thundered over the cobble stones, and railway-van drivers were thundering at each other, and at the market beadle, and at the Corporation generally, such uncomplimentary language as vexed railway-van drivers will. Certainly they were not without grounds for vexation. White Hart Street and Warwick Lane are the only carriage-ways into the market-square; and, when it is considered that the carriages are about seven feet wide, and that the roadway of Warwick Lane is little more than ten feet, and that of White Hart Street something less; that the vans contain over two tons of meat; that the uneven stones, moistened by November fog, afford to the horses' feet about as easy footing as would a pavement of buttered rolls; and that a market beadle (what does *he* know about horses?) takes the bridles into his hands and frantically "backs" van, carman, and all, or endeavours to urge the perplexed cattle forward by probing their flanks with his market cane and uttering small canary chirpings—it is no wonder that the carmen occasionally exhibit a little ill-temper. This uproar, however, has its advantages—it relieves a stranger's mind of the horrors that would beset it if, in the midst of gloom and the jaundiced light that gas and daybreak make, the vehicles were disburdened quietly and by stealth. Breathing the air of yesterday's shambles, the beholder would see long and broad packages, mysteriously shrouded in sackcloth, borne up dark passages or stacked before the unopened shops, and it would require some more powerful counteracting influence than the big, innocent-looking wicker baskets in which the mutton is packed to assure him that the canvas sacks contained nothing more dreadful than sides of beef.

This muffled beef—much of it from Aberdeen and other remote regions—was almost all in "sides;" that is, the hind-quarters with the whole of the ribs attached. Economy keeps shoulders of country beef out of the London market; for, taxed with carriage-dues, such inferior portions of the ox would not be able to compete with that which is killed in London. This rule applies also to mutton, and goes far towards elucidating the mystery that hangs over metropolitan mutton-chops. There are scores of taverns in the City where hundred-weights of chops are cooked daily. I know of a butcher's shop in Chancery Lane, and of another in Threadneedle Street, and of another in Cannon Street, which daily exhibit the loins of as many sheep as go to make an average flock; but I never saw at either place a twentieth of the number of legs needful to carry the loins; and as for breasts and heads, half-a-dozen sheep would be entitled to them all. Now, as no breed of sheep was ever yet known to yield more than a certain number of chops, what becomes of the other portions of these animals? I used to entertain the notion that the mutton-chop merchants disposed of the rest of the sheep to poor-neighbourhood butchers, but inquiry convinced me I was in error. I have perambulated the byways of the City Friday after Friday (that being the day on which the little butcher restocks his shop), but never yet discovered any other mutton but entire and fresh from the rearward slaughterhouse. However, my friend the marketman solved the riddle in a twinkling. He informed me that many tons of saddles of mutton *only* arrive in the big wicker baskets weekly from the country.

Early as it was, the market taverns were open, every one of them. The windows of the "Old Coffeepot" were brilliant, and the gaslight within, shed on rows of bottles, cast seductive, ramhorn rays into the raw, foggy air; the portals of the "Salutation and Cat" were ajar; the "Bell" was up and doing; the "Market House" blinked snugly behind its red curtains; the "Dark House" was already deep in its matutinal rum-and-milk; and at a certain hybrid establishment—half-beerhouse, half-coffeehouse—known as "Mother Okey's," and a house-of-call for disengaged porters and out-o'-work butcher lads, the windows were streaming with the exhalations of the mocha brew. I peeped in at "Mother Okey's," and was surprised, considering how precious is market space, to find that lady's premises so extensive. Her forms and tables covered more ground than many of the leading salesmen can afford. At the tables, deeply scored with lines necessary to the game of "shove-halfpenny," were seated a troop of out-o'-works and porters at breakfast; and, from the prevalence of juicy steaks, I am inclined to think that many an in-work mechanic fares worse than an out-o'-work butcher.

Apropos of the scantiness of market space, the rents exacted by the Corporation for such miserable hovels as go to make up the market, almost exceeds belief. For the privilege of hanging a board—about two feet wide and seven long—beneath the window of a public-house, and the use of a shed opposite, capable, if converted to its proper use, of holding a couple of tons of coals, my informant pays a *hundred pounds a year!* and this in the worst part of the market. "And not dear either, as prices go here," said he. "Why, if I could move my premises to the other end—say to within twenty yards of Bonser's (the chief firm in the market, in the main entrance from Newgate Street), I'd give two hundred a year for them willingly. Salesmen in that quarter are giving more for less accommodation than I possess."

The friendly marketman and I then went to breakfast,

and when we returned the wholesale marketing was in full swing.

In the space of half an hour a marvellous change had taken place. Shops no longer existed, nor wooden walls, nor benches, nor bulks, nor posts even; neither were there any taverns. The "Bell" was choked—dead and buried—by pig meat, the "Dark House" gasped for breath beneath a crush of beef, and "Mother Okey" was overwhelmed with veal and mutton—her very doorway reduced to a mere crevice between two carcasses. The monsters who rushed about with filthy nightcaps and "knots" in their hands, crying "Here I am!" "Who wants me?" and "Now, my masters!" were nothing but meat; the hair on their heads was felted with fat, their vision was impeded by it, their wrinkles "stopped" with it; their hands were animated steaks, and their flimsy garments were by its agency rendered impenetrable as tarpaulin. The great sides of beef, now unshrouded, hung naked and rosy on giant hooks; and sheep that had left their fleecy coats three hundred miles behind them, were delivered from the big wicker baskets, and ranged in clustering rows. Then there were the butchers. West-End aristocrats, with spotless jean coats and Gibus hats; half-and-half dandy butchers, with blue half-sleeves and ribbed aprons; and real, practical, working butchers, in blue coats and market leggings. By mere pinches or pokes with the finger, they decided on one-hundred guinea purchases in less time than your cautious reader or I would take to choose a quarter of lamb; and, making their way through the wall of flesh to the watch-box counting-houses behind, paid down their crisp bank-notes and clinking gold like true British butchers.

So for some hours the wholesale marketing continues, and not without peril may the uninitiated in market ways mingle amongst and note these things. When once caught in the meaty maze, to get out of the way is impossible. Every man's meat is against him. His ear is rasped by the jagged vertebræ of an Aberdeen ox, "by leave" as he is informed by the giant on whose back the offending joint is borne; and, while he is turning to inquire by *whose* leave, the sharp, icy paw of a defunct pig wriggles itself between his neckcloth and the back of his neck. So situate, he is unable to avail himself of the warning "Hi!" and takes the consequence—a headless sheep applied battering-ram-wise at the small of his back, and he hardly knows whether to kick or thank the man with the meat-truck who, by a mighty rearward push, extricates him from his dilemma. Nor is he less morally than physically outraged. To him it seems that barefaced, wholesale thieving is being practised on every side. The sootty and knotted ruffians before mentioned are the delinquents. He sees them without the least reserve march up to a row of "sides," help them on to each other's backs, and decamp with them through the rush without let or hindrance; another, turning square out of the press, seizes a sheep off a hook and runs off; while a third, before the very eyes of the market beadle, is plundering a wicker basket of saddles of mutton. Even if the stranger were made aware of the true state of the case, it is doubtful if he could be convinced that the property was perfectly safe in the hands of the market porters; for it frequently happens that the purchaser's cart is a long distance from his purchase, which has to be wriggled and pushed and pulled through a dense and opposing mob before the said cart can be reached.

The heat of wholesale traffic at last subsided, and, it being Saturday, the retail buyers came straggling in. My friend, however, informed me that at least an hour would elapse before anything worth calling business would be doing; so I reminded him of a celebrated sheep-slaughterer he had before mentioned, and proposed to beguile the hour by an inspection of the said slaughterer's premises. Directed by my friend, I made my way to the shop of Messrs. Venables and Dixon, near the market-square.

In a great wooden box, rude as a rabbit-hutch, sat a polite gentleman at his ledgers. He couldn't ask me into the hutch without himself getting out of it, so we chatted through the air-holes. He told me that the number of sheep slaughtered by the firm averaged five hundred a week through the year, but that during some parts of summer as many as a thousand a week "were turned out." He further informed me that each sheep passed through four pairs of hands, and that he employed two such gangs constantly. The two gangs of eight men could kill, skin, and properly dress a hundred and sixty sheep in twelve hours, which is little more than four minutes for each sheep.

"And pray, where may your slaughtering premises be situated?" I inquired, never dreaming that accommodation for such wholesale killing could be found within the market precincts.

"There is our slaughter-house, sir," replied Mr. Wilson, jerking his thumb toward a doorway behind his hutch, and from which a cloud of opaque vapour was issuing.

There indeed it was, and this was what I saw on approaching the doorway from which belched the stifling smoke. I saw a barn no larger than a drawing-room, in which were eight men gory to the elbows, and with their faces speckled red. But, limited as was the room, the eight men did not have it all to themselves; there were likewise in the room at least fifteen sheep—alive, half dead, dead, and half undressed, and hanging from beams completely muttonised. By the door there was a great sweltering pile of fleecy hides, and in an extreme corner was a hideous wooden tank, with bars across the top, and along the bars was a row of freshly-slain sheep. As fast as the dressers lugged one from the crimson bars to the stone floor, a hot and saturated giant, looking hideous through the gloom that lurked in the place, plucked another from the frantic live ones, who were penned against the wall, and who, having the blood of their fellows before their eyes and on the floor, causing their feet to slip, stared about them and uttered sounds such as I never before heard sheep utter; except one, and that was in Old Smithfield Market, and I heard somebody say that had been kept without water till driven mad. I trust I am not mawkishly sentimental; but when I saw emerging from that dismal den, foggy with the steam of blood and departing breath, and contrasted the sad, limp bodies of the poor animals with the rosy carcasses that came from the country in the wicker hampers—when I saw the former, borne along on the butcher's back, wag their heads mournfully, and as though aware of their ignoble appearance—I could scarcely forbear wagging my own sympathetically.

Gladly I escaped to the comparatively Arcadian air of the market, where the retail business had now commenced in earnest. The leviathans of the market, such as the Messrs. Bonser, despise petty huckstering, and are close shut up an hour ago; still there are shops and stalls displaying abundance of meat—some prime and handsome, and some very, *very* ugly. Were I made market inspector for a single day, I should doubtless provoke the law by sending tons of this fresh-smelling, but skinny, blood-shot meat to be burnt in the knacker's yard at King's Cross. But I suppose the inspector knows best, and the meat is all perfectly sound and wholesome. Whether or no, it all finds purchasers. The newly-married young shoemaker, ninth son of a managing mother, brings hither his little wife, and instructs her how to invest half-a-crown economically; the family man brings his wife and an olive-branch to carry the basket, and bids, per stone, for meat enough to last an entire week; the hard-up man, his wife's week's charing concluded, brings her all the way from Camden Town, and they purchase enormous joints of veal at an absurdly low figure.

But what I have seen of the retail business of Newgate Market disposes me to believe that if you want sound, nutritious, animal food, you can't do better than patronise the butcher round the corner. The meat that goes so wonderfully cheap in the market, the butcher round the corner would not keep on his premises. But folks like to dabble in the "wholesale." I do. I'd have my pen'orth of apples picked from the tree if I could; as I can't, please serve me from a full bushel basket. Therefore, why should I blame Mrs. Jones for liking to pick out her nine pounds of "brisket" from as many tons?

A DOG SHOW.

IV.

A DOG SHOW.

ESIDES cattle shows, and poultry shows, and fruit and flower shows, and rabbit shows, and Punch-and-Judy shows, and the annual showing of the Lord Mayor, there exist throughout London, in at least fifty different "slums," and corners, and crooked ways of the great City, establishments devoted to the "showing" of dogs. By name I have all along known of the existence of these places—knew that they had been in vogue since the days when there were public cockpits at Westminster and St. George's-in-the-Fields, and when hideous bulldogs drew badgers and aristocratic audiences at Hockley-in-the-Hole. With this extent of knowledge of the subject I should, doubtless, have remained content, had not a philanthropic soul, yearning to establish a dog-hospital in a toolshed at Canonbury, inclined my sympathies doggishly, and resolved me to find out what a "dog show" meant.

The columns of *Bell's Life* revealed more than a dozen invitations of the sort I was desirous of complying with. East, west, north, and south of the metropolis were the exhibitions to take place; and, in at least nine cases out of ten, Sunday evening was the time appointed. Of the advertisements the following is a fair sample :—

"A Treat for the Fancy!—On Sunday evening next a Show will be held at Mr. Lerinke's, 'Duck,' Bethnal Green—chair taken at eight o'clock, by Mr. Abrahams, faced by Billy Cool. Mr. Abrahams will produce his splendid stud of toy terriers on this occasion. Mr. Lerinke has a terrier, weight three pounds and a half, open to kill with any dog in the world at his weight."

The programme issued by the landlord of the "Lurcher," Waterloo Road, and mine host of the "Crown," Fiddler's Alley, Haymarket, and half-a-dozen others, all more or less resembled the above. My ignorance, however, put anything like choice quite out of the question; and I selected Mr. Lerinke's establishment simply because it was first on the list.

Passing Shoreditch church, just as the good folk were flocking out therefrom, I took my way up the High Street till I came to a black, narrow gap in the face of it, between Church Street and the railway station, and into it I turned;—through Club Row, where the Sunday bird, and rabbit, and goat, and guinea-pig fair is held; past the "King of Clubs," where every evening, including the Sabbath, prize-fighting goes on, the fighters being chaffinches, and goldfinches, and canaries, the weapons their well-trained voices, and the prizes a "ten-pun'ote" or a German silver "waterpot," just as the birds' owners or backers may agree. Past these, through a lane or so, through a long alley, too narrow so to be called, and more like an accidental chink—a warp in the foul brickwork—and there was "Duck Street" and the "Duck" tavern, and the name of Lerinke written over the door. Following a man who wore a kennelish countenance and a close-fitting hairy cap, and who hugged something bulky within the breast of his coat in a manner highly suggestive of stolen goods, I crossed Mr. Lerinke's threshold and stood before his bar.

It was not a handsome bar. The wooden front of it was at least as dirty as the floor, and exhibited symptoms of long familiarity with hobnailed boots and lazy knees, while the grimy, battered metal counter was chequered with a chain-pattern of glazy rings. About the walls in glasses were preserved specimens of canine monstrosity, from the span-long terrier to the bulldog in all his full-blown hideousness. Men and dogs filled the space before the bar, and behind the bar were Mr. Lerinke and Mrs. Lerinke, and a barmaid.

I was surprised at Mr. Lerinke's appearance. Knowing that he fought dogs and held stakes for amateur pugilists, and kept a rat-pit, and was frequently in the pit and up to his eyes in rats, I had expected to see a brawny fellow, with big muscles, and a way with him that even a bulldog could not mistake; on the contrary, I found him a small man, with an everlasting smile and an oily voice—the sort of man, in fact, you would expect to find carrying the big banner in a "total abstinence" procession, or cutting bread and butter at a love-feast, rather than ruling among savage vermin and hobnobbing with bulldogs and bulldog-men. I don't know the sort of breed it is, but there *is* a dog one occasionally meets in the street, a brown dog, one part spaniel and seven parts kennel cur; a dog with lean loins, and an inquiring nose, and pursed lips, and a bewildered where's-the-next-meal-to-come-from expression about his eyes; he plods along the road with a business air, as though, having at last argued down the proud little bit of spaniel in him, he was bound on a begging errand to a West End relation. Now and then, however, he pulls up short and dead—"skidded," as it were, by that rebellious one-eighth of respectability—shakes his head miserably, and then forges along once more. Mr. Lerinke reminded me of this dog instantly. He looked exactly as it would have looked—just as beseeching and make-believe pleasant—if you had offered it meat on a skewer, and wickedly amused yourself by pricking its nose with the sharp end before you threw it down. As for Mrs. Lerinke, she looked contented and happy; and the few small Lerinkes to be seen about the place seemed soundly booted and breeched, and well fed. In ordinary cases this would not have been remarkable, but in this case it was; inasmuch as it was hard to understand how a man with his heart so thoroughly set on dogs should trouble himself much about such trifles as wives and children. That his heart *was* set on dogs was clear. The loving sidelong glances he cast on them when he thought nobody was looking, the kindly purring noise he made while tenderly handling baby dogs, and the way in which he scratched their tiny polls and clucked to them, were ample proof of it. Conspicuous among the stuffed specimens on the walls was a murderous-looking bulldog in a handsome mahogany-and-glass case. The fate of this brute Mr. Lerinke was explaining to a gentleman who wore the head of a Skye terrier out of his coat-pocket as swells of the lower order occasionally wear their handkerchiefs. Had the defunct dog been an only son, the little man could not have exhibited more emotion. He would not, he said, have taken fifty pounds on the nail for it; indeed, he had had forty-five pounds ten offered for it; but it warnt likely! You might as well have offered forty-five ten for his biggest kid, or—this in the lowest whisper—the missus herself. Well, sir, he was pisoned! He was the best in the world—too good to live—so the vagabuns pisoned him. On a Sunday morning it was hearty and well one minute among their legs in front of this bar, and the next minute, hallo! on this side of the bar dead as paving-stones! Proosick acid did it! On a bit of meat!

The gentleman with the Skye terrier was so affected that he swallowed all his rum at a gulp, and hurried to a flight of stairs in the corner, and, thinking it probable that the stairs might lead to the show-room, I followed

I had guessed rightly. When the door was pushed open there belched out a cloud so warm, so dense, so redolent of rank tobacco and spirituous liquors that only that a man came up close behind me laden with a snarling cur I think I should have retreated. In I went, however, and this is what I saw:—A long, narrow room, shallow from floor to ceiling as a church vault, and (by reason of the foul vapour) as gloomy, although there were several jets of gas burning. At the end of the room the flooring was raised a foot or so, and on this was the chairman's chair; and at the other extremity of the room was the chairman's "facer," proudly nursing a dreadful brute, with its jaws bound up with thongs of leather, and which I was confidently informed "was the handsomest brindled bull for miles round." Round the walls were more stuffed dogs and pictures of fighting-men and running-men, and of dogs killing rats, and of dogs and cocks killing each other. At one side of the room, and visible now and then through the many pairs of ragged legs that hemmed it in, was a great roaring fire, which was needful, for the night was very cold, and the draught came in at the gap at the bottom of the door, and in at the crazy windows, and in at a great hole in the ceiling from which the plaster had tumbled down.

Concerning the company. In my rambles round about the great metropolis I have fallen in with some curious company. I have passed an evening in a room with a large number of women and men, and where, had it been known that I was anything but a thief or a scoundrel at enmity with the law, I stood an excellent chance of being thrown out of the window or having my head knocked against the wall; I have supped with tramps and beggars in a Kent Street kitchen; but, with few exceptions, I never before saw congregated so many faces with "hulks" branded on them, so much brazen blackguardism, so much bare brutality, as was exhibited by Mr. Lerinke's guests.

There were, I should say, at least fifty of them; some with black coats and hats with curly brims, some in caps and flannel jackets, some with smocks and "ankle-jacks" —all, or nearly all, bull-necked, heavy-jawed, and with the hair dressed after a fashion known among its patrons as the "Newgate-knocker" style—that is, parted in masses on each side of the head, and turned under unnaturally. Every man possessed at least one dog, and as he sat at the table the animal was squatted by the side of his pot or glass, with his arm round it. These, however, were the "toy" dogs, marvels of shape and size—so small, some of them, that their weight is reckoned by ounces, and with limbs but little thicker than the stem of a tobacco-pipe, with beautifully-formed heads, and eyes full of intelligence. One could not help reflecting, after gazing first on the dog, then on its keeper, what a pity it was that the former should be tied to such a low-bred companion!

How did these beautiful little creatures come into the hands of their present owners, is a question little less difficult to answer than another. Of what use are they to their masters? One may understand how affection may attach an honest man to an honest dog, or a ruffian to an able-bodied, ruffianly "brindled bull;" but what gratification can a big, coarse-minded man enjoy by the possession of a "toy?" a thing without bark, or bite, or a single other quality assimilating with any one he himself possesses. One would as soon expect to find him keeping white mice or silkworms. "What is the value of that little dog?" I asked of a young man in a tattered jacket and a very dirty shirt, who was "showing" his terrier—weight two pounds and a quarter—against another. "I don't want to sell her," the young man replied; "twelve pounds is her worth—ten I'm offered for her."

Had there been no other than dogs of the "toy" school in the room the business of the evening would have been, no doubt, carried on in a much more quiet way. As it was, however, there were shrill-voiced ratting dogs, and fighting terriers, and fighting bulldogs, struggling and straining their leashes to get at each other, with their red eyes starting from their heads, and their black lips curled back from their fangs, howling, yelping, barking shrilly and spitefully, or growling with a deeper rage from the bottom of their wide, red throats; while their masters, savages as themselves, roared out horrid blasphemy, and staked their eyes and limbs on the swaggering lies they uttered, and struck their great fists on the table to show they were in earnest in the wagers they offered to lay, and clapped hands together when the wager was made; while others, who had come on purpose to make a match and found a difficulty in "getting on" with any one, sat apart, stirring up their dogs to show their mettle, or clenching their muzzles and holding still their writhing limbs when for business reasons it was desirable that their tremendous courage should not be made too public.

Apart from the bustle and the uproar sat two or three of the most miserable objects that could be imagined,—ragged, thin, and anxious-looking, and each accompanied by a gaunt, hollow-sided bulldog. I didn't ask their condition. It was too apparent. Like the poor fellow to whom some kind Indian acquaintance sent an elephant which he could not afford to keep, which nobody would buy, and which the authorities would not allow him to kill, so were each of these wretches afflicted with a bull-dog, the only difference in the cases being that a fatal desire to belong to the "fancy," and not the whim of a friend, brought the calamity upon them, and that not sanitary considerations, but infatuation, obliges them to bear about the dreadful burden. So will they drag on a miserable existence, half-starved, and cordially hating each other, till the workhouse-doors, or others still more inexorable, part the wretched pair and break the spell.

V.

THE NIGHT COFFEE-BOOTH AND ITS CUSTOMERS.

IT is often my fate to ride home from Fleet-street by the last Islington omnibus. At about thirty minutes before midnight this vehicle arrives at the "Angel," and at that point it is my custom to alight. I need not mention that sometimes the night is fine, sometimes otherwise—very much otherwise—foggy, snowy, rainy, windy; so that the street lamps rattle and waver, and even the accustomed policeman holds his hat on; or so bitterly cold that the night cabmen on the ranks shut themselves within their carriages and have to be knocked up before they may be hired.

Hail, blow, shine, or snow, however, there is one spectacle I rarely miss as I step from the omnibus, and that is a large hand-barrow laden high with some poles and some sailcloth, and some forms and a table, and a big wicker-basket, and a great bright tin boiler with a brass tap, while from the bows of the barrow there swings a cylindrical and perforated firegrate and a jolly, glowing coke-fire. A very decent-looking old fellow pushes at the shafts; and walking at his side, and lending a friendly hand at up-hill and stony places, is a tidy, buxom little woman, with a pippin face, snugly tucked up in a shawl and a woollen comforter.

The nature of their avocation was evident—they were the proprietors of a night coffee-stall—a common enough nocturnal feature of the London highway; still, like most folks, I had been so accustomed to associate all that pertained to night life in London with the raffish, the sharkish, the blackguardly, and the idiotic, that to see such decent people embarked in it seemed not a little singular and worthy some little inquiry.

So I kept the barrow in sight from under the lee of my umbrella (it was raining and blowing pretty hard) till it stopped near a piece of waste ground in front of a tavern, the gaslights pertaining to which were by this time all but extinguished, and the barmen busy hustling out into the rain and the mire the most pertinacious of their customers (who implored "another quartern" with all the eloquence of paupers at the door of a relieving overseer, and were, it is but just to add, as gruffly refused), and the potman was hoisting up the broad shutters. With marvellous expedition the old people relieved the barrow of its load, rigged up the tent, arranged the forms, lit the bright swinging lamp, perched the tin boiler on the fire, and spread the table with a white cloth; the table they quickly adorned with cups and saucers and a big loaf and a cake withdrawn from the basket; so that, within a quarter of an hour, the little cabin was built and invitingly furnished; and when the old lady had cut up a stack of bread and butter and another of cake, and the coffee-boiler began to steam, I experienced much less embarrassment than I had anticipated in crossing the road and requesting to be served with a cup of coffee.

"Is there anything else I can do for you before I go, Sam?" asked the old woman of her husband as I began to sip his really excellent mocha.

"No, my dear, thanky; I shall be pretty comfortable now, I think," replied he, looking round the cabin critically; "good-night, missus, I shall be home soon after light."

I believe he would have kissed her had I not been present; but he compromised the matter by adjusting the comforter about her neck in the most solicitous manner, and then she, returning his "Good-night," and bidding him take care of himself, toddled off.

"Your wife does not stay here with you?" I observed.

"I'd be werry sorry to see her," replied the proprietor; "it might be all right in general, which it is, even with the worst of them—the unfortnight ones—civil, bless you, sir, as can be; still, now and then we have a orkard customer, much more orkard than I should like a missus of mine to be a witness to. Besides, it's better for her to be abed than a breezin' and a blowin' out here."

Having complimented my coffee-man on his good sense, and ordered another cup of coffee, which I likewise praised, we fell into a very interesting conversation, which, however, was unfortunately more than once interrupted by the occurrence of a customer, and, as coffee-stall customers were the topic of our conversation, it was convenient to drop the subject whenever one appeared. Still, those I had at present seen were of a most ordinary sort, as I took opportunity to remark to him.

"Well, you see, it's early yet," replied he; "the curious sort don't drop in till about two, and then they keep dropping in till about five; then the reg'lar working trade begins, men and lads who are obliged to be at shop, and make a quarter before breakfast-time. Ah, I have often thought what a remarkable book it would make if I was to write down all the queer customers I serve."

I, myself, could not help reflecting on the exceedingly remarkable volume my friend was capable of producing under the circumstances. Still, the notion, in a limited sense, was not without its attractions, and before I bade the coffee-man adieu I had arranged a little plan with him. With a pencil with which I provided him, and on some leaves torn from my pocket-book, he was, on the following night, to make note of his customers and what they were like, together with such brief comments on them as he thought necessary. In the course of the day following he was to leave his notes at my house. He brought them. Here they are:—

"Half-past Eleven, at which time we began to put up the stall.—Had a customer (if you could call him such, poor fellow) waiting till it was ready. It was the blind man as you might have seen on the canal-bridge reading the New Testament, with cockled-up letters, by the touch of his fingers. He had only took threepence-halfpenny since tea, which was four o'clock, cold weather being bad for him, on account of people not stopping to listen. The missus was ready to go when he had finished his cup, so she see him across the road. 'Cept a cup to a night cabman, and ditto with cake to an unfortnight, and giving the policeman a light, nothing done till half-past twelve.

"Half-past Twelve.—Never thought to serve two blind people in one night; but so it was. This time a little boy about six years old, with his father, who, although it ain't for me to talk about looks or to judge, was not a nice sort of person. He seemed out of sorts, and turned over the bread and butter for the thickest, in a way that made me speak about it. 'It ain't no more for sitting, I spose,' said he, taking up the boy and slamming him on to a form. 'Didn't I sing it properly, father?' presently asked the little chap. 'As proper as you'll ever sing it,' snapped out his father. Then turning to me, says he, 'You're jolly pious in this quarter, ain't you?' 'Not that I ever heard,' says I; 'what makes you ask?' 'Just this,' says he, 'you must know that my little boy, who is as blind as a stone, and likely to be a burden to me as long as he lives, has got a tidy voice, that is for the comic style—"Dark girl dressed in blue," "Mrs. Rummins's Ball,"—that sort of thing, you know; well, I takes him of nights, you know, to concert-rooms, 'specially where there is a bit of a platform and a piano where he can show off, you know. If the company likes to take pity and club round, it's optional. I don't ask 'em, not I; I sits down and smokes my pipe like another man. Well, we goes to-night to the "North Star" close here, and says I to the chairman, "Perhaps the company would like to hear a little blind boy sing a song." "I dessay they would," said he, and, after tapping the table, he announced it. Well, I 'spose because he was blind they thought he was going to strike up the Old Hundredth, or something in that line; but he didn't, he sang "Mrs. Rummins's Ball," and when he had done, instead of clapping and knocking as he deserved, they fell to hissing like steam, and in a minute a waiter comes, and says he, "There's somebody as wants you in the next street, sir." A pretty canting lot you must be about here!' and then he flung down the price of what he had had, and, jerking the blind boy off the form, walked off with him. Four cups to the night street-sweepers, and a goodish many spilt, if not drank, with five spoons bit in two for a wager, and a saucer broke, by three tipsy gents out of the Belvedere, who handsomely paid a shilling each for damages, making up the time till half-past one.

"Half-past One.—More call for pickled cabbage (which, you must know, I was asked for till at last I kept) than anything else, by married men, and them as are single, and live in quiet lodgings, that they might go in something like sober. I've had as much as a shilling give me for a pull at the vinegar in the jar before now. At a little after two I sold my last pen'orth of pickles, and then begins to come in my very worst sort of customers: they who, in consequence of having something short of the price of a lodging, walk about till two, and then come and dribble and drabble their bits of ha'pence in coffee and bread and butter just as long as you can put up with 'em. Bless you, if I encouraged it, I shouldn't be able to get near the coffee-tap. They'll come in, trying to look as promiscuous as possible, and call for threeaporth of coffee, and sit down close to the fire; but I'm so used to 'em, that only by their lingering way of stirring it I know what their game is. If I don't take any notice of 'em they are asleep in a jiffy, and when I wakes 'em they order a slice of bread and butter, and then they're off again. I wakes 'em again, and again they order another slice, till I'm thankful when their last halfpenny is gone, and I can say, 'Now, sir, what can I serve you with?' 'Nothing more, thanky.' 'Then, good morning, sir!'

"But these lodgingless ones ain't all 'sirs,' and that's the worst of it, the other sort being much more frequent and harder to get rid of. I've had 'em come and say, 'Mister, I want to sit by your fire till the morning: don't turn me away—for God's sake don't!' So, for God's sake, I give 'em shelter, which it's what a man ought to do, no doubt, specially when he comes to consider that that very night may be their last in that unlucky lane to which there seems no turnin', and that, by the help of another day's seeking, they may find the reward for remaining honest against such heavy odds.

"Half-past Two.—Three unfortnights, two of which are old customers and sisters, for coffee and cake. 'Don't you wish he sold rum, Polly?' asked one. 'I wish he sold laudanum,' replied she, 'and was bound to make me swallow a quartern of it! I feel as though I was standing up to my knees in ice.' 'That's a very wrong wish of yours, aint it, miss?' says I to her. 'You be hanged, you old fool!' said she; 'what do you know about it? I'd like to see every man in London choking in a ditch with a stone round his neck.' Just then comes up two navigating-looking men, with bundles at their backs, and asks if they were on the right road for Uxbridge. 'You ain't going to Uxbridge now, are you?' asked the one that spoke about the laudanum. 'Right away, miss: the young 'uns and the missuses are there, where we left 'em to try for work at the new shore up here; but it's no go, and the sooner we gets back the better.' 'You might have rode home for eighteenpence,' said Polly. 'That's the identical sum we set out with, three days gone,' said the navvy, ruefully. 'Come in, men,' says Polly, 'and pitch into the bread and butter and coffee; I'll pay.' So in they came; but I'm proud to say that they used her like honest chaps, eating a tidy lot, certainly, but not half, no, nor a quarter, as much as they could; and then went off shaking hands with her, and thanking her, and steadfastly denying the sixpence she wanted to press on them. Cabman brought a drunken gentleman, who swore dreadfully because I had no new-laid eggs; said he was well known to Mr. Cox, of Finsbury, and would take care that the thing was looked into. Polly, the unfortnight, who was not yet gone, asked him to stand coffee; on which he threw what was in his cup all over her, and called for the police, who turned 'em all out, and the gentleman got into his cab, and was drove clear off without paying. The fire-escape man looked in, and I smoked a pipe with him, while one of the homeless ones, mentioned in half-past one, edged close to the fire and dozed for half-an-hour.

"Half-past Three.—Being market morning, the drovers begin now to come along, and for the next hour, off and on, the stall is filled with them and their dogs, which makes it uncomfortable; and all the more so because they bring their bread with them, and like their coffee so very sweet. They're a dreadful rough lot, and their talk is something awful; but I darn't open my mouth, or over would go my boiler in a twinkling. I'm thankful that I only have their company two mornings in the week.

"Half-past Four.—Plenty of unfortnights, who have been a waitin' and a watchin' about for the drovers to go, now come in and spend their ha'pence, and take it in turns to warm themselves. If you was to peep in and see me behind my table, and the stall filled with a dozen of these customers, mostly pretty, and dressed out so gay, you might think me lucky; but if you was to hear what I hear in their talks one to the other of their poverty and wretchedness, their brutal usage, and their hatred of themselves and all the rest of the world, I think you would alter your opinion. So there they stay, taking it in turns to stand at the fire, till five o'clock strikes. At that hour they know, as I have before told you, that my regular morning working customers drop in, and so, without being told, they then clear out.

"You might wish to know what sort of a night's work this makes. Well, I've sold three gallons of coffee, and I get two-and-threepence out of that, tenpence out of my bread and butter, and ninepence out of my cake. That's three-and-tenpence, and rather over than under the average; and I leave it to you to say if it's earned a bit too easy."

VI.

CONCERNING MUFFINS.

"My dear," said I to my wife, dutifully saluting her as she adjusted the top button of my overcoat, "we will have muffins at tea this evening."

"But, my love, there are no muffins to be had yet awhile," replied she.

"My precious, there will be muffins this afternoon: listen for the tinkling of the bell just before dusk."

She shook her head incredulously, and observed, "We shall see."

We did see. As I deposited my umbrella and my life-preserver in the hall that evening I experienced the happy sensation that invariably attends the man the correctness of whose prognostication is proved. The air was fragrant of buttered muffins, and in another minute were revealed to me the luscious discs, blushing a dainty straw colour in the cheery firelight.

"Did I not tell you so?"

"Truly," replied my wife, regarding me as the head of a household likes to be regarded; "but how, in the name of goodness, you came to know that it would be so is more than I can imagine."

"Your silly little head cannot be expected to know everything," I replied, with an offhand air of superiority, and seemingly unconscious of the glance of prideful admiration that was directed to me on account of this last proof of my profound wisdom. I let the discussion drop, and gave my attention to that which had originated it.

Perhaps I ought to be ashamed to confess that my wife's simple and confiding nature had been imposed on. The fact is, I knew as well that the muffin "season" would commence that day as when the next Good Friday would fall. I know all about muffin boys, and men, and bells, and trays, and can give the names and addresses of the chief muffin merchants, east, west, north, and south.

I attained my muffin knowledge in a purely accidental way. Possibly the reader may know nothing of the neighbourhood of Shoreditch, or his knowledge at most may be restricted to the highway part of it where the railway station is; there it will be useless for me to specify by name a certain narrow, tortuous, miry thoroughfare, with a rutty road and pathway for not more than two abreast, that leads from the main street to Curtain Road. Anyhow, that was the street, or lane, or whatever they call it, it was lately my lot to traverse, and there, keeping my eyes about me, as is my wont, I was struck by a somewhat singular announcement stuck in a shop-window.

It was a mysterious-looking shop. The name over the door (which was close shut, and, as might be seen by the broad mud splashes that crossed the chink of opening, had remained so for several months) was Toomey, but of Toomey's trade there was not even a hint. You naturally turned for the required information to the contents of the shop, and there you saw a great stack of empty ginger-beer bottles; and for a moment your mind was at rest—only for a moment, however, for a second glance disclosed several flour barrels and sacks, that could not possibly have to do with the ginger-beer trade; added to this the written announcement, "The season commences on Tuesday," was clearly against the bottles, for, as common sense dictated, the call for the exhilarating beverage contained in them becomes fainter as the summer wanes, and at the present season of the year, with the wintry wind blowing and the rain falling, could be in no demand at all.

Happily, in the midst of my perplexity, there sauntered past Mr. Toomey's premises two intelligent-looking but sparsely-dressed youths of the neighbourhood. Their industrious eyes at once found out the mysterious notification, and they halted simultaneously to discuss it.

"Oh, 'mences on Toosday, do it," was the observation

of one of them, as he screwed up his mouth and reflectively fingered the lobe of his left ear.

"It do so, aperiently, William," said his companion, "which it is later by three weeks than last 'ear. How do it find you, William?"

"It don't find me werry well," responded William. "I sees my way to the apron and sleeves; the old 'ooman will look arter them—it's the bell as floors me. It's been away since the Darby, which the money as was got on it went, as you werry well know, to buy a close-brush. Let us see, June, July, August, Siptember, 'Tober, 'Vember" (this on his fingers), "that's thruppence, and thruppence as they lent on it, that's just a 'sprat' altogether. I wish I might get a sprat to spare atween this and Toosday."

As the youth had mentioned two threepences as equivalent to a "sprat," it was pretty clear that the name of the familiar little fish was "Shoreditch" for sixpence—a sum the attainment of which by William within the prescribed period was so utterly hopeless as to be inexpressible in words. A few steps of a hornpipe, however, seemed to meet the case, for after its serious performance, William so far dismissed the subject as to be able to devote his entire attention to a sugar-tub that stood at a grocer's door adjacent.

I was no longer at a loss to understand the import of the placard in the dingy window. Without doubt the "season" alluded to was that of muffins. What else could an apron and sleeves in connection with a bell point to? What the flour-sacks and barrels? But how was the opening of the season inaugurated? Was there a procession of muffineers with green baize banners? and did Mr. Toomey himself announce the momentous event by clang of brazen clapper? Early in the afternoon of the Tuesday advertised I once more visited the spot where William had bewailed his want of a "sprat."

Mr. Toomey's premises had altered wonderfully in appearance. The ginger-beer bottles had disappeared, and in their place—in the place, indeed, everything else had previously occupied—were piles and mounds of muffins

and crumpets. It was not a lofty shop, but it was very
long and tolerably wide; and yet, with the exception of
a narrow passage, it was chokefull of the ware in question; while at the end was a stack of muffin-trays, all
bright with fresh paint, and reaching from floor to ceiling,
each one bearing on its front ledge the name of Toomey.
There was one thing that rather astonished me : here were
the goods meant without doubt to be buttered and consumed that very afternoon; there were the trays ready
for conveying them away; but where were the vendors?
Presently, however, directed by a Babel of tongues, I discovered by the side of the muffin merchant's premises a
spacious yard, and in the yard, and pressing about the door
of what I suppose was the bakery, was a mob forty or
fifty strong of decent-looking old men, and boys ranging
in age from ten to sixteen, each attired in a snowy apron
and sleeves, and bearing in his hands a bell and a piece
of green baize. Presently an old fellow came leisurely
towards the gate where I was standing, and observed,

"What's the use of 'em scrouging? There's enough
for all of us, I'll be bound, and they won't get served
before three o'clock, that's a certain thing."

"But why three o'clock?" I inquired.

"Blest if I know," replied the old fellow; "I only
know it is so, and always was; if you was to go the
round, both this and the t'other side of the water, you
would find just this sort of game—this pushing, and
driving, and scrouging to be first, going on at all the
master muffin bakers."

Then ensued a conversation between myself and the old
muffin man, in which he informed me that the "season"
was regulated by nothing more reliable than the whim
or convenience of half a dozen muffin merchants, established in as many obscure streets in and about the metropolis;—that he, on whose premises we now stood, regarded
the districts of Dalston, Islington, and Highbury as exclusively his;—that Belgravia and the aristocratic parts
of Chelsea were supplied from the insalubrious vicinity of
Strutton Ground;—that the seat of the southern muffin
interest was Kent Street. My informant was particu-

larly desirous that I should understand that these (he mentioned their names) were the leviathans of the business, and ruled the "season;" for, said he, "of course you, as a gentleman, don't want no telling that the season for a thing *is* the season, and that the crumpets as you buy of a 'fectioner in July ain't no more in season than is green peas at Christmas."

"Pray, is it a profitable business?" I ventured to inquire.

"Profitable enough to him, I'll wager," replied he, intimating who "him" was by a jerk of his thumb towards the muffin-shop; "I've known him empty twenty sacks of flour a week."

"And how many muffins would that make?"

"How many muffins?" repeated the old man, slowly, and gazing mazily up the street and down the street, and up at the gables of the tall old-fashioned houses. "Goodness knows. You could never count 'em. Look here, your edication will find it out quicker than mine. How much batter—werry thin batter—will twenty sacks of flour make?"

The arithmetical problem thus suddenly put so fairly staggered me, that I could merely shake my head, and ejaculate "Ah!"

"Werry well, then," continued he, "half a pint of batter makes six muffins. Now you've got it. Besides," continued he, sinking his voice confidentially, "he's got two seasons. He's got a ginger-beer season as costs, as I know from my lad as works here, £70 a year for corks and twine alone. Bless you, old Toomey's a warm man— never drinks nothing but brandy-and-water!"

Seeing that he expected it, I was much impressed with this last item of intelligence, and for a moment was overwhelmed with silent amazement.

"About being profitable," he broke out again presently, "why, you know, fourpence out of a shilling ain't bad, and that's what we get. Mind you, he don't change your stale, and at that figure you can't expect it. But muffins have been frightful slack these three seasons. You see the butter's all against us."

"The butter? I beg your pardon."

"Oh, no offence, sir; none in the least. It ain't *your* fault, but it's none the less true, I as‑ure you. When one's up t'other's down. You don't catch 'em runnin ckal together; no, not one season out of six. Nobody thinks of eating dry muffins, or muffins with marmalade. So, you see, with butter at fourteen pence a pound, it's good-bye muffins."

Three o'clock just then struck out from the neighbouring churches, and, with a nod, the old muffin-man turned on his heel and hurried towards the now open door of the muffin bakery. In less than a quarter of an hour the bells gave tongue, and the welcome news that the muffin season had commenced was spread through the town.

THE HORSE REPOSITORY.

VII.

THE HORSE REPOSITORY.

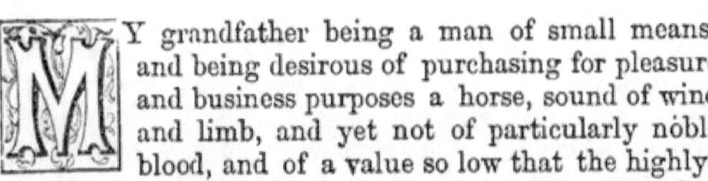

Y grandfather being a man of small means, and being desirous of purchasing for pleasure and business purposes a horse, sound of wind and limb, and yet not of particularly noble blood, and of a value so low that the highly-bred hammer of Tattersall could not possibly descend to "knock it down," experienced considerable difficulty in suiting himself. He might wait for the annual horse fair at Barnet; but to select a decent beast from among the best of unkempt quadrupedal savages assembled, required an amount of subtle calculation and sagacity peculiar to purchasers of growing crops and cargoes of cocoanuts in the husks. There was Smithfield, and had he been a butcher he would not have had the least hesitation in proceeding there alone to buy an ox or a score of sheep; but, had any friend suggested that he should visit Smithfield's chartered and officially-recognised weekly horse sale, the said friend would have been regarded as a simpleton unacquainted with metropolitan pitfalls, or as a wicked, practical joker.

There were several other courses open to my grandfather, all more or less objectionable; and among the latter the "auction-yard" of Messrs. Betty and Martingale, and Mr. Spavinger's weekly horse sale. Mr. Spavinger's premises were not splendid; they were not even commodious, nor particularly clean. The entrance was a low archway, about the mouth of which lounged and leant any number of seedy, tight-breeched blackguards—shrewd villains, most of them with a knowledge of horseflesh almost amounting to inspiration, and astute readers of the human countenance, enabling them at a glance to tell the simple visitor from the knowing, and so to shape their behaviour. At the same time, I am ready to believe that, except when brought in contact with equine nature, these unlucky dogs are as honest as the majority of us. They are like the terrier—if that respectable dog will pardon me—who is of peaceable disposition, just in his dealings with his own species, and all other animals except the rat. Only show him a rat, and he at once abandons his pacific demeanour and becomes a furious, mouthing little savage, anxious only to rend and tear and make havoc. So it would seem to be with certain of the human species, that, being from their childhood thrown into horse society, and having ample opportunities of observing that, compared with the intelligence of the brute, their own low, loose minds appear to little advantage, gradually conceive a violent hatred to Equus, and resolve to devote their entire lives to persecuting it, and to convincing the arrogant beast which is master. These worthies are like the terrier, inasmuch as they eat and drink with their fellows, and that without sponging or filching the bread or the beer: if they have wives and little children, they will dutifully carry home such of their earnings as are left from their spendings; they will even turn the mangle should their wives possess such an instrument; or, at least, nurse the baby while she turns it. So far are they docile, harmless creatures; but show them a horse—that is, a horse whose owner wishes to dispose of him—let them but catch scent of one such, and his disquietude will begin. This peculiar species of individual will nose about here and there till he discovers it, when he will eagerly offer his services to the seller—he "knows a gen'leman as wants jist sich a mare," if you'll allow him to take it round to the gentleman's stables; he will not take no for answer—he has suggestions to make concerning the animal's appearance, and hints the difference a little "touching-up" would make; all the while fussing about his four-legged enemy, pulling open its eyelids and staring impudently into its eyes, wrenching its jaws asunder and examining its teeth, poking its withers, and investigating its hoofs. Decline his services flatly as you may, an uncontrollable itching, a right of further handling of the beast, possesses him; and though he be absolutely driven away, there presently he is again, hovering about your quadruped like a baffled bobfly.

To return, however, to Mr. Spavinger's horse auction. Penetrating the gloomy archway, you come to a sort of open court, paved with those ingenious instruments of torture "cobble" stones, which, when trod, yielded with an unpleasant and inodorous oozing. Flanking one side of the auction-yard was a row of squalid stables, and flanking the other side was a double or triple row of such carriages, and carts, and trucks, as were ordered for the day's sale. The company, with a praiseworthy endeavour to avoid the slushy pavement, mounted the various vehicles, while Mr. Spavinger, seated in front of an old cab, rested the catalogue of the goods against the dash-iron, and knocked them on the driving-box; while his clerks sat within, and took the purchase-money and gave receipts through the window.

Bad enough as all this was, it was still possible that fair dealing might have come out of it had the auctioneer been an honest man and the company *bonâ fide* buyers and sellers. This, however, was far from being the case. That ancient and mysterious institution known as "knocking-out" held freer sway at horse and carriage auctions than any other, and before it the sale became a sham and the bidding the merest waste of time. "Knocking-out" at carriage and horse sales of the old school prevails to this day. There is a rough, ignorant man residing in a squalid street in the London Road, Southwark, who may be regarded as one of the chiefs of the knockers-out. He, however, does more in the vehicle and harness than in the horse branch of the business. His experience of carriages commenced with costermongers' barrows. He builds them and lets them out at eighteenpence a-week, and at certain seasons of the year has as many as seventy so engaged. Not only does he let the barrows, he also stocks them with any sort of fruit with which the market happens to be glutted. Should contrary winds so retard the ships that bring cargoes of pineapples that the fruit is damaged before it reaches the consignee, the barrow-letter is the first at the Monument Yard sale, ready to buy damaged pines by the cartload to the extent of a hundred pounds' worth. The same with oranges and cherries. This fruit is farmed to the costermongers on the simple plan of "thirds"—that is, a fixed price is set, and the stock weighed or counted out to the vender before he starts in the morning, and again when he returns at night, the produce being apportioned, two-thirds to the costermonger and a third to the proprietor of the fruit. During a good season the barrow-master's troop will easily take among them £30 a day; out of this he takes ten, besides the rent of the barrows and the original profit on his wholesale purchase of the pineapples or cherries.

Lucrative as this "game" must be, it is inferior to that of "knocking-out," which gives much less trouble, is accompanied by no risks, and continues summer and winter. It is conducted as follows:—The before-mentioned barrow-letter and a few choice companions meet at Mr. Spavinger's on a sale day. There are cabs, and phaetons, and horses and harness to be sold; and the merry little troop of "knockers-out," although they have not the slightest intention of retaining a single article, intend purchasing at least half the goods presently to be submitted to public competition. The value of the goods on which the knockers-out have set their heart, say, is five hundred pounds; the knockers-out, among them, are not prepared with as many shillings. That, however, is not of the slightest consequence. If Mr. Spavinger and the knockers-out are friends, so much the better; if not, they "work" before his very eyes, and in defiance of him; they have done it a hundred times and will do it again. They have done it so many times that the habitual resorters to the horse and carriage auction know them, and at the same time know that there is not the slightest chance of buying a single article "wanted" by the banded "knockers-out." They may bid if they please, but the confederates will bid against them—will bid and buy a horse for twenty pounds worth ten. So the obstinate, honest bidder may compel the rascals to pay pretty dear for their whistle, bearing in mind one little circumstance—that when the obstinate bidding has gone five pounds further than prudence dictates, the knocker-out may suddenly pause, and allow the honest bidder the privilege of taking the disputed "lot" at half as much again as it is worth.

The key to the knocker-out's success is a fear on the part of the legitimate buyer that he may be suddenly left in the lurch as above described. The only way, therefore, to obtain what he wants at a moderate rate is for him to consult the conspirators before the sale begins. Says the buyer to one of the knockers-out, "Mr. Blinkum, I want lot 21, sorrel mare."

"You can't have her," replies Mr. Blinkum; "I've got her down" (whether he has or no, of course).

"I'm going as high as £17 for her," persists the buyer.

"Well," replies Mr. Blinkum, well knowing that she may be bought by the gang for £14, "if she is knocked down to me, you shall have her at that price."

So the game goes on till the sale is over, and then the gang adjourn to the nearest tavern and the "knocking-out" commences. Say there are six in the gang. Each one produces his catalogue, with the articles knocked down to him notified. The case of Mr. Blinkum and the sorrel mare, however, will illustrate the whole proceeding.

"Lot 21—anybody want it?" asks Mr. B.

Nobody wants it. One of the clique, however, remarks that, since it was knocked down at £13, Mr. B. could afford to stump up handsomely for his bargain.

"I'll give you a crown each to go out" (out of the transaction), remarks Mr. B.

"I shan't take it," observes a conspirator.

"Then take the mare, and give us a crown each," retorts Mr. B., "with a pound to me for buying her."

This, however, does not meet the objector's views, and he finally agrees, as do the others, to "knock-out" on consideration of receiving seven-and-sixpence, which Mr. B. pays, and has still left a profit of over two pounds on his bargain with the private buyer. In all probability the gang have at least twenty lots to discuss, resulting in the division of a very pretty spoil.

Thus it is that so universally is that near relative of the rogue family, Jeremy Diddler, supposed to be the patron saint of the genus Equus and all that pertains thereto, that he must have been a bold man who first ventured to embark in the horse-dealing business with the steady determination to elevate it to at least the ordinary standard of commercial respectability, to establish a public auction differing from that of Messrs. Betty and Martingale, and Mr. Spavinger, inasmuch as a man utterly unknowing in equine matters might venture in and buy a horse or a carriage with the certainty that he will not be chaffed by stable ruffians or fleeced by the common horse-sale shark; and that, whatever he may pay for his nag, he will be made thoroughly acquainted with its faults and failings, if it have any—a repository where the seller may with confidence bestow his property and regard its careful keeping as guaranteed. No little perseverance was required to convince the public that the St. Martin's Lane Repository was only superior to old Mr. Spavinger's yard as the gambling hells of the Haymarket are superior to the skittle-ground attached to the " Pig and Whistle ; " while the host of " knockers-out " and " chaunters " and " copers," hearing of the scheme, set it down as the old dodge with a new cloak, and imagined that, by washing their faces and wearing white neckcloths, they could entirely meet the new rules. They have, however, discovered their mistake long ago, and gone back to Mr. Spavinger's, while the public are brought to understand that the purchase of a horse does not necessarily involve meddling either with edged tools or foul ones, and that by the exercise of ordinary discrimination the first essential to equestrianism may be obtained as easily as a new coat or a pound of cigars.

VIII.

THE BOAT OF ALL-WORK.

IT didn't rain "cats and dogs" nor "pitchforks;" it simply rained very hard, indeed; likewise it blew very hard; and having doubts about the stability of the ribs of my umbrella, I turned into a little archway in the Strand to wait till the bluster abated a bit. Though narrow, it was a deep archway—so deep that vision was baulked by the gloom that crept up from the latter end of it, wherever that might be. There was shelter for fifty people at least; and, standing there alone, I could not help thinking what simpletons the drenched pedestrians were not to do as I was doing.

"Now, sir, the boat!"

Full tilt against the notion that I had the archway all to myself, the observation rather startled me; but, finding that it emanated from no more formidable individual than a wizened old fellow in an overwhelming tarpaulin coat and a sou'-wester with ear-lappets, I at once recovered my self-possession, and addressed the lunatic, "Which boat, my friend? what about a boat?"

"Every quarten 'our, and it's just up, if you're agoin'," issued from between the monstrous ear-lappets. Then, seeing that I was still somewhat perplexed, he good-naturedly explained: "The *Perseverance* and the *Grasshopper*, and them—the 'a'penny boats, don't you know? Down here takes you to 'em."

Down there? Absurd! My first impression was the

correct one. The poor old gentleman was deranged. Some ancient waterman, once jolly and young, but ousted from his occupation by steamboats, and devoting the remnant of his life to the burking of his enemy's adherents. Gazing awfully down the murky, vaulted lane into which the villain had endeavoured to entice me, I pondered for a moment on my lucky escape, and then, casting up my eyes thankfully, saw—

Saw that I had been shamefully unjust to the little man in tarpaulin. This *was* the road to the halfpenny steamboat pier; a board at the entrance to the cavern announced it, and that no mistake might occur, furnished a painted hand, with a finger pointing spectrally into the impenetrable gloom. I no longer regarded the old man as a dangerous enemy, but as a true friend. Thanks to the weak ribs of my umbrella in the first place, and him in the second, there was about to be elucidated a mystery that had troubled me for years.

So many years, indeed, is it since the matter began to trouble me that I was still so small a boy as to be unable to look over a bridge without climbing on one of the recess seats. So elevated, many a time have I watched the plain, low-squatting steamboats in question, ever dingy, ever slow, ever freighted with men who wore shabby jackets and who smoked short pipes, and by women just so lip-laden, and who wore cast-off coachman's coats in the winter, and silk pocket-handkerchiefs on their shoulders and inverted bonnets on their heads in the summer. Strewn about the decks of the boats, invariably, were big bags of old clothes and boots and shoes, and pyramids of scaly hampers bursting with soles and other fish, and baskets full of oranges and all sorts of nuts.

Of course there was nothing mysterious—nothing remarkable even—in all this; but what *was* remarkable (without doubt it would occur to a child sooner than to a man) was the air of *drudgery* that pervaded the length and breadth of the vessel. On working days it is, of course, the rule to find the bees of the world's hive wearing business airs as well as business garments, but work is by no means incompatible with cheerfulness. Moreover, public conveyances are regarded as mediums of pleasure as well as business, or why does the 'bus-driver wear a rose at his button-hole, or steamboat captains indulge in cigars when a pipe of humble birdseye would afford them as much gratification, and at a much cheaper rate? Why is the scraping of fiddles, the twanging of harps, and the dulcet notes of concertinas allowed on board steamers that ply between the bridges, if the proprietors are not aware that idle, aimless pleasure-seekers comprise a fair percentage of their passengers?

On board the *Perseverance* and the *Grasshopper*, however, things are managed very differently. No harp and violin, no cigar-smoking captain, no busy venders of "comic broadsheets;" all dull, and dreary, and weary-looking, as men are when unremuneratively "hard at it." For all that the "captain" looks like one, he might be a hardworking lighterman recently pressed into the service; and as he pensively rests his big hairy arms on the pipe through which he converses with the sooty man who, buried in the bowels of the vessel, feeds the roaring fire and tends the engine, you might fancy him pining for a haul at a pair of stout barge-oars. As for the passengers, they are either going to market, and full of anxious wonder how they will "find things," and how far their bit of money will go, or else they are returning from market, and, having made good bargains, full of business anxiety to get home and realise; or, not seeing their way very clearly in the matter of their recent purchase, plunged in a slough of arithmetic, and endeavouring to extricate themselves by hideous contortions of countenance and by all sorts of nervous outspreading and handling of their dirty fingers and thumbs—it being no uncommon thing when the numbers, by reason of their exceeding ten, become embarrassing, for a man to borrow a digit or so of his neighbour, or for himself to mark farthings and fractions with a bit of chalk on his various knuckles. The good ship, meanwhile, as though conscious of the dead weight of work—of the sweating and bone-grinding for bread ever burdening her—seems to have altogether lost her spirits and the buoyancy natural to the boat tribe, and to have settled down a hard-working cobbler—(no, not a cobbler; cobblers whistle at their work and play at skittles on Mondays)—a hard-working tailor of a steamer, bending low at its work, and content to fag from morning till night for the small consideration of a boiler full of water and an occasional feed of coals.

The melancholy aspect of the business alone at first occurred to me; its wonderful feature did not strike me for some time; when it did, this was it. The *Perseverance* and the *Grasshopper*, and one or two other drudges of the same family, were ever busy, ever humbly wriggling their way with their heads to the east or to the west; but whither were they bound? At what point on the Thames coast did the fish and fruit mongers take ship, and where did they disembark? My inquiries on the subject led to nothing definite. I learnt that the "'a'penny" ones owned but two piers on the river, and that one of them was "near Hungerford," and the other "just a stone's throw from London Bridge." So instructed, I have sought diligently for the places in question, but never could discover them. About London Bridge were steamboat piers enough; but the cheapest of them had the fare—one penny—so conspicuously displayed as to make inquiry mere impertinence; "near Hungerford" my explorations were equally diligent and equally fruitless. Having so far explained the business, the reader will the better understand the pleasure it gave me to find myself fairly on the track of the mysterious vessels.

Adopting the guidance of the spectral finger, I plunged into the gloomy alley, but, alas! speedily wished myself in the open Strand again; for, by-and-by, tiring of the length of the dismal lane, and fearing that I had mistaken the road, I turned off into the first opening that presented itself, and went blundering on till I found myself involved in that horrid vaulted maze formed by the "dark arches" of the Adelphi. There, looming through the foul murk that enveloped the dreadful place, were the carts and waggons in which slept, till ousted by the police, the tramps and the houseless beggars. In sly nooks and corners were little heaps of straw and tan where the "regular" dark-arch lodgers slept. Here and there upon the arch-walls were green brands left by the river at its last rising, and more than once the squeaking and scrambling of rats were plainly audible. Thankful was I presently to arrive at a gap between the arches where the blessed light of day shone down, and there I resolved to wait till somebody happened to pass, and of whom I could inquire a way out of the pretty pickle I had got into.

I had not to wait long. First came the footsteps and voices, and then the forms of a troop of men and women with fish-baskets and fruit-baskets, and crockery such as is bartered for old clothes from door to door. "Pray," asked I of a man who, having but a little load of fish, could afford to pause for a moment, "Pray, is this the way to the halfpenny steamboat?"

"Well, this is *one* way," replied he. "This is the way we coves comes, 'cos it's a near cut. 'Spectable coves, like you, comes down Ivy Bridge Lane, side of the clock-shop in the Strand. Howsomever, 'taint worth while to go back. You keep straight down, and turn to the left, and you'll get to where they takes the 'a'pence."

Following his injunctions, I finally arrived at a mite of a public-house propped, as it were, on stilts out of the river mud, and embowered in some sort of verdant mass that probably was ivy, but it was so enveloped in the substantial fog peculiar to certain parts of the Thames shore that I could not see very distinctly. I could just make out the sign of the house, however. It was the "Fox under the Hill."

Nearly opposite to the "Fox" was the hutch where sat the man who took the steamboat halfpence. If the business stirring that morning might be taken as a fair sample of halfpenny steamboat trading it might without hesitation be quoted as "brisk." It quite dazzled the sight to watch the dirty paw of the cashier within the hutch ever darting like a nimble, fine-legged spider at the halfpence pitched with that air of freedom that distinguishes the British costermonger on to the little board fronting the pigeon-hole. Likewise, if the passengers about to embark in the *Endeavour* represented a fair average, the charwomanish aspect of that worthy vessel at once ceased to be wonderful. Starting on the service in the most cheery way, and with every plank and spar about her as lithe and elastic as the sole use of ash and yew could render them, a score of trips could not fail to bring her to her knees, spiritless and jaded as the most elderly "slop hand" in the employ of those celebrated merchant "clippers"—A 1, and copper-hearted—Noses and Sons.

As I expected, I found no nonsense on board the *Endeavour*. The fittings were painted an appropriate lead colour; the forms were square, thick-legged, and substantial; no absurd caution decorated the base of the funnel concerning the impropriety of smoking abaft it; while as for any announcement advising you to abstain from conversation with the man at the wheel it was rendered quite unnecessary by the sullen and melancholy that characterised the steersman's purple visage. Looking down into the engine-room, you at once saw that the frivolities of rottenstone and polishing rags were despised. The *Endeavour's* engine, as the stoker who came up for a moment's breath of fresh air informed me, was meant for work, not to be laughed at by old women and bumpkins from the country, when I mentioned to him the fact that the day before I had seen on board a penny boat the engine rods and valves lustrous as plate-glass, and wearing in a handy chink a sprig of sweetwilliam, as a well-got-up and ponderous swell might wear a flower in his coat button-hole. The stoker growled a derisive laugh, and remarked that he expected soon to see the captains of "they boats a wearing of cocked hats, and the call-boys with welwet tights and calves."

To return, however, to the passengers. There were big brawny men, with their garments spangled with the stale scales of fish, and wearing broadwise deep baskets likewise scaly, but speckled red by yesterday's strawberries, the owners, as it will happen when there is "nothing at the gate" (Billingsgate), being driven from his customary fishy path to invest his market-money at the "garden" (Covent Garden). There were big, brawny women, with great baskets, bound for Shorter Street, Spitalfields, the chief mart for all sorts of flawed and damaged crockery, to be bartered for "old clo'!" "Old clo'!" made its appearance in tremendous quantities in casks, and bags, and bundles, from the fashionable bonnet shapelessly crushed, but still brilliant, to mildewed castors, boots, and slipshod dancing-shoes. Beside the blousy and freckled traffickers in these and other sorts of goods, there were others, scores of them, who surely had no money to take to market, nothing to buy, nothing to sell, but who, tattered, torn, and hungry, were bound to the docks or thereabouts to see if a job might be picked up. Being hungry, say you, why not avoid the luxury of riding and tramp it afoot, comforting the belly with a little bread the while? Because, after calculations as profound as those of men who buy and sell money as though it were taken in nets at sea, or who dabble up to their chins—up to the very steps, and over and above the chimney-pots of their Brompton villas—in tallow or palm oil; because, having pondered on their empty condition, and on the inability of man to hoist and carry huge weights when foot-weary as well as empty, they resolve that to part with the precious halfpenny is to be a gainer; or, perhaps, having regarded the approaching dissolution of their patch-fretted boots, it is evident economy to ride in a steamboat at the rate of a farthing a mile.

IX.

THE BONES OF LONDON.

WHAT becomes of them all? Assuming that the weight of an animal's skeleton is a twentieth of its entire carcase, and that the weekly consumption of beef, pork, and mutton, in London, averages 10,000 tons, the question is a little more puzzling than at first appears. It is a question, however, that concerns womenfolk rather than men, and womenfolk answer it. "It is easy enough to explain what becomes of the nasty things," says the mistress; "they are Betsy's perquisites." Betsy experiences no difficulty in advancing the inquiry another stage, and in a way equally lucid and satisfactory as her mistress.

"They goes to the rag-shop," says Betsy. So they do, O paragon of all-work! That, beyond dispute, is a phase of their career, whatever else may happen to them. They may be hoarded by the thrifty, thrown into the dust-bin by the improvident; they may come to the dogs, even; but to the rag-shop they are inevitably carried.

Who cares what becomes of them after that? With the "picking" of a bone its existence as an article of utility is popularly supposed to terminate. Nothing of the kind. Its career is, as it were, but just commenced; it had not even attained its proper growth till the day when it ceased to be a sheep's leg-bone and became a leg-of-mutton bone, and the basket into which Betsy casts it is not its coffin but its cradle. Don't despise the unwholesome, mildewed-looking thing should you by accident encounter it a month after it entertained you at dinner. You can't afford to despise it. You may meet it again under very different circumstances. In a gorgeous brown crackling coat it may yet grace your dining-table; you may be under obligations to it for the exquisite flavour of your next spring lamb. You will, moreover, be pleased not to regard this resurrectionist warning as a low and greasy attempt at funny writing, but as a serious fact, and one vouched for by chemists and philosophers of all schools and classes. Bone manure is, of course, at the bottom of the secret.

However, the preparation of bones for manure was not the commencement of the business—that is, of the business I saw transacted at the factory I visited. It is not often a public scribe gets the chance of a subject all to himself; but, from some unaccountable reason, a popular description of bone crushing, and dissolving, and boiling has not hitherto been written. Perhaps the inodorous nature of the business may have to do with it. Well, I confess that, as I approached the waterside premises, and was greeted by a remarkably high-flavoured breeze, and saw looming in the distance the grimy chimney-shafts and the long row of waggons and carts waiting their turns to be delivered of their osseous burdens, I began to feel faint-hearted and inclined to retreat. I may here state, however, that in this case, as in many another of a like kind, beyond the unpleasant smell, there is nothing objectionable. Dr. Wynter informs us that men and women employed among the apparently pestilential heaps in dust-yards enjoy even more than ordinarily good health; and that twenty tradesmen called promiscuously together, compared with twenty "sewer-flushers" (the reader has doubtless seen these fellows with high boots and big lanterns who descend into the bowels of the City through iron-capped traps in the pavement), the flushers were found to be sounder and healthier as a body than the shopkeepers. In the case of this bone-factory at Lambeth, the proprietor for more than twenty years has lived and brought up a large family in a house at the end of the yard, and surrounded on all sides by crushing-sheds and boiling-sheds, and immense ranges of buildings where the raw material is stored. Some years ago, when this factory-owner was indicted as the perpetrator of a public nuisance, he triumphantly brought forward a blooming flock of big and little boys and girls who had breathed the factory atmosphere from their birth. The workmen about the premises fare no worse than the resident proprietor. I have it from the lips of the men themselves—and many of them have laboured at the mills and the boilers for ten and fifteen years—that illness is extremely rare amongst them, and that during the last terrible visit of cholera—nowhere so destructive as in the low-lying parts of Lambeth and Vauxhall—not a single "hand" at the bone-mills was affected. An ignorant man, however, averse to scientific explanation, and led by the nose, might be pardoned for entertaining an opinion at variance with that to be deduced from the above facts. Entering the factory-gate, the evidence offered his visual organs might reasonably lead to agreement with the verdict already arrived at by his nose. The place is paved with bones, walled with bones; there are mountains of them to the right and to the left, and breast-high they hedge avenues leading to the various departments. One of these departments is devoted to cookery. It is a long, low shed, and may be called the kitchen of the establishment. The cooking utensils are a row of immense coppers capable of containing, I am afraid to say how many gallons, and the cooks are big, hairy-armed men, in heavy woollen frocks and coarse sack aprons. Ladles and spoons are dispensed with, and their place supplied by pitchforks. As I stand at a respectful distance, and, peering through the rank mist that fills the kitchen, see the great cauldrons foaming, pitchy black, and their heavy lids heaving and stirring uneasily, I find my faith in the innocuous quality of the business flagging,—staunch Dr. Wynter even serving as an imperfect comforter. I am not reassured by the proprietor; for, says he, "Don't go closer; you may find the ammonia too much for you." Yet there were the cooks as contented and as cheerfully busy as bees in a hive.

Another department was the mill-room, where the

bones, after their gelatine had been extracted in the boiling process, were reduced to atoms. Here there was nothing to offend the nose, for the material divested of its fatty matter is as innoxious as wood chips; but the ears suffer dreadfully. The mill is simply an arrangement of toothed iron rollers, among which the bones are swept by a man who stands by a sort of slanting stage above, on which the bones are heaped, and from which he scrapes them with an iron scraper. Nevertheless, the unfortunate particles of skeletons, in passing through the revolving teeth, emit a sound of crushing, and crunching, and grinding, impossible to anything but bones, and terribly suggestive of corporal suffering, the extraction of firmly-bedded molars and incisors not to be forgotten.

The value of bone as a manure, although discovered more than a hundred years since, has only been taken full advantage of since about 1815, when bone-mills were established in Yorkshire. Previous to that, on estates where bone manure was used, the material was reduced to handy bits by the application of a hammer, or else it was strewn in the cart tracks to be crushed by the action of the wheels. How it is that the chief substance that enters into the composition of bone is good to fatten the land is easy of explanation. The principal chemical ingredient in bone is phosphate of lime — fifty-three in a hundred of its parts are so composed. Vegetable life is largely dependent on phosphates for its growth and maintenance: so largely, indeed, that should the soil become exhausted of that principle, the crops raised thereon are sickly and weak, and scarcely worth the harvesting. This was the case in Cheshire at the end of the last century, and was doubtless occasioned by the constant and long-continued drain of the soil of its phosphorus in shape of corn and dairy produce. The rich red sandstone loams of the district were worn out—sucked dry, as farmers say. More by way of experiment than as a certain remedy, the exhausted pasture land was dressed with bone manure at the rate of a ton to the acre, and in less than three years the value of the said land was doubled. The turnip hungers for phosphates more than any other vegetable. It has so small a seed that the quantity of phosphates stored round it for the nourishment of the roots and leaves of the young plant is in a poor soil by no means adequate to the demand; hence the necessity of concentrating by artificial means the vital element about the tiny seed, else those other essentials to turnip life — carbonic acid, water, and ammonia—may abound to as little purpose as a windmill without wind. So it comes about that your discarded mutton bone of to-day nurses and comforts next spring's vegetation, and the ox eats thereof—the tender grass, the matured hay, and the juicy turnip—and waxes sturdy and stout of limb, and fat enough to be brought to market, and to be bought by Mr. Brisket, your butcher, who sends you a joint of the beast, and you are afforded an opportunity of renewing acquaintance with an old friend.

In 1839 Liebig suggested that the efficacy of bone-dust as a manure might be vastly increased if it were dissolved in sulphuric acid. A part of the Lambeth manufactory is set apart for this purpose. Here is sunk a deep pit containing a great iron tank, in which the mixing takes place, 15 cwt. of the acid being added to every ton of bone-dust. The result of the incorporation is a heavy slate-coloured soft powder, worth from five to eight guineas per ton As, however, the animal matter still remaining in the bone-dust is a hindrance to the blending of the acid with the earthy matter, there is mixed with it a considerable proportion of bone-*ash* from which every particle of gelatinous matter has been extracted, and which materially assists the sulphuric acid in its action. Bone-ash is obtained by the complete combustion of bones in an open furnace, where the oxygen of the air burns away the organic matter, and leaves the earthy constituents as a white friable mass. If, on the other hand, the bone—say a shin-bone—be immersed in an acid sufficiently diluted to prevent its injuring the animal membrane, and yet strong enough to dissolve the phosphate of lime, the remaining matter will still retain the exact figure and dimensions of the original bone, and yet be rendered so flexible that it may be tied in a knot.

It must not be supposed, however, that all the bones that pass through the gates of the Lambeth factory are either ground or melted as manure. Some of them are much too valuable to be so used; as, for instance, the leg bones of the ox. I was shown tons of these with the knobs at the ends sawn off, some in cisterns sunk in the floors and still undergoing the bleaching process, and others stored in great barrels, as beautifully white as ivory. Large quantities of these are sent to France and other parts of Europe, and converted into handles for tooth and shaving-brushes, children's gum-rings, knife handles, and cheap combs.

A considerable portion of the Lambeth bone-works is adapted to the manufacture of soap from the fatty matter obtained from the bones. Did space permit, much interesting matter might be written concerning the various processes; of the coppers, broad and deep enough to drown a dozen men, and of the mysteries of "mottled," and "yellow," and "primrose," together with their comparative merits. One little bit of information that I gleaned concerning soap may be of value to the thrifty British matron, and she is heartily welcome to it. Beware of cheap soap, however proper its appearance may be. "This," said the worthy soapmaker, handling a "bar" of unexceptional "yellow," "is as good as the article can be. This"—he took down another sample, seemingly of equal quality—"is cheaper by at least a third." "Inferior material, of course." "Nothing of the sort, sir! The same material exactly, with this difference—the cheaper sort (people *will* have cheapness, you know) contains a compensating amount of *water*. It is so full of it that it is a difficult matter to cut the great block into bars, but the bars are immediately subjected to such a heat as dries the outer surface and cakes it hard, giving it the sound and substantial appearance it now wears."

X.

MR. DODD'S DUST-YARD.

AS the ground was covered with snow, and the weather so bitterly cold, that had the mercury in the glass grown six degrees taller freezing point would still have had the start of it, I was in doubt whether Mr. Dodd's "eliminators" would be at work. So I intimated to the "yard foreman," at whose house I called one morning at the extremity of the year. As, however, that polite person pronounced that "nothing but rain licked 'em," I buttoned up my great coat, while he lit his pipe and rolled up the sleeves of his blue guernsey, and we set off.

There are several "yards" connected with the establishment; but the one I wanted was that devoted to dust, and I found it between the stabling department and another, set apart for the reception of monstrous slopcarts and all else pertaining to scavengering. The dust-yard was, as near as I could guess, about a hundred and fifty feet wide and seventy broad, one end opening on to the main street and the other to the Regent's Canal. Flanking one side of the yard were a score or so of upreared dustcarts, and on the other side, extending almost from the outer gate to the water's brink, were great mounds of ordinary dustbin muck; and in the midst of the mounds—literally, so that in many cases part only of their bodies were visible—were thirty or forty women and girls. In view of the canal, the surface covered with big slabs of yellow ice,—with a rasping north wind blowing continuously through the yard, and with frost and snow everywhere to be seen, there sat the

MR. DODD'S DUST-YARD.

"hill-women," girls of sixteen and old dames of sixty, each holding before her a sieve as large as the top of a small loo-table, in which she dexterously caught the huge shovelful supplied by the "feeder," all as busy as bees, and as cheerful.

As a body, the females evinced by their attire little taste and less premeditation: indeed, in most cases they presented an appearance of having crawled through a bundle of rags, trusting entirely to chance as to the part of it from which their heads might emerge. It is only just, however, to mention that the above remarks applied chiefly to elderly parties, ladies who had outlived the frivolities of youth; but maidens there were much more scrupulous, wearing the bonnet fully trimmed and fashionably off their heads, revealing tresses copiously oiled and evenly parted. Respecting this latter feature, the advantage of having light hair was plainly manifest; in all such cases the parting was plainly distinguishable as a dusty lane between two hedges; whereas with ladies of raven locks all that was observable was a centre channel, suggestive of the system of drainage patronised by our forefathers, and still to be seen in ancient alleys. Most of the ladies wore coarse, fingerless gloves, and all of them had great lace-up boots, such as carmen wear, and great sackcloth aprons, such as few carmen would care to be burdened with.

Conversing afterwards with a gentleman in the employ of the firm, said he, "How they exist is marvellous. They are here these bitter mornings before half London have left their beds, and they stay here till dark. I suppose they have some sort of breakfast before they come, and something more when they get home; they'd need, for all they get to eat between times is hardly worth mentioning. Meat is entirely out of the question. A lot of them club together, and about twelve o'clock one makes a fire of breeze and brews an old kettleful of weak tea, and this, with a slice or two of bread, or at most a herring, is their dinner, year in and year out." To look at them, however, such a suspicion would never enter one's mind. I have been amongst factory-workers and "mill-hands," and market-garden women, and assistants at City establishments, but I never yet met a body of female labourers looking so thoroughly healthy and jolly. Every one was fat, every one was rosy, and laughing and singing as though it were capital fun to grovel among the refuse of the town out in the open air—a Siberian air, bleak and withering. The least likely-looking of the company was a corpulent lady, aged about fifty, and with her jaws bound round with a red rag; but even she was not so poorly but that she puffed away at a hideous little pipe with an appetite, and which, without taking her hands from the sieve, she dexterously shifted to the corner of her mouth so as to admit of her swelling the chorus of a ditty a leather-lunged young Irishwoman was at the time singing.

I have since ascertained—and I am thankful for the discovery—that my impressions as to the healthiness of these toilers amongst filth and ashes were not erroneous. I have Dr. Guy's authority for stating that, despite their constant and immediate contact with the most loathsome refuse, they are among the healthiest of our working population. The medical authority in question states them to be a "healthy, ruddy-complexioned race—the healthiest set of men I have ever seen. I do not think, whether in town or country, such another body of men could be brought together, except by selection. It is not going too far to assert of them that, if the comparison were limited to the inhabitants of London, or our large towns, no score of selected tradesmen could be found to match the same number of dustmen brought casually together." It would seem from this startling statement that sanitarians who protest against neglected dust-heaps do not know what they are talking about, and that the Board of Health is quite mistaken in prosecuting owners of reeking dust-bins. It should, however, be borne in mind that, during the operation of sifting, the dust is exposed in an open space. Despite the well-known power of ashes to absorb every sort of noxious emanation, if the hill-women pursued their labours in a covered building the results would doubtless be very different. To return, however, to the dust-yard. I observed that every sifter had near at hand two or three old baskets, and that each time she called out "sarve," and a youth, by tipping into her ready sieve a shovelful from a "raw" heap "sarved" her, she gave the fresh supply a handy twist, so as to spread the material over the entire surface of the sieve, and proceeded to deal with it in a way that I could not readily understand. Resting the outer edge of the great sieve against the heap before her, and its other extreme on her knees, she dived into it with both her hands, and went through a series of evolutions that, for rapidity, were unmatched by any conjurer I ever yet saw. Whatever it was she plucked from the sieve, was tossed over her left shoulder, over her right shoulder, and under either arm, and never failed to find a lodgment in one or other of the baskets.

"What is she picking out?" inquired I of my guide.

"She's picking out heverything," replied he. "She's picking 'hard-core,' and 'fine-core,' and rags, and bread, and bones, and bits of metal, and cabbage-stumps, and that sort of awful (offal), and bits of iron, and old tin pots, and old boots and shoes, and paper, and wood, likewise broken glass. After that's done, she can get along with the breeze and ashes straightfor'ard."

"She retains the scraps you have enumerated as perquisites, I presume?" I observed.

"Oh no, she don't!" replied Mr. Scorch, shaking his head vigorously. "She retains only what's give to her, and that's the wood. She don't retain nothing else—leastways, not if *I* know it."

"Oh, indeed! all claimed by Mr. Dodd, eh?"

"Wrong again, sir; it's all claimed by *me*, and I'll tell you how it's worked. Mr. Dodd employs so many 'collectors'—dustmen as you call them. They go about the parts the governor contracts for, getting ten shillings a week, besides what they have give them, and being obliged to bring in so many loads a day. For a certain sum I undertake to sift every load and get out of it, for the governor, the breeze, the ashes, the manure, and the 'core' (broken crockery, oyster-shells, broken bottles, &c.,

used for the foundation of new roads). All the other stuff my women find in the dust belongs to me."

"And you find the rubbish worth saving, eh?"

"Rubbish! worth saving!" ejaculated the foreman. "Well, I should *rather* say I did. You see that building over there?" pointing out an extensive brick edifice, crowned with a tall chimney. "Well, the *rubbish*, as you call it, is so well worth saving that our master went to a precious many hundred pounds' expense that it might be made the most of. It's my warehouse, that building is, where my rag-sorters, and rag-washers, and rag-driers work, and where I store everything that is found out here that may be turned into money. Come and look at it."

He led the way through the great yard, and close to the edge of the canal I found the building with the tall shaft he had pointed out in the distance; and, ascending some steps and pushing open a door, we entered. With a creak the door banged to, and suddenly I found myself in the most curious of all the curious places it ever was my fortune—good or bad—to set foot. There was no need for tedious exploration in discovering the wonders. As soon as your foot crossed the threshold of the building, there you were in the midst of them.

"Mind the hole!" sharply ejaculated my guide, and not without reason; for there, dimly revealed in the twilight that filled the place, and within a pace of the door, was a black gulf, broad, wide, and of unknown depth, filled within a few feet of the floor's surface with old shoes and boots!—thousands, tens of thousands of them; all sorts, all sizes; baby's first little strapped shoe, hustled into and peeping out at the gaping toe of the dilapidated "Wellington," the huge "ankle-jack," the tramp's boot, with the iron-plated heel worn all aslant, the heavy uppers botched with twine-sown patches (a wayside job, evidently), and mutilated "tongues," now lolling at rest above the leather thongs, but plainly revealing the derivation of the patch-pieces; the dainty satin dancing-shoe cuddled into the russet, lime-burned foot-casing of the burly brickmaker; the still substantial gouty shoe, longer lived than its master; the narrow-waisted, fashionable abomination, cursed through its life, and at last joyfully kicked off because of its corn-inducing propensities: here they were, some blue with mildew, some still bearing traces of a polish, and some half eaten by rats; here they were, as many shoes and boots at the very least as there are legs at a gallows show.

"Of what use are they?" inquired I of Mr. Scorch, who evidently regarded me as curiously as I regarded his old boots.

"Jews," responded Mr. Scorch, with a mysterious wink, "they knows what to do with 'em better than we do, mister. What do you think of this lot?"

The "lot" in question consisted of crumpled-up paper of every texture and colour, about a ton in weight, and all of it tolerably clean. I thought it a rather valuable heap, and told him so.

"You are right," said he. "I get half-a-crown a hundred for it." Mr. Scorch again winked, and in a very artful way, as he named the tremendous sum; but when I reflected that the price he received for his waste paper was fifty shillings a ton, and that of the article re-made ranged from forty to seventy pounds for the same quantity, it seemed to me that by looking about him he might possibly find a better market.

The next article he introduced to my notice bore so unsightly and valueless an appearance that the affectionate way in which he patted and poked it considerably surprised me. It was contained in a huge basket, and more than anything resembled odd corners and chunks of muddy wood, or broken, half-burnt bricks.

"We find a tidy lot of that, and I wish we found a lot more," said he. "It's first-rate stuff, that is."

"For burning?" was my natural observation.

"Oh, no," replied he; "for eating. It's bread—pigs' wittles!"

"Come down here," said Mr. Scorch, leaping down into the shoe-gulf, "and I'll show you my wash-house."

Not without a twinge of nervousness I too leaped and strode after him towards a dark passage. Just, however, as

XI.

THE COUNTY COURT.

THE first and last and only taste of law I ever indulged in was at a County Court. It is a long time ago, and I was new in the brain market when Judas M'Swill, the publisher, demurred to the liquidation of a little account of mine. Litigation was never to my mind, and it was not until I had seriously impaired a pair of double-soled shoes in " calling again," that I appealed to one of her Majesty's Commissioners, who promptly cited Judas and I to appear before him that the matter might be settled. It *was* settled. Judas paid the money, and has I hope by this time recovered the painful extraction. I have spent the money, and forgotten even what I bought with it, so we will say no more about it. Indeed, the little affair would never have been mentioned at all, only, as I was bound to account in some way for my presence at so undesirable a place, I saw no particular reason why truth should suffer.

About the ways of the Court, therefore, or the laws which regulate its working, I am as ignorant, as I should wish to remain. I don't even know for certain whether or no a man who owes a debt, and won't or can't pay it, may be remitted to prison from time to time for the term of " forty days," and for all the days of his life ; and am by no means assured of the accuracy of the popular belief that you may with impunity owe a man threepence-halfpenny, or threepence threefarthings even—that you may at once embark in the business founded by Jeremiah Diddler, and, while you keep your individual defalcations

THE COUNTY COURT.

at threepence-threefarthings, may laugh your creditors to scorn, and defy them to set the law at you. But beware of owing the other farthing. That is the other little coin that breaks the back of the law's patience. Threepence-threefarthings, if you please; throw in another fourth of a penny, and up goes the County Court Commissioner.

I certainly might have ascertained more about these matters if, instead of lingering about the lobby till the crier cried "Greenfinch v. M'Swill!" I had remained in the body of the Court and joined the bare-headed motley crowd that, thick as cattle in a cattle-ship, crowded the narrow space that fronted the judicial bar. Here again my ignorance of County Court practice bothers me. Ten o'clock is the hour at which the doors of the Court are opened, and at ten o'clock the whole number of plaintiffs and defendants concerned in the day's business—to the number of at least three hundred—are bound to attend; and, packed in the stifling justice-room, hanging about the stone-paved lobby, or beguiling the time at the public-house next door, and over the way, and round the corner, wait till their "case" comes on, which may happen at twelve, two, or four o'clock, according to the programme. The sum for which County Court litigants may set the curious machinery of the law in motion is certainly very low, and they can scarcely, while enjoying the sweet spectacle, expect first-class accommodation at third-class fare here any more than elsewhere; but why they should be condemned to corn-crushing and suffocation before ever their causes are tried seems, to an ignorant mind, somewhat inexplicable.

It was a curious mob that crowded that mite of a Court. There were placid-faced debtors, with whom owing money was a natural weakness, and one they were perfectly resigned to; and shame-faced debtors, who, perspiring freely, keep in the rear of bulky people, and who were in agonies when a move in the business shifted their screen and exposed their guilty presence to the majority of the assembly; there were saucy debtors, who from the shadow of their bonnets regarded their creditors defiantly, and with a wag of the head that plainly expressed, "Much good you will get by *this* business, my friend;" and meek, used-up, listless debtors, on whom the shadow of the "forty days" had already fallen, who were used to "forty days," and regarded their advent with dull eyes, significant of spirits whipped to rags by adversity. Of the genus *Creditor* the samples were as numerous. There was the hard-faced, bullet-headed man, looking as pugnacious at least as a "second" at a prize-fight, and who had come there to "have it out," who looked out constantly for the Judge's eye, and when he caught it smiled at his Worship in a friendly way, and winked softly, as much as to say, "*My* case will be on directly; if it don't astonish you, never trust me again." There was the smug-faced "tally" rascal, and his brother, the director of the Cent.-per-Cent. Loan Office, both to be known by the pencil behind their ears and the slip of paper in their hands, and each looking as complacent as might a fox that, having run down and lamed a rabbit, was content to lick his lips awhile and contemplate its picking. Then there was the nervous creditor (as was Greenfinch), whose debtor was cunning and eelish, and might be expected to glide through the meshes of the law, leaving the creditor richer in nothing but experience. Very curious, too, was it to observe the gulpings, and winkings, and mumbling of lips indulged in by plaintiff and defendant and witnesses, conning over the neat things they meant to say to his Worship when come to his awful presence. Ah! those gulpings and winkings! How much good conscience is swallowed and put to sleep during the process! It is terrible to think how much; for it may be safely assumed that in seven cases out of every ten that come before the Judge of the Debtors' Court, A. will solemnly swear that white is black and B. that black is white, so that the real evidence in the case is of no weight at all; and the Judge, on the strength of his experience, awards a verdict to the most modest perjurer of the two.

As a rule, however, when fiscal foemen pass the threshold of the justice-hall, personal feeling is tacitly sheathed, and no more formidable weapons displayed than figures, assertions that are more or less facts, and hard swearing. Decorum is insisted on. Mrs. M'Turvey, who lent her best shawl to Miss Donovan—a favour which that person acknowledged by mortgaging the garment for enough money to enable herself and the bridegroom to get dreadfully tipsy, and while in that state to fall on and maltreat the entire Turvey family—much as the outraged Mrs. M'T. may be stirred by a recital of her injuries, she does not allude to the aggressor in stronger terms than as a "woman" and a "person." The weak-kneed tailor who summonses Mr. Levy for $10\frac{1}{4}d.$, the price for making a pair of the celebrated "Peckham" trousers, is bound, in deference to his Honour's awful presence, to allude to his bone-grinder as "that gentleman." If you would see debtor and creditor *au naturel*, you must not go beyond the lobby of the Court. Here the shoemaker meets his tardy customer, and wishes to know if "things is to go on, or is he to be paid as a gentleman should;" and the general dealer meets the out-o'-work carpenter's wife, and discusses with her the payment of that long bread-and-butter score; and the bland undertaker meets the poor soul in black crape, that she and he may presently stand before the justice-seat to argue why an execution should or should not be levied on the widow's goods. Not that it must be imagined that County Court law is an instrument whose sole use is to aid the strong Right against the unfortunate Wrong, or to hamper the feet of those steeped in misery till nearly drowned. Without its intervention much roguery would go unchecked, and simple honesty go lean, while clever chicanery fattened. It is the disciples of this latter school, especially, who are anxious for "lobby" settlements. They evade the Commissioner as the sufferer from toothache evades the dentist, and, to get off quietly, will pay down their money rather than have it forcibly extracted by judicial forceps.

Within the lobby, and lurking about the outer steps, may any hour of the day be seen dodging and worming in and about the disputatious throng, restless as ants and impudent as flies, certain sharp-shanked, seedy sharks, who, having somehow picked up a few scraps of legal knowledge, set up as public advisers on a small scale. They don't pretend to fees (they know enough of criminal law not to risk *that*). Anything will do, a shilling or sixpence, or—or, indeed, anything but odd half-pence. The tactics of some of this fraternity are ingenious. Brown disputing an account with Robinson, endeavours to settle matters without going into Court. Brown doesn't succeed, and the disputants part company. Long-eared Shark has overheard something of the case and the names of the disputants. Two minutes afterwards Shark taps Brown on the shoulder: "I say now, Mr. Brown," says he, "let me prevail on you to come to some arrangement with Robinson: save hearing-fees, you know; and from what I know of the case, it will certainly go against you." That is, of course, according to his version of the story. "You could put a different complexion on the matter, eh?" "Well, well, don't mind me; I'm no more Robinson's man than yours—just a lawyer friend, who doesn't like to see honest men quarrel." Robinson's lawyer, thinks the affrighted Brown; and for his credit's sake proceeds to put the legal gentleman in possession of the facts of the case, together with the terms he will come to. "And suppose I bring him to accept?" inquires the Shark, significantly. Brown has heard of the constitutional roguery of lawyers, and thinks it nothing very dreadful to avail himself of the perfidy of Robinson's adviser at the expense of half a guinea. Straightway is Brown's overture carried to Robinson, who, making sure from the Shark's knowledge of the case that he is specially retained by Brown, comes to terms, and the business is completed.

As it is generally understood that County Court Judges are apt to favour the victims of the "tally" trader's machinations, and to dislike his representative within the Court, there is another to be found in the lobby with whom "terms"—say the expense of the summons and five shillings for the creditor's trouble paid down, and the weekly payments to go on as usual—may be made. Or perhaps the debtor's employer will be responsible for the debt, or one or two of the tally debtor's neighbours will "put their names" by way of security. I saw one of the above-mentioned Sharks who had pinned what seemed to be an engineer behind a pillar, and, being a little inquisitive to know the Shark's tactics, I leant against the other side of the pillar. "Oh, no!" exclaimed the engineer, "it ain't a tally debt—leastways it ain't *now;* but it was. Three pun' fourteen the bill was last Whitsuntide, and a weskit, and a shawl and a pair of military heels for my missus, was the things. Well, we brought it down to two pun' fifteen, and then I fell slack. Then he comes and he says, 'You're a respectable man; why don't you borrow the money?' Says I, 'I wouldn't like any of my people to know as I wanted it; besides, it ain't so easy to borrow as to talk.' 'Well,' said he, 'borrow it at a loan-office. I wouldn't press you, but I must make up a bill by Tuesday. Borrow it at Sloman's, and I'll be your security. Borrow five pounds, and then you'll have a little for yourself after you've paid me.' So I agreed. Let's see! Two pun' fifteen to him, sixteen and tenpence stopped for interest and that—well, I got about three 'arf-crowns. Now, you know, it stands this way. The tallyman, being my security, was obliged to pay the 'rears of the loan, which it's *all* 'rears, besides a jolly lot of fines; and now he summonses me, which of course it's his right, and I'll pay him if he gives me time. I've got work now, and I'll pay him five shillings a week, if he'll take it." "Ah, well," said the Shark, "I'll go and see what I can do for you." That he did something satisfactory I am pretty well certain, for, on passing up the street shortly afterwards, I saw the engineer and the Shark emerging from a public-house.

XII.

CHRISTMAS EVE IN BRICK LANE.

T is, of course, hard to say, honest poverty is so prodigiously wary of betraying itself; but, if certain signs and tokens are trustworthy, this will not be such a very hard Christmas with the poorest of our brethren.

Nor is this comfortable conclusion based on tabular statements and statistics. It is not because the casual ward of St. Grudgeabone's-in-the-East is not more than half full, or that, in happy consequence of a dearth of applicants, the soup-coppers at the charitable kitchen remain quite full, that I feel authorised to make the cheering announcement. It is because of the state of the market—of Poverty Market. I have spent an hour there, and have seen with my eyes and heard with my ears, and know all about it.

Of these markets there are more than two dozen, probably; but it makes no difference to me, and under the circumstances, for they are all alike—alike as oysters in a barrel. The flavour of one is the flavour of the whole, and the market-places of the poor may be as fairly sampled at a single dip. If Dutch plaice are three-halfpence each in Brick Lane, Bethnal Green, they will be at four for sixpence in Strutton Ground, Westminster—not a farthing more or less. If clod of beef is at fivepence in Leather Lane, a journey to Clare Market, with a view to buying it at fourpence-halfpenny, will be fruitless. The gin-shop doors of Whitecross Street, and the Lower Marsh at Lambeth, and at Brill Row in Somers Town, swing in unison, as though held by a single string; and behind the doors, and between them and the flashy ginshop bars, it is uniformly high tide of roaring, turbulent drunkenness, or dismal low tide and a silent shore—yellow, strewn with sawdust, like the sands of the beach, and waiting for the flood. At such times, when you see Mr. Speckles, of the "Upas Tree," nigh to Liquorpond Street, yawning in discontented idleness, you may, if you happen to be of a speculative turn, take small odds that a hundred similar licensed jaws are elsewhere as dismally ajar.

Or the depth of London poverty may be gauged by a little observation of the frequenters of either of these market-places. Wait until the gas is lit, and then (it should be on a Saturday night or a Christmas Eve) manfully make a plunge, and go with the human tide that rolls and surges through the narrows of, say, Strutton Ground, Westminster. Note the bricklayers, and the masons, and the carpenters—you will know them readily enough; and if you find amongst them a goodly sprinkling of those who, by the angle of their short pipes and the cock of their cap-peaks, are evidently breeches-pocket-proud, you may know without further inquiry that "things are fairish." Likewise, it is a good sign to see flowers in the bonnets of the women, and a "keeper" as well as a wedding-ring adorning the marriage finger; indeed, this latter is a very significant sign, as will be at once understood when it is explained—I have it from a credible party, and one who would not "lend his ears," or indeed anything else, except in matters that were reliable—that, "as soon as ever things get shaky, the 'keeper' and father's Sunday silk handkerchief are the first things put away. One or two may come at brisk times to admit of going to the play or an unexpected raffle, and go with the common run of business and without particular notice; but when they drop in three and four of a morning we know how things are going, and could tell you almost to a day when we should be pretty full of Wellington boots, and fancy waistcoats, and summer shawls and gowns. It's a long chain, if you take the separate links of it; but, lor! how soon it's wound up! If there's a largish family, they'll come at the clock in six weeks; and I tell you, sir, when you see a working man pledging his clock, you may know that he's pretty well wound up. Yes, sir, it's getting close to the wedding-ring then. That I look on as the *last* link in the chain; and it's curious, too, considering how they go together, as one may say, that the keeper should be the first link and the wedding-ring the last."

"Especially," said I, "as the value of this last link—I mean the pecuniary value—must be considerably more than that of many of the other links."

"Well, if you come to that, you know,' said Mr. Backitt, shaking his head dubiously, "upon my word, and although they're lumbersome and take up a deal of room which can be ill spared, I'd rather take in flock beds, and I've a good mind to say flat-irons, than wedding-rings. The worst of it is, the thinner and more worn the things are, there's the more fussing over them. They come cheerful enough sometimes; then they are good thick rings, without more than a year or so of wear taken out of them, and it is buxom young women who bring them, pleasant, and not unwilling to pass a little joke with one; it is the middle-aged and the old women who are the teasers. They never think of pulling off the ring before they get into the box, and there you may see 'em wetting their bony old knuckles, and trying to screw it off with their finger in their mouth, and perhaps piping their eye all the time. You might think the picture was a funny one by only hearing a description of it, but you'd be of quite another mind if you came to see it. The sums they'll ask on the thready old things, too, would frighten one if he was not well used to it; they never think that their wedding-ring is of less value than when they bought it; indeed, I really do believe they think it is *more* valuable; and they'll talk in that earnest way, bless you, that you'll find yourself lending quite the melting price if you are not careful. I generally get out of serving 'em if I can—turn 'em over to my young man—all a business fellow, sir, I can tell you, and will prosper. The old women don't come it over him. 'Now, then! how much on the old hoop?' says he, and then slips it on his little finger, and writes off the ticket as coolly as though he was taking in a dog-collar."

However, to return to my subject at the point where Mr. Backitt broke in upon it. If, as you elbow your way through the crowd in Poverty Market, you discover such signs of prosperity as I have mentioned, you may make your mind easy that business is slack at the workhouse bakeries within and without the city, east, west, north, and south. On the other hand, if the majority of the men you meet wear their heads deep in their capes; if they wear their jackets buttoned high and both their hands in the pockets thereof; if their eyes are downcast, as though good luck had somehow escaped from them into the gutter, and they were there looking for it; if such as have their wives with them allow them to press ahead a pace or so (the reader may have observed how that sometimes when a team came on a bit of heavy road the arrangement of the cattle will be altered, and, until the difficulty is surmounted, the great brown horse gives precedence to the little grey one, who, without half his strength, has six times his capacity for manœuvring and wriggling out of ruts); if the said wives have pursed mouths and eyes eloquent of arithmetic; if their thin shawls hang squarely at the shoulder parts; if at the greengrocer's a monstrous quantity of potatoes are shot into their big-bellied market-baskets, you may know that wherever you meet the poor man in and about London he is "hard up."

If throughout the year there is a season during which more than any other a poor man is in danger of getting "hard up," it is most decidedly at Christmas time. He is so much at the mercy of the weather. If he is a bricklayer or a bricklayer's labourer, or a stonemason, or a plasterer, or a navvy, or a gardener, or any one of a dozen other avocations which might be enumerated, a heavy frost falling in the night debars him from bread-winning as effectually as though fetters had grown to his wrists while he slept; and, without being either a gardener or a bricklayer, it is easy enough to imagine what it must be to the frostbound father of a numerous family, and Christmas within a few days' stage. How the enthralled man must find himself eagerly listening to his wife's prognostications concerning her corns and a change in the weather! How irritated he must feel to hear her grinding at the same superstition at the end of a fortnight, and the frost still pinning the earth with the tenacity of a bulldog at the throat of an enemy! How he must be tempted to kick that provoking cat, who *will* persist in sitting with her back to the fire, a sure indication of frost! Nor is frost the only enemy with whom the poor willing worker has often to contend against for his Christmas beef and pudding. Daylight is but nine hours long; and even though he allow himself no longer midday rest than suffices for the swallowing of his scanty dinner, "three-quarters" is all the time he can make. Cowardly coughs, and fevers, and influenzas attack his little children at their weak and worn boot-soles. The rent collector *must* clear his books, by hook or by crook, he says—and his tenant knows what *that* means—by the twenty-fourth. Dr. Bunney sends his lad with a sharp little note, reminding the already much-perplexed parient that little Charley, who has commenced cutting his teeth, has not yet been paid for! "It never rains but it pours!" says the poor fellow, as, after consulting his good lady, he returns written word by Dr. Bunney's lad that Mrs. Ginnypeg is not very well, and would be glad of a call when Dr. Bunney is coming her way; and that as regards the little bill it would be an accommodation if she is allowed to settle the two together. Poor Mr. Ginnypeg! It's all very fine for the carol singers to bawl "Let nothing you dismay!"

Nevertheless, and all things considered, I should judge from the signs and tokens already hinted at, that the poor man has known Christmases which have caused him much more dismay than the present one. My "market intelligence" is derived from Brick Lane, Bethnal Green; and, goodness knows, if there exists a market deserving the prefix "poverty," this is the one.

I have spent an hour among the fierce gas-jets, and the clash of butchers' knives and steels, and Babel of "Buy, buy, buy!" and I am of opinion that Mr. Ginnypeg's prospects of a Christmas dinner are at least "pretty fair." Mind, I don't by any means wish to convey the idea that I found Brick Lane overflowing with milk and honey—I did not expect to find it so; but, as an honest reporter, I am bound to say that, after all I had recently read of this plague-parish, I expected to find a leaner and more drouthy state of things than appeared.

The butchers' shops, from the first-floor windows to the stall-boards, were hung with ribs, and sirloins, and aitch-bones, and shoulders and legs of mutton fat enough to excite the admiration of an Esquimaux. At Mr. Faggotty's, the pork and sausage shop, there hung a pig of such vast dimensions that made it a wonder, the natural perversity of porcine nature considered, how they ever managed to drive, or back, or sling him through Mr. Faggotty's narrow slaughter-house doorway. There were fat geese, and fat turkeys, and holly-berry devices on bladders of lard in the cheesemongers' windows, and on the surface of half-tubs of butter. Good signs every one of them, and significant of feasting, but not the signs and tokens I especially allude to, for all that.

It was the *absence* and not the presence of certain eatables from Poverty Market that impressed me favourably. Chief of all was the almost entire absence of fish—of fresh fish, understand (of dried, in the form of haddocks and bloaters, there was an unusual quantity, which was satisfactory, inasmuch as it betokened luxuries for tea or breakfast). Now, any one at all conversant with the ways of poverty, knows that the quantity of fish it consumes is enormous. And no wonder. For sixpence a piled-up dish may smoke on the dinner-table; whereas, if the money was invested in butchers' meat, even of the coarsest and scraggiest description, a dinner-plate would contain it, with a fair margin for potatoes. At ordinary times the most conspicuous feature of Poverty Market is fish. Every third stall is a fish-stall; tons of plaice, of soles, and cod are sold in a single market-place in a single day. When fish fails, there is consternation among poor mothers, and general cheerfulness among butchers with mutton-scrags and offal to dispose of.

Yet, to be always having fish for dinner, even though he is fond of it, has about it a smack of poverty under which the poor man does not rest easy. With his fair five shillings a day, he will not object to fish for supper as often as you please; but he'll have beef, or mutton, or bacon for dinner. In fact, his patronage of fish lasts only during his "hard up" periods, and by this token to-night he is *not* hard up; the few straggling fish-stalls have no attraction for him or his wife; their sole attention is for the butchers and the abounding animal fatness about them.

Another ordinary feature of Poverty Market, now pleasantly missed, is the stall whereon is sold penny lots of vegetables for the pot—the three turnips, the onion, the half carrot, and the leak. These are the ingredients which, with a pound of scrap meat, form the family "stew." Doubtless there are worse things than a stew for dinner, but it is not quite the thing for Christmas. If nothing better may be had, why—— But, thank goodness, something better *may* be had this Christmas, and the penny vegetable lots are not wanted. I counted but four from one end of Brick Lane to the other, and even they had cheeringly added horseradish to their business.

Another good sign was that the lemon trade was brisk. Moses and Isaac, while they despise the great Christian festival, were not above making a shilling out of it, and elbowed their way through with their mat baskets over their shoulder and a double handful of the yellow fruit, shouting "two a peddy lebbod" as earnestly as though their lives depended on the sale. Now the lemon and destitution are not likely to be found together; one can scarcely imagine a dinnerless family sitting round a yearning firegrate sucking lemons. No; the lemon is good, for its peel sake, in the manufacture of apple-pies; it is desirable as adding pungency to the glass of grog. Probably it is useful in many other ways; but the two mentioned are enough for the purpose, and I can only repeat that when I saw so many lemons about I observed to myself, "Here's another good sign."

I might go on to a column's length in my enumeration of good signs. I might speak of the crowded state of the shops of the grocers at which pudding-clubs were held; of the prevalence of toy-sellers; of the prodigious quantity of holly and mistletoe about; of the roaring trade driven by the man with the newly-invented roasting-jack, and who exhibited a wooden goose revolving in the most satisfactory manner. I might discuss these things and many more, but I have no time; it is now nearly ten o'clock, and when I left Mr. Backitt, in the early part of the evening, he had said, "Just give me a look in about ten o'clock. *I'll* tell you what sort of a Christmas it is with 'em." So I made haste to Mr. Backitt's.

There is no affectation of gentility about Mr. Backitt's premises—no "offices next door," or boxes with catch-latches in the passage for shame-faced poverty with a watch to pawn; the space before Mr. Backitt's counter is nearly as large as that before an ordinary gin-shop bar, and as free. Like a gin-shop door, that of Mr. Backitt is kept ajar by a strap, and I give it a push, with the intention of walking in. But I could not push it far enough to squeeze in; the shop was crowded chiefly by women and girls; there was much gossiping chatter, a frequency of abusive remarks addressed to Mr. Backitt and his perspiring young man, and a strong odour of gin, so that the likeness of Mr. Backitt's place of business to a gin-shop did not cease at the strap-held door.

"Will you allow me to pass, Miss?" I said to a young lady of thirteen, who, although already borne down by bundles, was fiercely demanding another "Pashely shawl—name of Tigg!"

"No," said she, "I shan't! Give us hold of your tickets, and I'll give 'em over to Samuel, if you like."

"But I haven't any tickets," said I.

"Oh, you wants to leave," observed the damsel, laughing. "I wish you luck, old boy; they won't take anything in, bless you, while there's so much deliveries. It's as much as they'll 'part.' There was a poor soul, about half an hour ago, who wanted her old man's westkit away from his trousers, and do you think they'd let her have it? No! Mr. Jackanapes Samuel says, says he——"

"Shawl, three shillings; Tigg!" at that moment bellowed the young man in question.

"Here!" screamed Miss Tigg, poking up a long parcel, as an indication where she was to be found; and having secured the "Pashely," she went off, saying no more to me.

For full a quarter of an hour I tried hard to catch Mr. Backitt's eye, but in vain; it was as much, nay, more, than he could do to count up interest and take money, and bully the boy up the spout for not throwing down the parcels with greater expedition. Meanwhile the mob came swarming in, and the clamour became so deafening that I was glad to escape, without having Mr. Backitt's opinion as to "the sort of Christmas it was with 'em," it is true; but I much doubt if he could have regarded that till full of redemption-money, and pronounced Christmas, 1863, a very hard one.

XIII.

THE HIGHWAY PASTOR.

THE Gubbings family, of Twister's Alley, Seven Dials, and of Keate Street, Spitalfields, and of Kent Street, Southwark, will not go to church. Throw open the portals wide as may be, ring the most inviting peals from belfries, announce, in large type, that a bishop will preach, and, in larger type still, that no collection will be made; invite Gubbings specially by calling him "dear brother," or, generally, by proclaiming that the attendance of working men "in their jackets," and with their wives and families, is particularly solicited—it's all of no use. The Gubbingses, as a body, look on each endeavour as a "dodge;" and, though they may give you credit for extreme artfulness, are—to use their own expressive language—"not to be had." You may even take possession of Gubbings's theatre on the only evening of the seven that he can spare it, absolve him from the customary threepence, and admit him free to pit or gallery, set the footlights blazing, and fill the orchestra with hymn music; still Gubbings winks his superiority to your machinations, and presents you the back of his ragged coat.

Gubbings's present ways suit him; they are hereditary ways, convenient to meet, and requiring no exertion. He can lie till ten on Sunday morning, and enjoy till dinner-time—beyond if he prefers it—the luxuries of an unwashed and unshaven face, and tobacco unlimited. If he keeps pigeons he can go out and fly them; if dogs, take them to the sporting barber's (there is always a sporting barber in Gubbings's neighbourhood), and get their ears cropped, or their tails bitten off. Maybe he has his donkey to "clip," or a spoke to put to a wheel of his barrow; or he keeps a "battling finch" (a goldfinch pitted to sing against another for money), and, as the said finch is supposed to improve in tone and steadiness of voice if shut out from all distracting sights, Gubbings sets about blinding it by poking its optics with red-hot needles—cambric needles, five of them with their points clustered like a diamond, and lashed at the end of a bit of stick; if he be a humane man he merely scales the eyes of the poor little battler by scorching them till covered with a film, which after a time will wear off, and the tortured goldfinch regains his sight again. These are a few of the goods in which Gubbings traffics during church time. If you have anything of a more attractive character to offer, bring it to his door. He can't run after you. You are the seller, and you must wait on him if you want to deal.

Who is to do it? Where is the man so daring as to set up his tent in the midst of the Gubbings colony, and offer to the inhabitants new lamps in exchange for the blear-eyed stenching things that glow snugly in places unknown to the sun—goods shunned and cold-shouldered, and which cannot find acceptors or store-room till heaps of long-garnered and comfortable evils are swept out and abandoned? Who is the bold pioneer who will, all alone, penetrate to the very nucleus of these hotbeds of crime and ruffianism, and there taking his stand declare to the beetlebrows, and threatening eyes, and sneering pipe-laden mouths gathered around, that they are all wrong, and ought to be ashamed? Whenever you come across one such, you see a hero, and, considering the dearth of heroes in these nail-driving, man-shearing times, a man worthy of your respect. I, however, by no means promise that you will invariably find the highway preacher either a person of refined education or clerically attired. He may—nay, undoubtedly will—be found wearing a black suit and a white neckerchief; but ten to one, if the fingers that turn the leaves of the good book are not corned with the hammer and chisel, or scored and channeled by constant tugging at "wax-ends," or that the top of the middle finger of his right hand seems newer and cleaner than any other portion of his digits, because of its constant thimble sheathing.

Neither are the pills that he administers to the ugly-hearted Gubbings sugar coated. The horny sheathing that envelops Gubbings's understanding is nearly as invulnerable as the grimy cuticle that covers his carcase, which fact may go a long way towards meeting the charge of rant and bawling directed against highway pastors generally. Delicately-pointed logic will never puncture Gubbings's conscience; it will merely tickle it, and make him laugh. He must be speared—clubbed; his hard-set sin must be riven from him, as stubborn rocks are blasted with gunpowder. It's not the least use smoothing and patting Mr. Gubbings, and offering him a new life for his old in an affable whisper; he will certainly take it as part of the forcing-him-to-church dodge, and resist it as such. No; you must meet him on his own ground; you must—metaphorically, of course—take the collar of his jacket in both your hands, and, looking him hard in the face, say (supposing the sabbath question to be the one under discussion), "Now, look here, my friend. Suppose you were suddenly to find yourself hungry, and naked, and helpless in the world, and some one on whom you had not the least claim were to take you by the hand, and say, 'See; here are seven guineas. Take six of them, and therewith provide yourself with food, and lodging, and clothes; the seventh guinea is mine, and you must not ask it of me.' Don't you think you would be a great scoundrel to break into the good man's house and rob him of the remaining guinea?"

"I'd like to ketch anybody I knowed doing sich a thing," responds Gubbings with a significant scowl. "Nobody 'ud do it—it's agin natur," murmurs the audience, wagging their heads till their sparse hirsute crops so recently browsed on by gaol scissors quiver again. "I know it is against nature," retorts the loud-voiced preacher; "nevertheless, you do it, and worse, every week of your lives. It is of something a million times more precious than guineas of which the Great Giver of all things is robbed. Here is his written command, 'Six days shalt thou labour,'" &c., &c. Argument, of which the above is a weak and tame sample, appeals direct to Gubbings. Its immediate effect is that he regards you with the same sort of savage admiration with which he regards Detective Twitcher, when that admirable and ferret-like officer gains a clue as fine as a hair, follows it up, and knots it and weaves it till his man is netted in a net with meshes strong as cables. Maybe when Gubbings gets home and to bed, and is lying awake in the dark, he will turn the matter over in his mind— the object being to find a side of it that suits him ; and if he finds it, if you have not so roundly handled the said matter that there is still standing room for Gubbings's rough-shod feet, he will snort defiantly, and, dropping to sleep, awake yesterday's ruffian refreshed.

Very far, however, from the truth is it that the highway pastor's flocks are invariably Gubbingses. I know several spots about London where he holds forth as regularly as the parish parson in the parish church, and to audiences as sedate and devout as ever church doors closed on. At the obelisk in the Blackfriars Road, certain as the tolling of the Sabbath bells, are to be found a godly cabmaster and a hatblock-maker, and by the time the hatblock-maker's sister has taken her brother's hat, and the text has been found, and the windsor chair mounted, from every one of the six branching roads comes flocking the congregation, and, making a big ring round the preacher, listen sorrowfully to his preaching.

It must not be supposed that these highway gatherings arise from lack of church accommodation. I can positively assert that, in almost every case, in the immediate vicinity of the highway pastor's rostrum there is at least one church (frequently three or four) not more than three parts filled. How is it? The same religion is preached by the pulpit and the highway pastor, and the listeners to the former are accommodated with seats. If they have not a prayer-book, they may borrow one. When the weather is cold the building is comfortably warmed, and when the weather is hot it is cool and shady; whereas the highway preacher's flock is liable to sudden storms, to chill winds, and to an awful grilling in the summer's sun. Why don't the hot and tired mob pass through the churches' free portals and hear the gospel at their ease? Perhaps it is that among a few of us so strong a love of liberty exists that even an hour or so in the body of a church, with an awkward sensation of "hush" filling the place, and the boots of a cane-bearing beadle creaking grimly on the muffled floor, is irksome, not to say unbearable. Perhaps it is that there are a few, not a whit more sinful than the best of us, but in whom there is more modesty, who, having so long stayed from church, are shy of taking their long-accumulated burdens across its threshold, preferring to get side-winds of gospel comfort, doing penance the while bareheaded in the sun. I beg pardon of the numerous body of anti-humbugs for writing such twaddle; but indeed I *can't* believe that the highway pastor's congregation are to a man vile hypocrites, who mouth prayers and hymns in public solely that people may see. Of this I am sure. More than once, more than twice or thrice, I have seen round the preacher's chair blear old eyes lighted with a light strange to them, and promising as buds in spring, and careworn, wrinkled faces, with an expression weird and mysterious as mistletoe mantling the frosty crabtree.

The labours of the highway pastor are not invariably bounded by daylight. It was observed that when the evening service was drawing to a close, and twilight was deepening into darkness, there came sidling up to the outer edge of the ring a few terribly shy folks, who for the previous half-hour had been lurking in the neighbourhood reading stale placards, lounging with their pipes against walls and posts, or gazing with great earnestness into the shop windows, appearing as if, of all things, Gospel preaching was the very last they are thinking of. Yet, as I before observed, no sooner did a good screen of darkness prevail than with stealthy steps the shy ones approached the attentive circle to glean a few good words before the pastor closed his book and bade his flock good night. The condition of these outsiders, as it were, content to kiss the very hem of religion, resolved the highway pastor to hold meetings in the dark. The result was successful beyond expectation. In the Mile End Road, in Rosemary Lane, Whitechapel; in Shepherdess Fields, Islington, and half-a-dozen places in and about London, on Sabbath nights, and occasionally on other nights in the week, the preacher mounts his stand and scatters his good tidings to a congregation whose faces alone are visible through the gloom.

XIV.

EIGHT A.M.—THE MORNING POST.

IN one shape or another almost every department of public business has produced its Judas anxious to betray the trust of his employers, and to "reveal" such of the arts and mysteries of his profession as, by hook or by crook, he has become acquainted with. Thus we have had "Secrets of My Office," "Revelations of a Police Detective," "Tellings of a Telegraph Clerk," "Diary of a Physician," &c.; but at present the town has not been favoured by the "Peepings," or "Pennings," or "Peachings" of a postman. We have "rhyming postmen," whose poetic flights are bounded only by a handrail, and whose style is powerful, as might be expected in those who so constantly "indulge" in the double-rap-turous. But for a postman—a town postman—to become merely a poet is a wretched waste of opportunity. It may be very well for petty, unliveried, suburban carriers, with long, straggling beats, to rhyme on their letter-packets, and so beguile the time as they trudge along; to sing—

> "A letter I've got for Sarah Jane,
> Who housemaid is at the end of the lane,
> Where the flower-pots stand on the sill in a row,
> And the hollyhocks and the sweetwilliams blow."

Or—

> "Another I've got for the person who dwells
> At the shop round the corner, and bacon he sells.
> The seal he will break, and read it, I ween,
> By the gas-jet just over the sausage machine."

But although this ringing of his mental mettle may

pleasantly tickle the ears of the underpaid peripatetic, it will draw no money into his purse. It is not enough in these sensational times merely to edify the public—it must be startled; and difficult indeed would it be to suggest a more decided startler than "The Peachings of a Postman." Really, when one thinks on the enormous sale of that book; when one, in fancy, reads the advertisement in the morning papers, "Notice! Ninth edition of Peachings just out!" and dwells on the fat checks arriving almost daily from his publisher, it is a temptation to persuade some friend in the G.P.O. to procure you a beat suitable for your purpose, and "go in" for book-building in the regular way, just as a man makes a trip to the Amazon or to Central Africa.

For my part, I should prefer a beat that was not too respectable; and for the very obvious reason that, in highly respectable neighbourhoods, the houses are furnished with letter-boxes, and I should have no opportunity, except now and then by a glimpse of an anxious face lurking behind the window-curtain, of making myself acquainted with the recipients of the momentous billets. If I might have my choice, I would choose a quiet, six-roomed-house beat at Kensington or Camden Town; and I should not care to make more than one round a day—the first round, at eight a.m. As far as the purposes of my book were concerned, it would be a mere waste of shoe-leather to undertake more than that single delivery. My gathering would consist entirely of the secrets of the *special* epistles of social life, and for these there is but one post—the eight a.m. post; nor is it at all surprising that it should be so. Take love-letters, for instance. Calf-lovers may look on all hours of the day as fit for the exchange of epistolary bleatings, and, possibly, it is as easy to "boo" passionately all over four sides of note-paper immediately after breakfast, and when the knife-grinder, and the chair-mender, and the cauliflower-vender are abroad, or even on a sultry afternoon and after a hearty dinner, as at any other time. Easier, perhaps. But your earnest lover never takes pen in hand till the evening. Sitting in his cell, amidst perfect stillness, he forges love-shafts of so exquisite a sort that the mere rattling of a window-shutter breaking in on their incompleteness would shatter them at once. His delight is to hear the lips of his pen kissing the dainty sheet, to catch its little rustling whispers as it spells out the loving words. This, if he is making love. He, however, may be breaking it instead. Well, quiet and seclusion are equally essential to his purpose. His malice is as exacting as hottest love, and it gives him joy to hear the tiny, black, wriggling snakes hiss as his pen gives them birth, and at every hatching—each one more deadly than the preceding—the monster pauses to grin and rub his hands, thinking how they will sting. No other hand but the writer's must consign such precious concoctions to the letter-box; indeed, if the eight a.m. postman is to deliver the adders, out he must go, letting himself out and in again with his latch-key, for both his landlady and Jemima have been a-bed this hour and more. It may be objected that in outward appearance the honey-pot would be exactly like the adder's nest, and I should not know one from the other. Maybe; but, as I before observed, I should not attempt to glean knowledge of the affairs of my customers by consulting their written names and addresses merely. I should look out for the face at the window or at the door, and make note of such trifles as trembling hands and wan cheeks, and eyes eloquent of joyful content or sad foreboding; for be sure the adders are expected, and Miss Alicom Payne is as certain of her honey-pot as she is that there will be marmalade on the breakfast-table.

The night being so far advanced, Piercy Beamisher's missive to Miss Payne does not fall into an empty letter-box. Other evening scribes have already made their deposits, and higgledy-piggledy lie invitations, acceptations, and rejections. There are one or two begging letters; and, as it happens, that addressed to Miss Payne falls plump atop of a shabby flimsy envelope, with the postage-stamp stuck at the bottom left-hand corner, and the superscription ill spelt and villanously askew. It is addressed to "Shandy Gaff, Esq.," and is the sort of letter that any one, let alone an experienced town postman, may see through with half an eye.

"My dear Shandy," writes Sarah Brown, "for dear indeed you are though not mine in the holy service of matrimony but which to make use of your own darling words doesn't make any odds in the eye of Him that sees all I couldn't but rite though against your wishes and to the house which you will say is madness and no wonder for so I am dear though far be the thoughts of blaming you. But what could I do with my close gone and not one farthing for the rares of the nuss who has brought him back poor little boy plump and beautyful as he was but now a complete Skelington through the feeding bottle and me with only power to set and cry to hear his wining through drying it away to go to service as you asked my love Her bringing him back made a row at the loging where I am likewise in rears and called such horrible names as would make your art ake to ear I pray to God that missus may not take this in and time the postin so that if possible it may come up with the shavin water I thought you was ill not having been able to ketch you going in nor coming out for over a week till this morning when seein you quite unexpected turn the wrong way from what you used caused the explanashun. It is all through not seeing you so long dear that I rite and only but for the poor little fellow I would brave it and rather die a 100 times So no more at present from yours for ever and ever, SARAH BROWN."

But the perusal of Sarah's letter opens my eyes to the difficulties of my position. My manhood chafes at my scarlet collar, and my impulse is to thwart the rascally Shandy by delaying the delivery of the note for just one little hour, when it will be handed to the traitor at the breakfast-table, and in the presence of the outraged Mrs. Gaff. "Yours for ever and ever," indeed! poor wretch. If you could only see the supreme smirk of contempt that for an instant distorts the handsome face of the poor little Skelington's father, as he arrives at this part of your message, you would be not a little dismayed for your future.

And what about *your* future, Shandy Gaff, Esq., and clerk at a Thames-street drysaltery, at a salary of a hundred and twenty pounds per annum? Beware that you do not treat miserable Sarah's pledges of eternal devotion too lightly. Recollect that there are two—nay three—to the bargain: herself, yourself, and the Skelington. *Yours* "for ever and ever" she may not be; but who says that you shall not be *hers?* You may shake her off—that you are bound to do if she will not fall away quietly; but if you only shake her into the kennel, where her love for you will rot and turn to pestilence, you may thereby be brought to death as surely as though she had clung to you during the shaking-off process—clung to you till she had strangled you. Consider her appeal before you crunch it up and wedge it between the bars into the fire with the toe of your boot. If, however, the poor scrawl is already consigned to the flames, at least spare a minute to watching its ashes. If you bring your mind's eye well forward you may make out some queer shapes. You may make out a draggle-tail, drunken drab, lying wait of evenings within a score yards of the threshold of your innocent house—a hiccupping, loud-mouthed woman, who is for ever demanding a shilling. If she makes her demands with nothing worse than sulky insolence you are lucky, because at times she is tearful, and so full of gin and gratitude as to be uncertain of her standing, and insists on clutching you by the arm and resting her blowsy bonnet on your shoulder. "Don't push me off," she says; "don't, my love, do such a cruel thing. I know my touch is worse than mire to you; but I'm still faithful and will be, s'help me God! till I die. I haven't come for your money, dear Shandy—only to tell you how true I feel towards you. Kiss me, Shandy, my dear." Do *what?* Kiss her—the hideous thing! Well, there's no help for it, dear Mr. Gaff. To get rid of her, you must either kiss her or call a policeman; and the latter you *dare* not to. One such evening a policeman came without calling. "Come, cut that!" said he to Draggletail. "If you don't leave go the genelman and be off I'll put you where I shall find you in the morning." "What do you mean, you beast?" asked Draggletail fiercely. "He's my husband; ask him if he is not?" "Yes, yes; that's all right, policeman," said you, and at the same time winked sheepishly at the man in blue and sneakingly proffered him a shilling, which he took without so much as thanking, and walked off with the air of a knowing man of business.

All this you may make out, gay, young Mr. Gaff, in the tinder of Sarah Brown's consuming letter. Nor is this all; the chimney draught carries away the front wall of tinder, and you get a further insight into futurity. There he is—a sallow, bony youth, with plenty of neck-handkerchief and no shirt collar, and with his greasy-cuffed coat buttoned tight at the breast, and with the stump of a dirty pipe protruding from his waistcoat pocket. This is the Skelington. He used to be very shy and respectful when he wore pinafores, and waited for you at a convenient corner in Thames-street, with a note from Draggletail; but since he has come into a tailcoat and a pipe, and is, to use his own powerful expression "on his own hands," his tone has altered considerably. Hear his voice in the crepitation of the paper embers.

"Didn't see me! cert'ny not! I'm too low and hard-up to see, I am. More fool me, not to show myself up and *make* myself seen!"

"What is it you want, William? Here on Tuesday evening, and now again?"

"What do I warnt? What do you think I warnt? Thunderin well you knows I warnt everythink. Gallus nice father you are to bring me and mother to this ere, and then chuck it in my teeth. I warnt wittles. I don't warnt kid gloves and meerschaumes, like *some* puppies as I know do, and have no more right, nor yet as much as I have."

"Then, why don't you work for what you want, sir?"

"Why don't I work? Cos I aint got nobody to shove me forward like *some* puppies that I know, and who I'm

the elder of. That's why I don't work.. You wouldn't
begrudge *them* a shilling to buy a bit of grub with if
they come and asked you. I aint a fool, don't you know?
and, what's more, I aint going——"

What the Skelington was not going to do must be
guessed, for at that very moment a puff of air carried
the tinder up the chimney. Why didn't it blow up
the chimney before? There would have been a little
remaining space to have discussed other sorts of letters
than this of Mr. Gaff's.

XV.

THE LEATHER MARKET.

THE supremacy of leather is, and ever was, maintained by the working Englishman almost as strenuously as Magna Charta, "An Englishman's house is his castle," and "God save the Queen." He regards it with the same implicit confidence as he regards his beer, and will no more accept gutta-percha or india-rubber as a substitute for the former than light French wines or lemonade for the latter. No matter in what shape the material appears, it elicits an equal amount of respect; and that the passion is deeply implanted in the Englishman is evident from the fact that it is one of the earliest to develop itself in the youthful mind. Long before the boy is out of pinafores and strap shoes he is anxious for a whip with a *real* leather thong, or choice is divided between that and one of those oozy leathern abominations known as a "sucker;" and if his first cap be furnished with a *real* leather peak, in place of a mean affair of japanned cardboard, he holds his head all the higher. True, we have degenerated from the ancient custom of casing our nether limbs in buckskin, but we still show an affectionate leaning thereto by miscalling our trouser-stuffs *doeskin*, and swathing our legs knee high in a refined and dandified preparation of horse or cow skin. Even the low-minded costermonger, to whom "wellingtons" are objects of contempt and derision, and who laughs to scorn galligaskins and knickerbockers, evinces the national tendency for leather by stipulating for "ankle-jacks" with "tongues" ample enough to overlap the lacings by at least three inches. There is no surer passport to the best room of an inn than a portmanteau of the orthodox brown colour, and branded "warranted leather;" if it should happen to bear the additional recommendation "*solid*," your high respectability is at once established. That it has been from time out of mind a material high in popular esteem is proved by that ancient but still choice stave the " leather bottel," wherein the champion of bull-hide, after lauding its superiority to delf and pewter, and even silver, is loth to throw it aside after it has well served its turn: after its mouth is so agape with age that its stopple shakes about loosely—after its sides are caved in and bulged out, and it rocks tipsily, and finally stands all aslant when an attempt is made to set it up—after its stout stitches have yielded to a thousand soakings of sack and canary, and the venerable leather bottle springs a leak; still, as prays the stave-writer, don't cast it off, don't put it away from you as a thing utterly useless, but

"Make it fast to the wall with a pin,
'Twill serve to keep hinges and odd things in."

I have been writing hitherto as though it were only among the lowbred and the vulgar—among costermongers and waiters, and tavern boosers—that leather is an article to swear by. We all know different. We all know that within a little year the commercial world—the merchants, and brokers, and bankers—were panic-stricken; that, indeed, many of them were clean knocked off their commercial legs through an earthquake in the leather market. It was not the fault of leather—such an excuse was never attempted; neither did the staunch fabric fail because of a " heavy run " on it. It was simply a case of leather worked to death—of advantage being taken of leather-worship by certain folks whose only aim was, like Jeremy Diddler, to hoodwink the worshippers and fleece them of their money. After all, however, it was probably but a righteous judgment. People—even golden-eyed, mammon-hearted people—were fast sinking into leathern idiotsy. No business transaction was so sure as a tran-

saction "with leather in it." A man might dabble in
indigo, in sugar, in tallow, and, though he wore the
wealth of a bank as a life-belt, sink and drown; but let
him but dabble in leather, and he was as buoyant as a
cork. You couldn't sink him if you tried. Did a man
wish to negotiate a bill—a tremendous bill, say a ten-
thousand pounder—it was cashed, and at a cheap rate, if
the acceptor were only assured that there was "leather
at the bottom of it." The number of bills about with
leather soles at that period was wonderful, almost as
wonderful—as the sequel proved—as the number of bill-
discounters "sold" through trafficking in leather bills.

Have men of leather yet recovered from the effects of
the earthquake? Consulting the *Times* lately, it was
found that hides were "dull," an announcement certainly
calculated to convey to the uninitiated in market slang
that they had not yet recovered from the melancholy
effects of the late crash. The leather-market report of
the same date, however, revealed that "butts" were
brisk and that "shoulders" were rising. To settle the
anomaly a visit to the said market was resolved on.

One would naturally suppose that the place set apart
for public dealings in an article of such national importance would have been as well known as Billingsgate, and
certainly as easy of access. Quite the contrary, however,
is the case. You might beat about Bermondsey from
morning till night, constantly led (by your nose) to
imagine that it is just round the corner, and so imagining
till the appearance in the streets of troops of dirty, lumbering, wooden-clouted tanners, carrying their tea-cans and
wallets, and smoking their short pipes, announces that
the business of the day is over. The better plan is to
make inquiries as soon as you arrive in the neighbourhood. "Up the archway 'side of the warehouses at the
end of the street," you are informed, but, on adopting the
said direction, find the archway so very clean and quiet
that you have your doubts whether you are not trespass-
ing and will presently be asked your business there.

Pursuing your way boldly, however, you presently
come to a great square, and then discover that the huge

range of building facing the street, and in which the archway is, is part of the leather stores. Along the whole face of the immense warehouses on their inner side —from floor to basement—loopholes and doorways present themselves, and, peeping in, here and there is seen such a wealth of tanned skins, in piles from floor to ceiling, in stacks from wall to wall, and in great rolls as tall as a bull is long, and as many of them as represent hundreds of thousands of bulls. At first sight one might safely wager that these sturdy pillars of leather were "butts;" but that they were or ever could be "brisk" seemed quite out of the question. Whether a slack day had been unluckily hit on for the visit, I don't know; but I must say that, as a British—as *the* British—leather market, the place was disappointing. Brisk, indeed! the head-quarters of the New River Water Company present a more lively appearance. There were the open warehouses, and there were the merchants, and there, leaning against the railings that enclosed the soddened, sad-looking green in the middle of the square, were three or four listless individuals, who might have been customers—might, indeed, have been well-known men of leather, who could by their joint weight send up the market or bring it down, exactly as it suited them. They might even have been engaged in one of these operations at the present time, or they might have been Fleet Street betting-men who had baffled the police and at last succeeded in finding a snug spot where their little game was not likely to be interrupted. So there they lounged, and about the warehouse-doors lounged the merchants —clerical-looking men, with sleek hats and speechless boots; and that was all there was to be seen. It seemed to me that the newspaper must be wrong, that "butts" were miserably dull instead of brisk, and that, if "shoulders" were rising at all, it could only be by way of a shrug at the flatness of the leather trade.

Through the leather market into the skin market. Here was another square, with a broad piazza flanking every side of it. Business was brisk enough here in all conscience. The square was chokeful of terrible-looking vehicles—terrible because not only the tires and fellows, but the very spokes of the wheels, were plastered with a red-brown substance, in which were matted scraps of hair and fragments of wool, dreadfully suggestive of slaughter and the shambles; as were the carters with their streaked hands, their speckled woollen leggings, and their oozy wooden shoes; as were the carters' whips, with the brass about their handles all lacquered red; as were the horses in the terrible carts—animals of high mettle and with sleek coats, who snorted and shook their heads as they sniffed the reek of the wet hides, much liking it.

Worming in and out among the carts was a swarm of busy men—buyers and sellers, and blue-smocked porters—while under the piazza were stacks of hides of Spanish, and Dutch, and English beasts, each to be distinguished by the length, or the breadth, or the width of the horns still attached to a bit of skull and hanging about the fronts of the stacks as though still vicious and daring you to approach. Besides these were heaps of innocent-looking calves' skins, and the skins of sheep and lambs, still so warm-looking and comfortable that one might imagine them new sheep-coats just come home, rather than cast-off garments, of no further use but to the fell-monger and the tanner. In addition to these there were several piles of hides that had been exported from foreign parts, and that had been salted that they might come to market wholesome.

But I wanted to learn something about the business of the market, who was responsible for its proper working, and how much work was done there, and I must, therefore, take especial note of the workers in this busy square. Prowling about the red hides, like so many jackals, were several little boys, in ragged blue smocks, and evidently coming of a butchering stock, but whose business (and they had a business, for every one of them carried a knife) at the skin market was not at all clear. Skipping about the roof of the piazza, and listening attentively to the price of hides as discussed below, was a gigantic raven, sleek and well-fed, but with a broken wing. What about the raven? Nobody could tell me; nobody had time to discuss this or any other matter with me. So I came away, very ill-satisfied indeed!

So ill-satisfied that by ten of the market clock on the following morning I was once more in the hide market. Its aspect was marvellously different from that of yesterday. The square was blank and empty, save and except that some market official, with well-polished galligaskins, lounged about idly, closely attended by the broken-winged raven, who hopped sedately as the official walked, and when the latter paused so did the bird, nodding and winking, and evidently on the best of terms with its reflected self in its friend's highly-polished leggings. Under the piazza was nothing but a few piles of skins uncleared from yesterday's sale, together with sundry hillocks composed of sheep's feet, and looking at a distance like some newly-invented material for paving roads. Something else, too, there was to be seen this morning under the piazza, and certainly it was the most inexplicable " something " the skin market had yet presented. I have before alluded to certain ragged little boys seen prowling through the market's crowd or dodging amongst the hide heaps with a manner that certainly betokened a sort of right to be there, but to what end was far from clear. Now, however, it was clear enough. There was the same ragged little flock, each with an ugly-stained knife in his hand, floundering knee-deep among the great moist skins, and turning them about and inside out, ever and anon darting at any hanging red scrap on the fleshy side and trimming it off. Nor was their attention solely confined to these flinders of meat, for some of them might be seen manfully clutching at one of the defunct beast's great horns, while with their knives they cut the ears off.

Nobody seemed to interfere with the children, not even the raven, whose perquisites market scraps of all sorts might reasonably be supposed to be. So far, indeed, from resenting the operations of the poor little grubbers as an infringement of his rights, he magnanimously hopped to a heap at which two boys were engaged, and, just pecking a morsel, passed on with a patronising glance, as though he rather admired their industry.

In the midst of my perplexity there came sauntering up to where I stood an old fellow, evidently a porter in the market. Jerking his thumb in the direction the leggings and their admirer had taken, he observed—

"Artful card that, Sir."

Not knowing whether the remark was intended to apply to the owner of the leggings or to the raven, I merely nodded by way of reply.

"The worstest prig out."

Again I nodded.

"Been about here, ah! Lord knows how long. Found a top of a shed hardly fledged."

Feeling assured now that he was speaking of the raven, I inquired to whom it belonged.

"Belonged, eh?" replied the porter. "I'd like to catch any one belonging to him. He'd soon let 'em know. Why, bless you, when he was quite a little chap, a boy about here wanted to belong to him. They had a fight for it. That's how he got his wing broke."

The conversation started, I took the opportunity to inquire what it was the little boys were cutting off the hides, when he shortly replied—

"Meat; they gets leaf from the salesmen."

"Ah! and what is it good for? for dogs, I suppose?"

"It's good for wittles," replied the porter, reproachfully. "They cuts off the little bits as is left on when the beast is skinned, likewise the ears; you may buy twopenny lots, and you may buy threepenny lots. In the hot weather you may buy penny lots. The hides it's cut off of is as fresh as a daisy—killed p'raps yesterday, or the day afore. I had threepen'orth of ears and bits on Sunday; and werry good it was."

I made inquiries respecting the heaps of sheep's feet, and was informed that they were going to the boilers: that there were only three "trotter-boilers" in London, and that the most famous of the trio was Jimmy Corderoy, of Wild's Rents, who it was that supplied every "trotter" seller in the metropolis. Jimmy Corderoy, according to my informant, employs a considerable staff of women, who, after the trotters have been scalded, take them in their laps and peel the hair off, preparatory to the final cooking process. The wholesale price of "trotters" is four a penny, but I was pleased to hear of Mr. Corderoy that he was "a genelman as wasn't particular to a trotter or so, and would quite as frequent throw in a few as not."

From trotters I endeavoured to lead my friend to the subject of skins, and all about them; but he declined to discuss the matter further than to assure me that "they went up and down, and down and up, like everything else," and with that bit of information I was obliged to leave him.

XVI.

THE LONDON HORSE MARKET.

WHY "Horse" Market? Or, if so, why not designate the great dépôt for butchers' meat in Newgate Street the beef market, Covent Garden the cabbage or grape market, and the mart for rags in Houndsditch the dilapidated waistcoat market?

It is a singular fact, but (and despite the title of this paper) there is *no* London horse market; that is to say, there is within the City bounds no space *specially* set apart and chartered for the public buying and selling of that important adjunct of our commerce — that four-footed friend of ours that attends us constantly in our every walk of life, in our business journeys and our pleasure jauntings, to our weddings and to our buryings — the horse. We have markets for leather, and hay, and corn, and tallow, and spices, and coals, and fish — places where the very best and the very worst of the crop of each kind may be bartered for. Pigs are sold openly, and bought without fear or suspicion; there is but one bullock and sheep market for Mr. Giblet of Bond Street and Mr. Blolam of Whitecross Street; but if you would purchase a horse, the last place to be visited is that provided by the Corporation for its public sale. Not that the Corporation is at fault. A stigma attaches to the unwarranted and promiscuous sale of horses that a Lord Mayor even of Sir Peter Laurie power could not "put down." Why is this? Is our morality so lax that it would assuredly break through under the overwhelming weight of temptation involved in horsedealing? Is it impossible to deal with the genus equus with as simple

THE LONDON HORSE MARKET.

and single a purpose as with oxen, or is there enveloped
in a horsehide some subtle essence that, brought into
contact with money and an irreligious mind, breeds
disease and roguery as naturally as the blending of
certain gases creates flame? A man possessed of just
enough intelligence to dress a calf or judge of the weight
of an ox by the breadth of its loins may jog to the market
with a hundred pounds in his pocket and be sure of returning with his money's worth, and a profit to boot; but
what would become of the same individual if, with the
same amount, he ventured to Smithfield on a horsebuying
expedition? He would be mobbed. The eyes of every
"horsey" man in the market would be either staring
with speechless amazement or winking to each other a
mute agreement to "share him amongst 'em." Just
imagine the precious string of spavined, weak-knee'd,
wall-eyed monstrosities the man with the hundred pounds
would bring home. The fact is incontrovertible. Unless
a man be awfully knowing—unless his vision be so acute
that the machinations of the "chaunters" and the subtle
tricks of the "copers" be to him as transparent as glass
—the Friday afternoon gathering at the New Smithfield
is no place for him to negotiate the purchase of a horse.
Hence the establishment of such places as Aldridge's,
where, if the auctioneer says of a horse "warranted
sound," you may take his word.

Let us, however, take a walk to the so-called horse-
market this Friday afternoon, and see what sort of
business is going on. First of all, however, we must
find it; for, thank Goodness! things are not now as in
days of yore, when the way to Smithfield could be discovered from any part of London—ay, even by a blind
man—as easily, though not so pleasantly, as he could
discover a bed of roses in a great garden. The obscure
position of the new market, however, is no very formidable obstruction to its being found. From whatever part
of the metropolis you may start you have only to scan the
road carefully, and if you should see, steering northward,
a horse with its tail plaited with straw and its hoofs
polished to preternatural splendour, or a costermonger's

barrow laden with old wheels and axletrees, or a lean goat harnessed to a fat chaise, or a man with currycombs, and whips, and whipcord, or one laden with fag-ends and tags of harness, you have only to follow, and you will finally arrive at the place of sale.

Business—that is, rattling, roaring business—has not yet commenced, nor will it till the chiming of the market clock gives assent. This circumstance is, however, not to be regretted, as it affords an opportunity of inspecting the goods and their owners before the press begins. First, as to the goods. A single glance around is at once convincing that the proper name for the place is not a horse, but an ass, market. Here, and here only, throughout London and for five miles round it, is it that the humble donkey is bought and sold. There are more donkeys than any other animals present; but this I may state—on the authority of a middle-aged person with a bison-skin cap and a capacious shawl wisped round his throat, and who evidently knew what he was talking about—is not the case all the year round. "It's like everything else," observed he, "it flucterates. I'll lay yer a a'penny that if sich a lot of donkeys wos to show about May they'd be caught up like mackril, six a shillin'. What's the reason on it? Why the fruit season's the reason on it. When you aint got nothing to sell, you don't want nothing to draw it about." The same authority further informed me that the difference in the value of a donkey in the spring and in the autumn was about twelve shillings—an inconsiderable sum as it at first seemed to me; but when he explained that, at the best of times, it must be "a right sort of donkey" that fetched five-and-thirty shillings, the sacrifice on the part of the vendor in the autumn was manifest.

There were other tokens beside the numerous donkeys that the costermongers' "season" had come to an end. Not many barrows, as a rule—these are merely hired; but plenty of scales, and measures, and pots (the latter with false bottoms and other cheating contrivances), and several big drums, instruments of late years adopted by the "cutting" cherry and apple "costers" as a means of gathering children and calling people to their windows to inspect their tempting wares.

There were present in the market other specimens of the donkey tribe beside the genus *coster*. There was the donkey used to panniers and respectable Brompton and Clapham society; there was the donkey late the property of the small laundress whose husband beat carpets; and the donkey—two, in fact—the cast-offs of some suburban assinine dairy. Curiously illustrative of that excellent maxim, "evil communications corrupt good manners," was the contrast the various animals presented. The donkey that had passed its life in the society of men of whom my bison-capped friend was the type, carried its ears aslant, leant negligently on three legs, and was a blackguard donkey from its impudent tail to the tip of its ruffianly nose; when the butt-end of the whipstock was brought down on its back with a noise like the banging of a barrel, it merely winked its eyes contemptuously and backed deliberately against the whelk man's stall, its close proximity to which had been the original cause of the chastisement. How different was the behaviour of the sleek Clapham ass, with its dainty white saddle-cloth and decently blacked hoofs! So of the neat laundry donkey, meeker even than its neighbour the chaise-goat, and only less bashful and seemingly washed out than the two unfortunates from the milk purveyors. What became of these two poor old used-up she-asses I should like to know. That they were not sold—at least that Friday—I am sure. Nobody seemed inclined to bid for them, or to think them worth bidding for. Once a big man, in a smock frock, sauntered up and punched the weakest one in the ribs, which act its owner construed to indicate a desire to purchase. "Wot for?" replied the big man; "I want a hanimal to work, I does. I ain't in the weal line myself."

Not only the animals themselves, but everything pertaining to their housing and harnessing could be bought in the market, and this as regards horses and goats as well as donkeys. Did you want an odd wheel, or a spring, or even a single plate of a spring, you could be served in a twinkling. Did you want simply a screw, or a screw-wrench, or a couple of linchpins, in a dozen different parts of the market there were tons of such things laid out on the stones for sale. This man had brought out to sell not only his beast and cart, but, piled in the latter, the whole of the building materials of his stable, together with the fittings, down to the pail and pitchfork. Here was a speculative little wheelwright, who had essayed the building of a van, but, having progressed as far as the body and the tireless wheels, had been brought altogether to a standstill for ironwork, and was now evidently and ruinously anxious to get the abortion off his hands. Here was a failure in the cats'-meat line—barrow (yellow, with blue cats' heads on the panels), knife and steel, and weights and scales, going for a mere song. There were perambulators by the score, goat-chaises by the dozen, and as for light pony carts and old-fashioned gigs (those ancient types of gentility), and light spring trucks, you could scarcely move for them. The cattle all undressed, and the harness festooning the various rails and posts, and the empty vehicles standing thickly about, gave one an impression of all the blackguardism of the City out for an excursion, and halting to rest, rather than of a public place.

The muster of horses, my middle-aged friend informed me, was about the average. As far as I could judge, there were about 200 of them, making such a pitiful collection as made one quite melancholy to contemplate. Certainly there were amongst the number several animals whose bodily condition was satisfactory, and which to the uninitiated were all that could be desired. But woe betide the innocent person who purchased one of them!— at least if there was any meaning in their nervously-twitching ears and nostrils, or in the fact that while a strong hand held their halters a clear space was always kept in the rear of their heels. These, however, were the few. The many were the listless and dropping-knee'd sort, whose dull ears had ceased to take alarm or pleasure at any sound that greeted them, and who carried in their eyes a droning, weary-to-death look that exposed the vamping and tinkering to which they had been subjected, if nothing else did. What a scandalous mockery it seemed to see them, old enough to be the great-great-grandfathers of horses, with their hoofs daintily blacked and shining—with their scant manes combed out and made the most of—with their poor old tails done up jauntily in a plait of clean straw—and their callous hides French-polished, as it were, and making by its gloss the stubborn row of ribs beneath the more apparent! It seemed worse to see the light horses served so than the big lumbering ones, who all their lives have never been hurried out of a walk, and who, being used to no better company than coalheavers and mudcarters, might reasonably be supposed to be dull brutes, incapable of comprehending a trouble too great to be buried in a nosebag. But the slim horses! what a wide field for speculation they afforded! Take that long-necked bay, blind as a bat, and with once sensitive nose now round and blunted against the grindstone of adversity, what does it think of as it stands on the market stones and hears the braying, and bellowing, and clatter, going on about him?—of the times when it was a joy to exert its nimble limbs that never tired—to bound, to leap, to gallop with the mere weight of a man on its strong back, to cleave the dull wind till its eyes tingled?—of the time when its fetlocks came to grief through failing at that tremendous "five-bar," which doomed it to the shafts? of its easy carriage life? of its dreary experience of omnibus life, during which it "went" at the knees, and at the eyes, and at several other points the 'bus driver knew not of, or he might have been more merciful? of its discharge from 'bus duty, and of its plunge into that deepest depth of equine misery, the shafts of a London night-cab? Now, however, there is an end even to that. As the night-cabman says, "his sarvices don't kiver his nosebag; that he moves pretty well while he is 'ot; but let him stand on the ranks an 'our or so, and you can no more stir him than cold lead with a wooden spoon." What's to come next? The blind bay, aware of his galls and sprains and unceasing aches, may be picturing to

I

himself, and with satisfaction, what a forlorn and wretched creature he must look, and how extremely unlikely it is that he will ever again be bought and set to work, the alternative being that the friendly horse butcher will presently take him in hand, and then an end to the weary business. Deluded bay! So excellent is the texture of your well-bred hide, so subtle the skill of the ruffians into whose hands you have fallen, that neither spavin nor gall are visible, and to all appearance you are a lean serviceable old horse, and as such will presently be bought, kept till the veneer wears of and the cobblers' work is revealed, again sold, tinkered, and botched, and bought again, till merciful sudden death puts you past repair.

Now the market clock chimes and the sale begins. What was just now simply a bustling, chattering mob is now a perfect babel. The horsey rogue with a patched quadruped to sell eagerly unties the halter from the rails and yells at the poor, tame beast, and twitches its mouth, and otherwise drags and cuffs it about that any latent spark of pluck remaining to the outraged animal may be roused and exhibited, the horsey one meanwhile exclaiming, "Who-o-o, blood! who-o-o, then! Gently, gently!" for the edification of some shy, half-resolved purchaser whom the horsey one has his eye on, and who is anxious to secure—as are all seekers of their "first horse"—an animal of spirit.

Hi! hi! clear the road, the animals are about to be run to show their mettle. This is one of the most singular parts of the entire business. An avenue is formed of about ten yards wide and a hundred long, flanked on either side by spectators. Within the avenue are the running horses and asses, and the men who, clutching them by the halter, at once guide and haul them along. But these other men in the running lane—where they come from or who pays them I know not; but you may meet them week by week going to the market, and you find them at the market, with no other goods than a long thonged whip and a capacious mouth for yelling. Distributing themselves among the cattle being shown, their business seems to be to give tongue in most Bedlamitish fashion, while they slash with their long whips and administer to every animal that passes them one cut or more as time permits. The lane being a hundred yards long, and the floggers certainly not more than ten yards apart, wooden indeed must the beast be that could not be urged into a trot. Under such usage my blind bay flung out behind and tossed his head in most gallant style; and even the two little dairy donkeys were so far frightened from their propriety as to allow themselves to be hauled and flogged along at the rate of at least five miles an hour.

XVII.

WATERCRESSES.

HE very best proof that watercress-selling is a miserable and unprofitable occupation may be gathered from the fact that, taken as a body, they who embark in it are either very old or very young—individuals whose shoulders are not yet broad enough, nor their muscles sufficiently developed, for a fair stand-up fight with the world for bread; and they who have fought through all their life's prime, and with variable success, but who finally, finding themselves breathless and spent, and unable any longer to continue the struggle, shrink aside out of the press, and, meekly going to the wall, seek a crust quietly and unobtrusively. You seldom or ever see a hale and hearty man or woman vending watercresses, or if you do, inquiry, in nine cases out of ten, would disclose the fact that the seller had a few hours to spare each day from some regular occupation, or else that, despite a robust appearance, some accident or malady rendered them unable to labour.

Why it is I can't tell; but there can be no doubt that the watercress is universally regarded as the last link in the chain of independent trade. While a man maintains his footing on the watercress rail of the social ladder he may claim to be considered a worthy man trading for a living. He may be but an inch removed from lucifer-matches, and such-like goods, hawked as an excuse for begging; but the said inch is well defined and understood, and to cross it is to launch into an altogether new phase of existence.

There is our watercress-man—a disagreeable, surly-looking old curmudgeon as ever carried a basket. I know how old he is to a day. He is seventy-eight come the King's (not the Queen's) birthday, and he has been a watercress-man three-and-twenty years. I know how he came to take to watercresses. By trade he is a working jeweller, but at last his sight got so dim that he was glad to accept the commonest work—none being the alternative—at which he could not earn more than eighteenpence a day. Consequently he grew "hard up," and shifted his good lodgings to poorer, and to poorer still, till he finally took up his abode in a house where a "crease" man resided. The "crease" man was doing so well that he could afford to come down to the old working jeweller's room of evenings and smoke his pipe, and drink his pint of ale, and stand little treats for supper; while the jeweller was obliged to stick to his bench, sawing and filing, and wasting what was left of his precious sight through his magnifying-glass and the wretched light of a tallow candle. At last the well-to-do cress-man's son, who kept a greengrocer's shop at Lambeth, offered his parent a home in his house, and then says the cress-man to the jeweller, "Tell you what, Mr. Wicks, if you like to go in for it, I'll sell you my basket and business for ten and sixpence, and take it by instalments;" which offer was accepted.

Mr. Wicks told me all this himself as he sat by my kitchen fire, and I must say he made his way there in a highly creditable manner. We hadn't dealt with him very long when one evening he was called to the gate, and what was supposed to be a penny handed to him in lieu of a pen'orth of cresses. In less than five minutes, however, there came a violent ringing, and we presently heard the voice of Mr. Wicks growling like a bear, and complaining as does a man who has received some deep injury.

"Ain't it enough," asked he, "to keep a poor feller on his legs from mornin' till night to earn a bit of bread, but you must make him come back the length of your precious long street to get his right money?"

I hurried to the gate at this alarming stage of the proceedings, prepared, I must own, to find our watercress-man attempting to swindle.

"What 'wrong' money have you received, my good man?"

"Why, 'arf-a-crown, instead of a penny," replied he, indignantly.

That transaction was the foundation of a friendship between Mr. Wicks and myself that has existed upwards of a month.

Through him I am possessed of information that would enable me to start to-morrow morning as accomplished a watercress-man as any in the trade. I am aware, for instance, that, having made my purchase, it is a good thing to have a pen'orth of hot coffee at the "stall" (I shall invariably find a coffee-stall in the vicinity of a watercress market), to fortify myself for the sloppy and unenviable job of sousing my goods at the nearest pump. Then I shall have to untie my unsold stock of yesterday and mix them with the fresh ones, unless, indeed, the stale ones are very "white," when I shall find it more profitable to throw them away and stand the loss. I am to be particularly careful never to buy my cresses by gas or candle light if I can help it, for it is at such times that the dishonest dealer palms off his ill-coloured stock. I am aware that he is not personally responsible for the colour of his cresses; that they were green enough when picked down in Sussex six hours ago; but it is the nature of the watercress, when very tightly packed (and they are as tightly squeezed into the big baskets as the pickers' arms can squeeze them), that they will "heat" like new hay, and emit such a steam when they are released by the consignee that you would think they were on fire. Whether they really would "fire" in time I don't know; but this (instructed by Mr. Wicks) I really do know, that, under such circumstances, the receivers of the big hampers have them conveyed at once to the market pump and there subjected to a drenching that, as Mr. Wicks says, "sends the colour out on 'em like cheap print."

One thing I am surprised to learn—that it may chance, after all, in taking to watercresses for a livelihood, I may still be subjected to an unpleasantness attaching to my present vocation. "Sir," said Mr. Wicks at our very first interview, "I'll tell you what is the 'licking'"— ("undoing," he meant; but he seems to have altogether forgotten how to talk like a jeweller)—"I'll tell you what is the licking of me, and has been for the past three months. It's that there hobnoxious bill."

"Not your son, surely," remarked I.

"No," said he; "I mean the Parliament bill—the repeal of the paper duty."

I should as soon have expected to find Mr. Wicks affected by the Church-rate Bill or the Bankruptcy Bill as the document he mentioned. His explanation, however, set the matter in a perfectly clear light. He had been for many years in the habit of serving with cresses, as they came out to breakfast and tea, the "hands" employed at a wholesale and manufacturing stationer's in Bunhill-row, St. Luke's. The usual number of workpeople employed at this establishment at ordinary times exceeds five hundred. Since, however, the paper-duty abolition has been pending, the number has been reduced to nearly a tenth, the watercress-man's receipts dwindling in the same ratio.

Among other wrinkles for which I am indebted to Mr. Wicks is one concerning the peculiarities of the green and brown cress. "Always buy the latter," urged he. "They will keep in good selling condition, with a little care and soaking in clean water, for nearly a week; whereas the green ones will hardly keep through a night, though stowed in a wet sack and laid in the cellar. Besides, if they do keep green, they don't smell very pleasant" (make a note of that, good reader, and *smell* your cresses before you buy them), "and the stems go so soft that it takes twice as many as it should to make a decent bundle." Moreover, Mr. Wicks, after inquiring if I knew what "brooklime" was when I saw it, broke up a bundle of watercresses and showed me several leaves of the weed in question. The said leaves are rather sharper than the watercress, and have a mottled appearance. People wouldn't buy the cresses if they knew there was brooklime with them, Mr. Wicks said; but that it was so harmless that I might, if so inclined, "eat a bushel" with impunity; and, moreover, that it was a capital medicine for jaundice.

Having thus far initiated me as to the sort of cresses to buy, Mr. Wicks magnanimously offered to show me where and how to buy them. Having, however, some time ago perused a detailed account of the ways and means of the watercress-sellers in "London Labour and the London Poor" (in which the writer had made known to the public the most minute particulars, even to the fact that the pace indulged in by the cressman was exactly *two miles an hour*), I was enabled to inform Mr. Wicks that I knew where the cresses were bought wholesale—in Farringdon Market. "That's one of the places," replied he; "but there are two others—one at Hackney and one at Waterloo Station. You get better served at Hackney than anywhere, because you buy them fresh out of the water; and, if you don't mind cutting them yourself, they ain't particular to a handful. The worst of it is, it is such a precious long way from St. Luke's, where I live; and if you ain't there very early—by four o'clock, say—you may stand shivering about the wet grass till your toes are numbed."

As far as I could understand from Mr. Wicks, the cress-beds in question are in the vicinity of Hackney Marshes, and that any morning scores of decrepid men and women, and tiny, ragged-headed, shoeless children, may be met, hours before daylight, trudging along with their baskets and old teatrays, towards the inhospitable region above mentioned, for the sake of buying "first hand, and saving, perhaps, twopence in the shilling," or, as it would undoubtedly happen in at least half the cases, a penny in sixpence—the extent of the stock money. And there they stand shivering in the bleak morning air, or saunter up and down by the chilly, cheerless stream, till the cress-cutters, walking knee-deep in the water, have time to give them their "turn." Something pretty it is to read about " cresses from the brook," isn't it? Quite refreshing to know that, though the cress-seller's gains are small, his labour is light and delightfully healthsome!

"I've been up at Hackney," said Mr. Wicks, "on an early February morning, when all the water, except the running streams in which the cresses grew, was frozen as hard as iron, and when it was so dark that the cutters had to have lanterns to see by. It's no use taking a basket for your stock at them times; you must take a bit of blanket or sack. Then it ain't much use: by the time you get your cresses home they are all frozen in one lump, and you have to lay them in the fender before you can pull 'em apart and tie 'em in bunches. 'Oh, dear!' says the people, 'what little bunches! why, it is like eating money!' 'Pon my word, it is enough to make a man cut the business, and go into the work'us."

Mr. Wicks was particularly anxious that I should accompany him one morning to Hackney Marshes, and witness the operation above described, starting at a quarter-past three (two good hours before daybreak); but, having a bad cold, I was obliged reluctantly to decline. I, however, compromised the matter by agreeing to accompany him to Farringdon Market the next time he went there. The "next time" came in an alarmingly short period, and at a ridiculously early hour.

Two mornings after that on which the subject was broached there came a ringing at my bell, and at the same moment four o'clock came booming through the murky air in muffled tones, as though the bell in the bleak belfry spoke through the folds of a "comforter." I am afraid I did not feel very well disposed towards Mr. Wicks at that moment. I had to picture in the most forcible colours what was the old gentleman's age next birthday, with his white hair and bare throat and chest, loitering outside in the dark, chilly morning, before I could bring myself to a sense of what was his due. In a few minutes, however, I was with him, and trudging towards "Farringdon."

It was barely half-past four by the market-clock when

we arrived, and still quite dark. Nevertheless, the great square and round wicker baskets had already made their appearance in the railway cars, and were unshipped and ranged in a row outside the market railings, at the Stonecutter Street entrance. The cress-sellers had not yet arrived, but the buyers had, and in considerable force; indeed, shock-headed, slovenly, and apathetic, they lounged about the posts or squatted in dreary threes and fours upon the market stones, as though, having nothing better to do, they had lodged there all night. Never was seen such a wretched lot of buyers. They were all so very old and so very young, there were so much rags and grey hair, and rags and wizened codlin'-faced poverty, and rags and bare mites of shoulder-blades, and tiny, horridly-dirty crimson feet, that it seemed that any one capable of taking from them the few halfpence they might have for watercresses, on any excuse whatever, was worthy of instant arrest and imprisonment.

Presently, laughing and chatting pleasantly, there came up the dark street the salesfolk. Evidently they had come up with their cresses by the midnight train, but had deferred business till fortified by a comfortable breakfast. What a contrast between them—they were chiefly women—and the poor wretches waiting to be served! It would be hard to find a contrast more extreme: the saleswomen warmly clad, ruddy and bright from the pure Sussex and Kentish air, and with that easy deportment that marks the well-to-do individual, on the one hand; while on the other was life in its ugliest shape—squalid, hopeless, ailing poverty.

The advent of the market women, however, and the opening of the big basket-lids, and the lighting of candles (thrust ruthlessly among the cress-stalks) at once roused the dormant loungers; and with their baskets and cold rusty tea-trays under their arms, they picked their way through the wicker avenue, shrewdly eyeing the various lots, giving here a dig with the fist to see how loosely or tightly the cresses are packed, or taking up a spray the better to judge of the colour. There seemed to be two ways of buying the cresses: by the "hand"—that is, as much as can be grasped by the forefinger and thumb—and by the "lump." By the former process the sales produced but little excitement. A penny a hand was the settled price; and either it happened that the hands of the saleswomen were much of a size, or, what was much more to the purpose, they were all equally kind-hearted and tender in their dealings with the ragged ones. The only grumbling that occurred was when the question of "blessing" came to be discussed. The "blessing" is a few cresses thrown in over and above the measured quantity, and evidently a "hand" bargain was never completed without it. I think it would conduce considerably to good understanding between the market-woman and her customers if the number of stalks of cress making a fair "blessing" could be adjusted. The wrangling on this point is incessant. "Is that me blessin'? Shure, it will take sivin sich to fetch a penny!" "Can't afford a bigger blessin' on threepen'orth, Kitty. Put 'em down if you don't like 'em."

Buying "in lump," however, involves considerable excitement, and just because the spirit of speculation, or, more properly, gambling, enters into the business. You may see half-a-dozen dirty faces clustered near the candle-lit cress-hamper, which is perhaps two-thirds empty; or there may be a "remnant" of just enough to pave one side of the basket.

"How much the lot?" has already been asked, and answered, with the invariable addition, "Have 'em or leave 'em."

The owners of the dirty faces are in a painful state of perplexity about the matter; they hobble off a short distance and compare opinions.

"I'm afeard they ain't very solid."

"They're Sussex creases, and the big stalks tells up well in bundling."

"Let us stay a bit, till it grows lighter, and be sure about the colour."

You may see these important conferences going on in half a dozen different parts of the market at one time, accompanied by all the lip-biting and chin-stroking and winking and other facial contortions peculiar to extensive speculators. Mr. Wicks, however, did not go in for a "lump" of cresses. He bought ten honest handfuls with a good blessing for tenpence; and I left him going cheerfully to the pump to wash them, while I went home to breakfast.

THE SONG-BIRD MARKET.

XVIII.

THE SONG-BIRD MARKET.

THE London-bred man, escorting his cousin from Shropshire through the metropolis, pauses in the middle of handsome New Oxford Street or Endell Street, the broad and long, and observes, as he points out the six inches of glittering watchchain and the bunch of seals pendent from his friend's fob, "Ah, John! you wouldn't have found it so easy to step along here with that dangling before people's eyes twenty years ago. We are in Saint Giles's, John; on the very ground where one time o' day existed nothing but thieves' dens and beggars' haunts, and where a man with a pound in his purse would no more dare venture after dark than he would, unattended, perambulate the depths of an Indian tiger jungle. It's all over now, however. St. Giles is knocked on the head and dead and buried, and, instead, we have the broad and handsome thoroughfares you see before you."

Innocent relative of the Shropshire man! St. Giles is still alive, dwindled by old age certainly, but still in the flesh, kicking up his heels and crowing lustily. Alive is St. Giles as when the wife of Henry I., the good Queen Maud, pitying the many lepers that were shunned and hounded through her husband's dominions, caused to be built, "nigh Bleman's ditch, to the west of London," a sanctuary for the accommodation and maintenance of forty of the stricken wretches, dedicating the building to "the Athenian Saint Giles." Where the parish church now stands then stood the pesthouse, isolated and all alone, on forest land, bleak and boggy, as is evident from the prevalence of ditches and brooks or "bournes"—Oldbourne (the modern Holborn), Woe-bourne, West-bourne, Tye-bourne, &c., &c.

Whatever obligation we may lie under to saints as a community, we certainly have small cause to be grateful particularly to Saint Giles. More than two-thirds of a thousand years has he sojourned amongst us, and ever has the parish under his special control been a blot and a plague-spot on the face of the city. When, in 1413, the gallows standing at "the elms in Smithfield" was thought too ugly an object to exist so near the city, it was taken up and transplanted at the north corner of St. Giles's Hospital wall, between the termination of the High Street and what was then Hog Lane, and is now Crown Street. At that period originated the "St. Giles's Bowl." A bowl of ale was provided by the master of the Leper Hospital, and the man about to be hanged halted at the great gate and quaffed his last refreshment. When the gallows was removed to Tyburn the presentation of the bowl was not discontinued; it was upheld as long as the Leper Hospital stood, which was till 1547, and then a neighbouring innkeeper, that so good a custom might not become extinct, undertook to have ready the ale-bowl whenever the hangman's cart might halt at his door. It was on this gallows of St. Giles of the Lepers Lord Cobham was hanged.

To St. Giles's parish attaches the melancholy celebrity of originating the Great Plague of 1665, two Frenchmen residing at the upper end of Drury Lane first dying of it. Another plague likewise dates from this ill-favoured locality—viz., the plague of toll-gates. In 1346 King Edward III. granted a commission to the master of the Leper Hospital and to John de Holborne, empowering them to levy tolls at the rate of a penny in the pound on their value on all cattle, and the merchandise drawn by the same, to defray the expense of keeping the roads in proper repair. It would seem, however, that the revenue derived from this source was insufficient for the purpose, for so long as two hundred years afterwards Stow writes —"High Oldburn, leading from the bars towards St. Giles's, is very full of pits and sloughs, and perilous and noisome to all that repair and pass that way, as well on foot as on horseback."

The Seven Dials—the core of the evil apple that has been so repeatedly pared—remains still intact. It was a villanous place long before the "Dials" were erected, and was known as "Cock and Pye Fields," and as the constant resort of all sorts of blackguardism, from duelling to dog-fighting. At length, however, at the latter end of the seventeenth century, the land was purchased for building purposes, and, says Evelyn in his "Diary," under the date of the 5th of October, 1694, "I went to see the buildings near Saint Gyles's, where Seven Dials make a star from a Doric pillar placed in the middle of a circular area." Then began the most respectable period of St. Giles's existence. Monmouth Street was built and christened after the earl of that name, who resided in Soho Square. Dudley Court contained the mansion of the Duchess Dudley, and in Lloyd's Court Lord Wharton and Lord Lisle took up their abodes. Compton Street was built and christened after Sir Francis Compton, who there resided. Sir John Brownlow, Sir Lewis Lewkner, and other celebrities, likewise occupied houses in streets branching from the Seven Dials.

How the neighbourhood fell from its high estate, how it passed so completely into the hands of the Irish, history sayeth not. The thousands of French Protestants who on the revocation of the edict of Nantes passed over to this country, and took up their residence in places where house-rent was cheap, may perhaps account for such places as Seven Dials growing less respectable, but it certainly does not dispose of the Irish question. It is, of course, an extremely foolish idea; but when one sees nobody but Irish people, never Scotch, never Welsh, the sole inhabitants of localities given over to filth and squalor, one is almost brought to entertain the question—is it the Irish that make wretchedness and depravity, or is it wretchedness and depravity that make people Irish?

Let it be how it may, one thing is certain, the Irish have got hold of Seven Dials beyond redemption. St. Giles's and the Irish are identical, and I seriously believe it to be the popular impression that the saint in question as properly belongs to Ireland as does St. Patrick himself, and at present there is little reason to suppose that the memory of the one will die out a day before the other. St. Giles die, indeed! Not he. Assailed as he has been for seven hundred and fifty years by leprosy, by plague, by fire, oppressed by the weight of the gallows, and stripped and routed by the officers of the law, and the Sanitary Commissioners and the Board of Works, he is as cheerful as ever. He is like an eel, and has been treated as one—beheaded, and chopped into little bits, but every bit is still full of life, and leaping.

There is one particular bit of this loathsome eel—a very little bit it is—lying between Earl Street and Castle Street, and known as Neale's Passage (Neale was the individual who set up the Doric pillar that Evelyn saw). It was broad noon when I paused at the mouth of the passage, and, attracted by the sound of music and rejoicing, looked down. Midway in the grimy thoroughfare (which contained about twenty tall houses), and reclining on a costermonger's barrow, were two Irish pipers—real Irish pipers, such as never in my life before have I seen in London—with genuine long-tailed coats, and tall, jauntily-cocked hats, piping an inspiring tune, while swarming the road and pathway were a great number of the female sex, some dancers, some lookers-on. Some of the females were hideous, yellow-fanged, and smoke-dried hags, wearing nightcaps with full and flapping borders; some were muscular creatures, brawny-limbed, and middle-aged, with a manly expression of countenance, and with their hair first twisted into a wisp about as smooth, and certainly as thick as a hayband, and then bundled up and secured by a substantial knot behind; some very little, old, slovenly-bosomed, draggle-tailed women of sixteen; while others again, were straight-limbed, comely damsels, with teeth defiant of neglect, and with rosiness of a strength superior to all opposition. These latter, for the most part, wore handkerchiefs over their heads and tied under the chin.

From almost every half-glazed, rag-stuffed window

in the face of the tall houses protruded a head, sometimes two heads, more or less hideous, the lips, as a rule, bearing a filthy little pipe. Equally as a rule were the upper windows garnished with reeking rags, suspended to dry on the thrust-forth clothes-prop, or with ropes of onions, or with shreds of dried cod, or some other such dainty, the outer wall being the only place beyond the reach of the picking and stealing digits of little children, hungry as wolves in mid-winter. Some of the down-looking heads were haggard and wan, and nightcapped, engendering a suspicion that the unseen bodies were lying abed helplessly; while other lookers-out, bright-eyed and eager, and strumming on the window-sills the tune the pipers are playing, looked as if they would willingly have joined the merry party below if they had aught else to cover their shoulders than the scrap of blanket or bed-quilt that now adorns them.

Only two of the dancers—there were ten or a dozen of them—danced at one time, while the rest squatted on the thresholds of the wide-open doors, or leaned cross-legged against the walls, or sat on the kerb and regained their spent breath, while at the same time they cooled their slipshod feet in the gutter. With the exception of the pipers there were no men present, which went far to show that it was neither wake, wedding, nor extraordinary merrymaking, but merely an ordinary afternoon's piping by the ordinary St. Giles's pipers, whose Christian names were familiar in the mouths of the dancers, who ordered Barney to play "fashter," and rebuked "Mike Sullivan, bad luck to yez!" for keeping incorrect time.

Being within a stone's cast of Monmouth Court, it occurred to me to go and see how fared the prince of ballad-mongers, the dying-speech merchant-printer, John Catnach. Narrow is Monmouth Court—scarcely so wide as an ordinary chamber doorway—and so low at the arched entrance that the tall policeman who emerged as I entered, slackened at the knees involuntarily. It astonished me but little to find the great publisher in such dismal quarters—great firms seldom court publicity, and, although it had passed from the hands of the original founder, that the firm was still great, was evident from the existence of a board at the entrance, announcing "Thomas Fortey, late William Ryle, sole successor to J. Catnach."

Alas! a cruel surprise awaited me. Instead of the extensive premises, instead of the creaking of the "crane," the tick-tack of the packers for exportation, and the heads of the ledger-clerks visible above the opaque bottom row of counting-house windows, I found the renowned Catnach printing and publishing establishment to be as dismal-looking a little den as it is possible to conceive. Of the decline of the dying-speech business I was already aware, but to find it as completely all over with halfpenny ballads one was hardly prepared. So it is, however; at least judging from the samples of "stock" exhibited behind the grimy little panes with which is glazed the shop of the successor of the immortal Catnach. The singing public has kept pace with the reading public; and two songs, or two and a half, even though they be of the most pathetic character, printed on seven inches by five of dirty white tissue-paper, could hardly hope to realise a halfpenny while five-and-twenty square feet of politics and police news can be had, hot from the press, for a penny. No! The singing public has burst the chains that bound it to the flimsy halfpenny ballad, and will be pacified with nothing less for a penny than a "Giant Warbler," or a "Doodah Songster," or a "Concert Companion," sixteen pages at least, and with a coloured illustration. Not to be behind the times, these Mr. Fortey provides (there is an entire row of specimens in his window, together with farthing "Cock Robins," and "Goody Twoshoes," and penny "Norwood Gipsies"); but if he has, as he must have, any considerable number of the shabby little ballads by him, he will do well to take my advice, and refrain from disposing of them at a sacrifice on the speculation that they may one day again come into fashion. Why not? When I was a very little boy the current cheap literature of the day consisted of "Varney, the Vampire," "Claude

Duval, the Dashing Highwayman," "The Patch of Gore," &c. Gradually, however, there grew an army of wholesome periodicals that did battle with the vampires and the dashing highwaymen, and routed the miscreants, and ruled in their stead. Vampire literature came to be regarded as a curiosity belonging to a past and barbarous age, and, whenever an odd volume of the kind was discovered in the fourpenny box at a bookstall, was bought as such, to be laughed at and ridiculed. Will Claude Duval ever more hold his weekly levées? Will the people ever again consent to assist at the Vampire's "feast of blood?" Ha! ha! preposterous! Will tinder-boxes again come into fashion? Will folks believe in witchcraft, or the broth of a boiled mouse ever again be looked on as an infallible remedy for whooping-cough? If the question had been asked me ten years ago I should have replied, "Certainly not;" but when, in the year 1861, I see Women with Yellow Hair, and Blue Dwarfs, and Modern Jack Shepherds, vigorously rearing their ugly heads, I decline altogether to hazard an opinion on the subject.

From Monmouth Court to Monmouth Street, the atmosphere. of which is thickened and soured perpetually by the exhalations emitted from great stores of mildewed shoe-leather and ancient clothing, passive and disturbed by renovating processes. The houses in Monmouth Street are tall and spacious, but from the last-mentioned cause the uppermost chambers are as murky as basement floors in salubrious localities. Below the hazy attics are two and even three floors, then the shop, and beneath, so deep that a flight of fifteen wide-apart steps barely reach from the street pavement to the bottom, are the cellars—mere black pits—swarming with inhabitants, not chickens nor rabbits, nor rats or other sort of vermin, but human beings —babies and grandmothers, and broad-shouldered men, and hoary-headed men, and little old women, and matronly dames.

It should be distinctly understood that when I speak of these underground dwellings (several feet below the sewers) as cellars I apply to them no other than their proper and recognised appellation. They have just the ordinary double flap one sees closing the entrance to the beer-cellar of a public-house, and when one becomes vacant, "This cellar to let" will be chalked on the said flap. It would seem that we are indebted to St. Giles for this amongst other eyesores, for the books pertaining to the affairs of his parish bear the earliest record of cellar-dwellers. "To prevent the great influx of poor people into this parish," says an entry dated 1637, "ordered that the beadles do present every fortnight, on the Sunday, the names of all new comers, under-setters, and persons that have families in cellars, and other abuses." For more than two hundred years then has the doctor scrambled down those cellar-steps to let more life into the world, and the undertaker has grasped the muddy rail, shouldered out of the deep hole the coffined dead to lay it nearer the earth's surface than ever it was —for any length of time—while in life. As I looked down at broad afternoon there burned (as I suppose ever has burned) the flickering yellow-flamed candle, and there, bent by labour and age to the shape of a beast, squatted the lank-haired tailor (as I suppose he has ever squatted), plucking the needle from the seam as though a life depended on each stitch, whilst his wife was suckling the baby, and sewing the buttons to a pair of trousers, and toasting a herring for the tailor's tea; while from the far depths of the cellar's gloom came the hilarious voices of the tailor's many children; and ever and again their half-naked forms might be dimly distinguished flitting, goblin-like, round the turn-up bedstead, the many hangings of which waved feebly in the breeze they created.

Through White Lion Street and into Great St. Andrew's, where the bird market is, and to see which was the prime object of my visit to St. Giles's. Such a babel of bird music! In an atmosphere composed chiefly of pestiferous exhalations and the choking steams that rose from the rank pans of the Jew fish-fryers, there they were, with their cages closely packed on each other—starlings, and blackbirds, and thrushes, and finches of the "chaff," and the "gold," and the "bull" kind; and English larks, and foreign canaries, fiercely yelling out their music, as though they had all gone stark mad. Perhaps they had. I almost hope so. Bird music is so intimately associated with hedges, and orchards, and cornfields—the little feathered songsters have credit for such elevated sentiments—that to discover, after all, that a lark will sing as well in a fried-fish shop as when sailing in the sun over a clover-meadow would be unpleasant. No! The birds of St. Andrew's must be insane, every lark and finch of them.

Birds of song were not the only sort vended in St. Andrew's-street. There were in big wicker-cages Aylesbury ducks and Spanish hens, and bantams, and suspicious-looking cock birds, sleek and small of breast and spiky of spur, and geese and pigeons of every size and shape, and ravens, and parrots. Then there were houses for song-birds, from the threepenny wire-and-deal edifice to the magnificent pagoda-cage with mandarin-bell, for genteel canaries. Bird-food, too: "German paste," hampers full of snails, and many-legged meal-worms animating horribly the measure of bran in which they were kept.

The bird-merchants dealt likewise in rats and dogs. "Rats bought and sold" was advertised on boards hung against the door-posts; and, if you peeped within the stinking little shops, there you saw scores of rats in iron cages, clambering over each other, and hurrying ceaselessly round and round, nosing at every interstice, in hopes to find one wide enough to squeeze their bodies through; while slim-waisted terriers, with jaws agape and straining at their tethers, fiercely barked their earnest desire that the vermin might presently be successful. There were other dogs besides the ratters—dogs for the "lap," great spotted dogs, stupid and flunkey-looking, for the carriage, and great surly hounds with pink eyes and hanging lips, faithful watch-dogs, and with sharp teeth for the calves of the midnight burglar. Every now and then, rising above the mad bird-music and the jabbering of the starlings, and the clucking of the cocks and hens, and the melancholy cooing of the pigeons, came the sharp howl of a dog in pain. I wonder what ailed him? Outside one of the shops was the picture of a terrier with a pair of big shears straddled over him, and the legend, " Dogs trimmed, eightpence," underneath. Was the poor howling wretch undergoing the trimming torture? I hurried from the dreadful place, followed by the fitful yelps, and almost fancying I could hear the horrid blades snipping off its poor little ears.

XIX.

A LONDONER'S CHRISTMAS.

MY name is Job Blunt. Probably you have heard of me before; if so, you are aware that I am not a sentimental man, nor an admirer of veneer, and stucco, and french-polish. They hide the true grain and breed speculation, and speculation, to me, is detestable. "Downright" is my motto, and I am entitled to it, for I ask no more than I offer. I am as plain as an oaken post, and as rough and as tough, and I hope I may say as stanch. I'm not ashamed of the nakedness of my hand, and I would'nt wear gloves if I was worth a thousand a year. I can find my way about without the aid of spectacles, and am quite content to follow my nose. It is a sound, homely, sagacious organ, and though, at present, it has not scented out the way to Tom Tiddler's ground, it has warned me of several paths promising enough to look at, but which turned out "no thoroughfare," being barred at the further end by a workhouse door.

I never take anything "for granted." If I don't see the way clear before me, I halt till some one is kind enough to show me a light. If a man doesn't understand a thing, he had better say so, and lay his case open to enlightenment.

Christmas is one of the things which I don't understand a bit. Don't misunderstand me. Why it should be a season of Christian rejoicing is as plain to me as to any other poor mortal with a soul to save; but either I am a dull, unemotional blockhead, or some people are dreadful hypocrites in their observance of it. There's that old Jobbling. I am a poor man, and live in a poor neighbourhood, and Jobbling keeps a porkshop round the corner. Jobbling had a goose club last year, and passing his shop early on Christmas Eve, I saw the porkman at high words with a poor woman, who had only paid up half her subscription-money, and who begged that she might have out the four shillings she had paid in bacon, that being, she declared, her only prospect of meat for her Christmas dinner. Jobbling would not let her have it; he referred her to the rules of the club, and fiercely told her that if she stayed there kicking up a row he would lock her up. Yet at church-time on Christmas morning I met Jobbling, looking as sleek, and as meek, and as sanctimonious as though Peace and Goodwill, in their search for worthy vessels, had lit on the porkman and filled him to the brim. Or, as though He whose birthday was celebrated just a year ago had died yesterday, and the new Prince, born when midnight had tolled and the merry bells began to peal, was too young to know anything of Mr. Jobbling's sinful ways of the past and many a previous year, enabling him to pass as a proper man if he only stuck well to his mask; that is, if it is a mask, and I am not a heathen. But, for that matter, I have observed the same behaviour in a dozen other men besides Mr. Jobbling. One would think that they held their lives on lease from year to year, from Christmas to Christmas, and that the only way of gaining a renewal of the lease was by a display of much humility and contrition, and shaking of hands, and charitable thoughts of distant enemies on the twenty-fifth of December. The next day, the new leaseholder steps into the world of weights and measures and chops and changes with less of the whites of his eyes apparent than was the case yesterday, and with the corners of his mouth at their accustomed angles. For a whole year the lease is stowed away—forgotten, buried; and this may be the true reason why the day following Christmas Day is called Boxing Day.

After all, however, and admitting that Mr. Jobbling's behaviour on a Christmas morning is that of a humbug, it remains a question whether he or they who made him so are most to blame. Who are they? Who are responsible for the wishy-washy sentimental nonsense that fills the heads of the people at Christmas time? Why, the story-writers: the literary gentlemen who, regularly as December sets in, take to saturating every journal and magazine in the three kingdoms with mystery and superstition, and all manner of unearthliness, a mere sniff at which, to weak minds, is as potent as chloroform. I've no objection to the writer of fiction; indeed, I can enjoy as well as any man a crisp, startling, rattling tale of adventure: but the stories of your Christmas writers are seldom or ever of this sort. They are artfully written, as though they were either the personal experiences of the writer, or confided to him by one who never would have divulged the tragic business that he had a hand in only for the "mysterious influence" of the season. The writer's aim is, not to amuse his reader, but to make him shudder—to give him the creeps; he cleverly insinuates "Who knows?" in the matters of churchyard warnings and visitations from disembodied spirits; it is his delight to make timid people afraid of shadows, and to mistrust the comfortable fire because of the "faces" that haunt it.

So far, I can only say that I *believe* the Christmas-story writer to be an impostor. I can't say for certain. There *may* be faces in the fire; the frost on the windows *may* take more fantastic shapes on Christmas morning than any other; there *may* be such things as ghosts. When I see 'em I'll believe in 'em. Perhaps it is only people that are more F. than R. who have the privilege of seeing such things, and of writing about them after they have seen 'em. If so, the Christmas-story writer is not so blameable a person as if he were more R. than F. I don't understand it; so will let this part of the subject drop.

What I do understand is what the Christmas-story writer has got to say about Christmas parties. In this matter I have no hesitation in saying that he is either a very ignorant person or a—well, I want a milder expression that will convey my meaning—a deliberate falsifier. I've seen three-and-twenty married Christmases, to say nothing of the six-and-twenty single ones passed down home: and I am bound to say that if the whole number could be squeezed in a press they would not yield a quarter as much sentiment, and romance, and pathetic incident—all due to the "mystic influence" of the season—as may be found in any one of the fifty domestic Christmas stories to be bought to-day at the publisher's shop. My name is Job Blunt; and, at the risk of being considered rude, I'm bound to express my opinion that the Christmas parties met in the Christmas stories are never met out of 'em; they're all bosh.

I believe I'm entitled to this opinion on all sorts of grounds. I flatter myself that I am not less wide-awake than most people, and that if any member of any Christmas circle of which I have made one had been seized with pathos, or sentiment, or anything of that kind, it would not have escaped me. For that matter, why should not *I* feel the "mystic influence" at Christmas time, since it's so much about? I'm ready! I'm not like an affected milksop who would shrink from it. Let it fall on me, or over me, or whatever it is, and when I feel it I'll up and say so like a man.

If not on me, why not on my family circle? It's a circle of the regular Christmas-story sort. Boys and girls, they count nine; and when they stand in a row the gradual descent from Thomas, who is a porter at a milinary establishment, to little Jess, the youngest, is very suggestive of a flight of stairs, which I believe is very often the case with Christmas-story family circles. My wife is a plump woman enough, and little, since the Christmas-story writers like plump little mothers of large families; and she has merry, brown eyes, which, as is known, they are likewise partial to. My father is an old man, with thin white hair, and a bent back, and a crutch stick (it is one of the oddest sticks you ever saw; made out of the ironwood paddle of a South Sea Islander's canoe, and carved from top to bottom with ships and whales, and pictures of cannibal customs; my father has been a seafaring man); he's a good-tempered old chap; and the young ones, when they know he is expected, are as pleased as Punch. He always spends Christmas with us. Then I've got an uncle a soldier, with a wooden leg, and a silver plate in his skull, both earned fighting in the China wars; and a nephew a middy in Green's service; and another nephew a warder at one of the London prisons. I could go on with the list a goodish while; but it isn't worth while, my only object being to show that the Christmas circle gathered in our parlour is one in which the "mystic influence," if it exists, might not unreasonably be expected.

Anyhow, we are jolly enough without it. If a man asks me to a party, I make up my mind to enjoy myself, relying that nothing on his part will be wanting to make me comfortable. I abide by the same rule. My Christmas guests may depend on good meat and good liquor, and as big a fire as they please. They'll find a piece of holly in the pudding and a bunch of mistletoe hanging from the centre of the ceiling. They'll find my son Tom, who, if they are inclined to singing, can accompany any of them upon the flute. If they are smokers, they'll find a good supply of the best birdseye and some straw pipes. But what they *won't* find, as I said before, unless they bring it with them, is the " mystic influence."

"It is there, nevertheless," Mr. Jobbling would probably say. "You ignorant man, it has not a corporeal existence; you can't catch hold of it; it's as subtle as air; it is air; your house is full of it; you breathe it and are full of it, you and all your family. Jolly enough? of course you are. It is the mystic influence that makes you jolly, and free of heart, and hand, and speech; it's that which gives a delicious flavour to the sirloin and that indescribable odour to the big plum pudding, and adds hops to the ale, and sets the fire roaring and crackling. What would the old stories and the old songs be without the mystic influence? What but it links the members of your merry-making circle so lovingly, and brightens dull eyes, and sharpens dull memories, and makes you speak and act as you only can this once a year?"

Speaking from the Christmas-story-book, this is pretty much what Jobbling would say. He might add, "Now, you take particular notice, next Christmas, of your own feelings towards other folks, and of their behaviour towards yourself; and afterwards tell me whether what I have said on the subject is right or wrong."

It is done already, Mr. Jobbling. I *did* take particular notice on the last Christmas that happened, and have much pleasure in presenting you with the result.

Besides my father and Uncle Haddock—he of the silver plate and the wooden leg before mentioned—there were invited the prison warder and his young woman, and my nephew in Green's service, and a shopmate of mine from the docks (I am a cooper, you will please to understand), and his wife and their daughter Rebecca, who, my wife will have it (it makes me laugh!), is sweet on our Tom. Eight, without our own flock, are as many as I can find table-room for. Bear in mind I have nothing to do with choosing the guests. With the exception of father and uncle Haddock, my wife invited every one. Since I wanted to put the mystic business to the test, I was glad that it came about so.

If any one imagines that I was prejudiced, he is mistaken. "A fair field and no favour" is my constant maxim, and I didn't depart from it on this occasion. Between eleven and twelve I went to bed, quite calm and easy in mind, and prepared to follow the humour the morning, the Christmas morning, brought one. But it happened that I was not to wait till the morning for my first observation of the mystic-influence question; about twelve o'clock there struck up some music close at hand. I don't know what else there was, but I could make out a cornopean, and a flute, and a concertina. It was the "waits." Now, everybody knows how beautifully the Christmas-story writers write about the waits, and their enchanting music. The musicians were just far enough away to make their performance pleasant and soothing to any one pleasantly half-asleep. I could make it out to be "The Last Rose of Summer" they were playing, and they played it so nicely that I was quite sorry when they had finished. They struck up again, however, and this time it was "The Light of other Days." Mrs. Blunt used to sing this when we were courting, and I was always pleased to hear it in any shape. I am bound to say that when I heard the waits playing this familiar old tune, it set me thinking. At the same time, however, I am equally bound to state that it always *did* set me thinking, more or less. I wondered if she, too, was listening and thinking. I nudged her.

"Hear the waits, Sarah?"

"Yes."

"Don't you remember——"

"Hush! How can I listen while you talk?"

This made me open my eyes. She is a rare woman for sleep, and mortally hates being disturbed; and yet here she was lying awake, listening to the waits! Did the magic of the music enthral her as the story-writers insist it does everybody? Was I enthralled? If I had thought about it two minutes longer I believe I should have been, but Sarah presently cut short my wondering as effectually as though it had been an egg and she had dropped a brick on it.

"There!" said she; "that's where he's out!"

"Where who's out, Sarah?"

"That flute-player," replied she; "I've got no patience with the new-fangled twists they put into tunes in these days. Our Tom plays six times better than that stupid." And with that she settled her head on the pillow, and in a minute after began to breathe in a way that convinced me she was fast asleep.

Next morning Tom awoke us—at least, he woke his mother by knocking at the door, and she woke me by calling out, "What do you want, Tom?"

"These precious boots," replied Tom; "I can't get 'em on. I've been trying this half hour. Dash the boots!" and Tom, whose foot I suppose was half in one of the boots (bought new on the previous evening), gave such a violent kick against the skirting of the wall that you might have heard it next door.

Tom had got up early, as he had promised to be over

at Rebecca's place at Rotherhithe to breakfast, and then they were all to come back to dinner together. It wasn't more than six o'clock, and pitch dark. To be hammered up in this way put me out a bit.

"Serve you right," said I; "you should be a little less dandified, my boy, and buy boots that fit you."

"So they did fit me when I tried 'em on," replied Tom, saucily; "so they would now, if my stockings were like another fellow's, and not all darned and seamy as these are!"

"Darned and seamy! you false-speaking boy, you——"

But there, we won't go further into the matter, Tom's boots and stockings being perfectly private matters, and of no sort of interest to any one besides himself. I shouldn't have mentioned them, only, having resolved to note my waking sensations, I was compelled. Did the row occasioned by Tom's seamy stockings scare away the mystic influence, and had Tom's boots gone on easy, should I have awoke placid and serene? Perhaps. But I'm pledged not to speculations, but to facts; and the fact is, I did *not* rise in a meek and charitable spirit, but rather inclined to give Master Tom a word or two of a sharp sort, if he hadn't contrived to get his boots on and set off to Rotherhithe before I got down.

So much for my waking on Christmas morning. There was nothing particularly noteworthy about the breakfast, except that the youngsters were allowed strong coffee and an egg each. After that the youngsters went to Sunday-school, just as they do on Sundays, and the two girls helped to clear up and cook, likewise just as they do on Sundays; the only difference being that there was more than common occasion to put the place to rights, and consequently more work to do, which I had a hand in by touching up the picture frames a bit, and giving the chimney-glass a polish. I tied up the mistletoe, and, being not quite sure about its being in the centre, called up the missus (she has got a wonderfully true eye) to have a look. I didn't tell her what I wanted her for, and when she came in at the door and saw, she for an instant looked a little cross; but then she laughed and said—

"Lor! the idea of your bringing me up from the kitchen for such nonsense! What an old stupid you are!"

She'll find out for the first time when she reads this that such a thought never entered my head till she put it there.

"You'll get the goose-fluff all over your black satin waistcoat if you don't mind," said she, and so I did; and the rum being on the sideboard, we each had a little drop.

This was about all that happened out of the general way till the old gentleman came. Grandfather, white-haired old grandfather, with his pockets crammed with toys for the youngsters, is almost as great a favourite as the waits with the Christmas-story writer. The father of the family in the Christmas story usually gives the old man a welcome in the passage, or at the gate even, the children swarming over him, and picking his pockets, and crushing his hat, and well-nigh strangling him out of gratitude. I knew that, however powerful the mystic influence might be, there was small chance of this happening, my father being a man very suspicious of fuss. Besides, the children had not yet returned from Sunday-school. The missus opened the door for him, both the eldest girls greeting him in the passage.

"Here you are, then, grandfather! Why, how well you are looking!"

"Yes, thank God! and I'm feeling well, except from my old complaint—you know. I wish you a merry Christmas, my lass; and you, too, my dears. Where's Job?"

"Here he is. When you've done kissing the women, come up, father."

"How are you, my boy? How well Sally looks!"

"Oh, yes; she's all right, I believe. How precious cold your hands are, father!"

"Cold! Blessed if I don't feel like a mouthful of frost-bite! Outside that precious Camden Town 'bus, Job—crawl, crawl! It was as much as I could do to keep from swearing. Thankee. Well, here's health and prosperity to us all! That's as tidy a drop of rum, Job, as I've tasted since I left the service."

Then we had a little to say about hot Christmases and cold Christmases; and then he went back to the subject of his cold ride on the omnibus, and from that we got to talking about railways, and of steam-boats, and of steam-rams, and of the war in America—just exactly as we should had it been Easter Monday, or Good Friday, or the most ordinary Tuesday or Wednesday. It was easy to see the mystic influence had not got over my father.

"The North can't do it, sir!" said he, bringing his fist down with a bang, as was his way when he argued about war. "The South will lick 'em into fits, sir; they might have done it months ago, but for their lady-like generosity, and sparing this, that, and the other, instead of putting it to fire and sword. They should 'mow as they go,' sir, as they did when I was a fighting-man. That's the way to put a quick finish to a fight, my lad! Why, look at that time when our little squadron was hammer and tongs with the Malayan pirates! 'Mow as you go!' was our motto there, sir; and——"

So the fierce old man-o'-war's man went on—about as peaceful and charitable as a mastiff. He kept it going till Uncle Haddock, and Joe Haddock, the warder; and Elizabeth, his young woman; and Mr. and Mrs. Cole, from Rotherhithe, along with their daughter Rebecca and my Tom (his feet having settled into the boots, he was all right now), arrived, and the dinner was ready.

It certainly was a capital dinner—as good a dinner as I ever sat down to. If the mystic influence had anything to do with it, I'm sure I am very much obliged to it; but, at the same time, it is only fair to state that it *ought* to have been a good dinner. Tenpence-halfpenny is a long price to give for ribs of beef; and when a man gives fourteen shillings for a goose, he can hardly be expected to be astonished if it turns out plump, and fat, and tender. Besides, my missus is a cook—a *real* cook, you understand. She was getting her sixteen pounds a year and perquisites when I married her, so I think I may make bold to say that the mystic influence wouldn't be able to put her up to much in preparing a dinner. It *was* a nice dinner; everybody said so. Everybody looked so hearty and happy that it seemed quite a pity to take the dishes away.

The Christmas-story writer seldom has anything to say about the afternoon (it's all nonsense to say that there *is no* afternoon between a poor man's Christmas dinner-time and his tea-time; his regular time being twelve, if he puts it off till two, it isn't a slight compliment), and I have nothing to say about it either. The ladies went one way, the young fellows another, and Uncle Haddock and father and myself shut the door and had a pipe and a glass, and fell off one after the other into forty winks round the fire. Likewise, the Christmas-story writer has nothing to say about the party at tea, and I don't wonder; I'm sure I am always glad when it's over. The mystic influence doesn't seem partial to it either, judging from the rare occasions of its touching it.

Now comes the crowning time. The small fry are put to bed (they only get disagreeable and lie about, making pillows of people's new trousers and silk frocks, if you are foolish enough to allow them to sit up), the candles lit, the fire stirred, the chairs set round, and the grog made. Here we are, then; this is the Christmas circle exactly as the Christmas-story writer pictures it, with the exception that a jolly big lump of Wallsend coal does duty for the Christmas log—which is a smoky, ill-looking concern, and I believe burnt more frequently in stories than in fire-grates—and that the grog is not in a bowl, but in tumblers. What next? There's Mrs. Cole and my missus talking in half whispers about the remarkable manner in which little Charley Cole is cutting his eye-teeth; there is Bill Cole and my nephew, the warder, talking about picking oakum and caulking; Uncle Haddock is swigging his grog, and explaining to father and myself how that he daren't drink because of the silver plate in his skull; while Joe Perkins, Elizabeth, and my eldest girls are giggling together, and observing my Tom and Rebecca looking so lackadaisical, and holding hands as though any one wanted to part 'em. Presently Tom discovers the gigglers, and wants to know if somebody is going to sing.

Then singing commences. Mrs. Cole sings "The Dashing White Sergeant," followed by that merry little old song, "When I lived in my Grandmother's Cot," by my missus; and then "The Wolf," by Joe Perkins, because Elizabeth asked for it. I don't sing; no more does Uncle Haddock; but my old father does—good old sea songs. He sings them—"Harry Hawser," and "The Death of Nelson," and "Hearts of Oak"—with surprising activity for so old a man; getting on his legs and describing the position of the enemy and the various incidents and catastrophes with his crutch-stick, and with such energy that after each song the family circle found itself a good deal spread out, and had to close up again before the next song commenced. He offended Tom, and his mother, too, a little, I think. Tom kindly thought to assist his grandfather with his music; and when the old gentleman, with a stamp of his foot, roared out, "'Twas in Trafalgar's Bay!" Tom began to tootle-tootle on the flute. The old boy stopped at once. "Drat it, Tom," said he; "if you don't understand the song, don't make a mock of it! It was a battle fought with cannon, my boy—cannon! not with pea-shooters! Put that farden squeaker down." It was with the greatest difficulty in the world that Tom could be prevailed on, after that, to sing "The Young Man from the Country," though he had had the song-book containing it as long back as October; but when at last he did, father was good-natured enough to heal the wound he had caused Tom, by joining in the chorus to his stupid song.

When we had had enough of singing, somebody asked somebody else the last new conundrum; but, as everybody knew, it was very soon answered. After a few old riddles, in the last one of which some reference was made to a strait-waistcoat, Joe Perkins told us a story about a fighting man who was confined in the prison infirmary with delirium tremens, and the dreadful work they had with him. After that, we ceased for a while to be a circle, and engaged in pairs and threes—Joe Perkins with

Elizabeth, Tom with Rebecca, Mrs. Cole and my missus, whispering, laughing, and joking, while Cole and I talked about the docks, and the old soldier and sailor about their pensions—all perfectly comfortable and jolly. Then a game at cards was proposed, and one and all engaged in a round and cheerful game at speculation, which lasted till supper-time, which ended the party.

As a merry party, as one that gave perfect satisfaction to all concerned in it, I'll back it against any in the land; but hang me if I could find anything of "mystic influence" in it from first to last.

XX.

THE GLEANERS OF THE THAMES BANK.

 RAGGED, tailless coat, minus the sleeves, buttoned over a shirtless back, a wonderful collection of materials and colours fashioned somewhat to the shape of trousers, and descending as low as the knees, with a pair of brown mud hose—said hose renewed at every tide, the new pair more often than not put on over the old—completes the costume of the mud-lark. A cap or old hat they have—we never saw a "lark" without one or the other—but the use of which an awfully towzled shock of hair renders quite superfluous; the article, in fact, is invariably used as a handy receptacle for the "lots" (bones), rags, and any other offal that falls in their way in their wanderings from the stock-basket or kettle, and saves the toil of dragging the whole of their findings with them in the operation of collection.

How the larks came by their appellation is a mystery; certainly no resemblance can be traced between the habits of the mud-lark, looking as he does like some extremely dirty amphibious animal, and the glorious little songster of the cornfields. No field is ever visited by the lark of the mud species; the only green thing that ever crosses his vision is the would-be antiquarian, who sometimes haunts the scene of his labour to purchase for a trifle the treasures and curiosities found in his peregrinations. Old *Roman* coins (shankless brass buttons—those of old Trinity men's coats preferred, on account of their size and the puzzling device on one side), ancient pipe-bowls,

&c., &c., form the staple articles of trade; it always happening that the wary lark has the "luck" to turn up something curious should a party looking at all like a buyer be in his vicinity.

We recollect a friend who happened to be walking the river bank near one of these treasure hunters, just in the nick of time to see him turn up a rare old Apostles' spoon, very massive, and still bearing faint traces of the Goldsmiths' mark. He eagerly secured it at the trifling sum of three and sixpence, and long cherished it as the gem of his cabinet, till, having occasion to visit a Sheffield warehouse, he found the same article could be bought, bran new, for two and threepence per dozen.

Still these are not genuine "larks," but birds of prey— the hawks of the tribe—and may be detected at once, by their extremely knowing look and comparatively decent clothing, from the stolid, almost idiotic expression of countenance, always to be found in the *bonâ fide* mud-lark. No matter the weather—blazing July or bleak December—there they are to be found as sure as the retreating tide, the same old faces, in the same squalid rags, from seven to seventy, raking their daily bread from the feculent shore of the Thames from Chelsea to the Pool. Gaunt, old-fashioned children, stalwart, brawny men, tottering old women, each may be seen daily battling with the rising river for a crust.

If there is a period when their position seems bearable, it is on a scorching August afternoon, when the pavement is hot to the tardy feet and the mind wanders to shady lanes and bathing places, when dusty errand-boys lean lazily over bridge parapets and envy the "larks" as they wade, leg high, in the cool river, and wish their fathers had 'prenticed them to watermen. But it is not August all the year round; and if those same boys should look down on to the shore a few months later (which they don't, for if they stand still on the bridge for a moment to look over, the north wind comes rushing up and cuts their ears off), in spite of the biting air—in spite of the masses of ice that are piled up here and there, reminding him of Esquimaux and Captain Ross—in spite of the frost-bitten craft that look like gigantic twelfth-cake ornaments—there are his envied friends of the summer, raking and poking, with never an extra rag to protect their crimson legs and arms. There they are, and there they will be, while tides rise and fall, and there is a pennyworth of anything to be found for the seeking on the river shore.

Great storms and sudden floods are the mud-larks' harvest times. When the usually black and sluggish "Fleet ditch," converted by the accumulated water in its long journey into a swift and roaring river, bursts its bounds, it crushes and carries away, in its fierce passage through the dens that abound in Clerkenwell, the floorings of cellars and underground dwellings, engulphing the squalid furniture of the wretched dwellers. Should it happen to be night-time, it is then may be seen the exciting spectacle of clamorous men and women in boats, surrounding the mouth of the great sewer, watching for the appearance of their goods as they emerge from over the top of the massive iron door that guards the entrance. Legless tables, broken chairs, fragments of bedsteads, butchers' blocks, and beams from underground slaughter-houses, the stock-in-trade of coopers and basket makers, tubs and trays, hampers, cradles, bowls, and baskets—all crushed and broken, and heaped in pell-mell confusion in the boiling river. "That's mine." "Murther! stop that table, good luck to yer!" "There goes me drawers and all the childer's things, ochone!" "Stop thief!" "Arter you with that there cheer," &c., &c., are the ejaculations heard on every side as the articles recognised shoot out into the open water, not always to be picked up by the legitimate owner. Something more awkward than ordinary will occasionally choke the way entirely, and then nothing will move till poked and eased with boat-hooks and long poles; then out they whirl again, and what with the darkness and confusion of tongues, a great part is lost altogether and gains the middle of the river, floating quietly down with the tide, and becoming easy prey to our friends the larks, as it settles ashore miles from its starting place.

Nor is this the only good this ill wind blows the mud-lark; for weeks after such an event he will, when he has the chance (it is not allowed, and the iron gate has been put as a preventive), drop from the top of the gate into the slush below with all the unconcern of a ditch rat, and there he will wade, feeling his way in the pitchy darkness, groping with his feet, as he proceeds, for anything that may have sunk to the bottom or still rests in the tenacious mud, following the course of the ugly sewer as it winds under the principal thoroughfares of the City. This sewer is all that remains of the clear, rapid brook that was once dignified with the appellation of the River Fleet, running between grassy banks and crossed by wooden bridges in its pleasant course from Highgate through Islington—through rural Clerkenwell—by the Clerks'-well and the Clerks'-green, near Field-lane, by the side of the Fleet-market, which extended the whole length of what is now known as Farringdon-street, and thus into the Thames. The many places named after it—Fleet-street, Fleet-market, Fleet-lane, and the old Fleet debtors' prison—will give an idea of its ancient importance. From various causes, its limits gradually narrowed until it became a mere sluggish ditch, occasionally overflowing its banks, thus being for many years a great source of disease to the citizens. It is now covered in from end to end; and it is only on the special occasions already mentioned that it bursts its bounds and asserts its claim still to the ancient title of river.

Mud-larks are of two kinds: the coal-finder and the bone-grubber. The coal-finder comes with his basket at each tide, and generally finds enough for a load; and as he can readily dispose of them in the very poor neighbourhoods, at the rate of sevenpence a load, he reduces his earnings, scanty though they be, to a kind of certainty. Not so the bone-grubber or "lot-picker," as he is technically known. The river bones, black as ebony, are quite useless for any other purpose than that of being ground for manure, and consequently are not worth more than half the article will fetch when fresh and containing fatty matter for the soap-maker; so that, although bones are his staple commodity, old rags, bits of iron, old rope, &c., in fact, anything that the marine store-keeper will buy, may be found in the "lot-grubber's" basket. Their most favourite resorts are the neighbourhoods of shipbreakers, to pick up the old copper nails and bolts; these are among the most valuable of their findings. They now and then pick up small treasures—old coins, ancient relics, &c., especially if it happen to be a very low tide; but taking the average earnings of the bone-grubber, his business may be said to be the most precarious and wretched of any. Certainly their wants are few: their clothing costs nothing, and their lodgings are the dry arches of the bridges or in the foundation of new buildings. The arches under the Adelphi are a favourite resort, on account of the advantages offered by the dry floors of the carts and vans which are to be found there. Sometimes—but this is a treat—a little straw will be left in them. The luxury of a bed is as little dreamt of as combs and brushes or soap, and it is only when he happens (happily for his health) to "sweep" (steal from) a barge, a practice he is addicted to when opportunity serves, that he has the advantage for a time of prison comforts—a warm bath, clean shirt, clean clothes, and a clean bed. "He didn't so much mind all the fuss," a mud-lark lately informed us who had spent the previous six weeks in the salubrious atmosphere of Coldbath fields, "only when you come to pull off the warm linsey togs, and put on your own ragged duds before you come out, it's wery cold and wretched, wery!"

When the grubber's trade is slack on the banks, he will venture up the mouth of the open sewers; and this branch, though more lucrative than any other to an experienced hand, is attended with much difficulty and sometimes peril, as the following story, current among the fraternity as having happened to an old grubber some years ago, will testify.

It was a bleak January afternoon, and the grubber's searching having been unsatisfactory along the shore, he groped his way into a sewer that emptied itself between London-bridge and Blackfriars; now through such low-arched passages that he was obliged to go on his hands and knees, and now through places so narrow that his sides brushed the slime from the wall, all in the thick, murky darkness, and feeling with the toes of his naked feet the useful from the rubbish that lay at the bottom under the mud. It was bitter out on the river bank, and the warmth of the place induced him to stop longer than he should. Evening came on, and with it so dense a fog as to deprive him of the little light he had from the few gratings above, or, should he get near the outlet, from the light of the fires aboard the coal barges at the wharves.

He lost his way; in vain, in his terror, he tried every opening he could feel up and down, bruising and tearing himself. He at last came to a standstill, breathless and exhausted; and to add to the horror of his position, he felt the semi-liquid mud moving about his legs, and he knew the tide was setting in. The place he was in was not more than four feet high, constraining him to keep in a stooping position, his hands resting on his knees. To move one way or another would have been useless, and if it would have helped him he could not have done it—the dreadful thought that, for aught he knew, the water would rise to the very roof, benumbed and paralysed him. Up rose the tide, slow but certain, till it was above his knees, and laved his hands; his legs shook under him, and he would undoubtedly have sunk down had not another enemy besides the rising river at that moment assailed him. A sudden squeal and a sharp pain at the back of his neck told him the rats had found him. A sudden writhe freed him from his tormentor; but as the water rose (it was now nigh up to his body) they, finding him helpless and defenceless, attacked him at all points. His ragged clothes were but a poor protection, and he had no way of killing them but rubbing their heads against the roof as they came squealing and scratching at his throat, and biting his hands through as he pulled them from him. But worse than all was their attacks on his naked legs and feet, compelling him to keep up a kind of dance, hopping from one leg to the other, and scraping them off as well as he was able.

He could distinctly hear the rumbling of the vehicles along the roads, and the church clocks strike out the hours, and had screamed himself hoarse in a vain endeavour to make himself heard. The place now became awfully close, and the stench dreadful, with the sewer water within a few inches of his face; he was very weak from loss of blood, and if his tormentors had ceased their sharp biting for one moment, down he would have sunk; as it was, pain kept him up.

At this moment a quarter chime rang from the church; in an instant he recollected the last hour they had struck, and he knew that in three minutes the water would subside—three minutes, and there was not more than nine inches of space between him and drowning. If he had been a mathematician he could have computed his chance of escape from the rate at which the water had rose during the last hour; but being only an uneducated " lark," he did his best to recollect a prayer or two that was stowed away in his memory years before, and so beguiled the long, long three minutes, and the great danger was over. With the turning tide the rats left him, and if he had not their biting to keep life in him, he had the strong hope of escape, which sustained him while the water fell, and the sewer was reduced to its ordinary low-water level, and then he sank to a sitting posture. He fainted clean away; and there he would have remained till the tide rose again, and he had become an easy prey for the monstrous rats, had not a friendly "lark," who had seen him enter and knew that he had not come out again, groped his way in with a light and dragged him out to the river side.

He had not been twenty yards from the entrance the whole time; he was frightfully maimed and bitten, and was taken to the hospital and cured of his wounds and his "larking" propensities for ever. He took to the crossing-sweeping—the mere mention of a drain (that is, a sewer) bringing his fearful night with the rats rather too vividly back to his memory.

XXI.

THE HALFPENNY BARBER.

NE of the most prominent of my early recollections is of a barber and a barber's shop. Who he was, or where his premises were situated, I have now not the least idea; I only know that, at my earnest persuasion, my uncle Peter (who was a seafaring man) took me with him one day when he went to be shaved, and that, during the forty years I have since lived, nothing has made such a terrible impression on me. I know I must have been very young at the time, because I have a distinct recollection of uncle Peter lifting me over the puddles, and purchasing on the route a broad sheet of bachelor's buttons in my behalf.

It was a queer little place, that barber's shop. Round the walls were fixed seats, and the floor was thickly strewn with red sand, which blinked and winked strangely in the ruddy glow of the charcoal in the brazier, over which was kept hot the shaving-water. In the centre of the room were two chairs, and about the legs of one of them, and matted in the red sand, were shreds of human hair—auburn, and black, and grey.

The shop was untenanted when we entered, but uncle Peter made himself pretty much at home, and seated me on one of the side benches, while he himself took possession of the chair that didn't have the hair about its legs. Presently, and with startling abruptness, the barber made his entry by a side-door, of the existence of which I had not previously the least suspicion. He carried a towel in his hand, which trailed behind; and he wore two long combs in his hair, which stuck out like horns.

Suddenly going behind my uncle, he flung the towel round his neck, and secured it at the back. I began to be alarmed. Arming himself with a stout brush, the barber next advanced to the pot containing the bubbling water, turned his back for a moment, faced round again, and then dashed the brush, all reeking with scalding water, at my poor uncle's mouth, and among his whiskers, in the most savage way, till the poor fellow looked as though he were in a violent fit. I slipped from my seat, and advanced timidly to the spot where these horrors were being perpetrated, just in time—Heaven above us!—to see the horrid barber seize my relative by the nose with one hand, whilst in the other he flourished a gleaming, wedge-shaped knife! He tilted my uncle's chin till his head fell back, and the peculiar little lump in his throat shone again!

Not a moment was to be lost. I flung myself on my knees, and offered the assassin the entire contents of the little pocket in my frock—twopence farthing, and four pieces of pencil—to spare my uncle's life. He laughed mockingly. I turned to my relative, and entreated him to exert himself—to burst his linen bonds and fly!

Nay, I volunteered, despite the dreadful wedge-shaped knife, to cling to the barber's legs, and hold him, so as to prevent pursuit. Finally, the barber yielded to my entreaty, and released uncle Peter, who wiped his mouth, and came out of the shop unshaven, as he had gone in. Oh, the rapture of finding ourselves safe in the open air again! How I congratulated my uncle on his miraculous escape, and comforted him with my few remaining bachelor's buttons!

I have laughed over this myself many and many a time, but it was some years before I could overcome my deeply-rooted horror of a razor. It was with feelings quite unnatural to a young man that I first noted the appearance of down upon my face.

Twice a week, after I had made the alarming discovery, did I stealthily abstract the scissors from my sister's work-box, and, in the secrecy of my chamber, shear my tender countenance, till my strong young beard, arriving at maturity, rebelled against such feminine treatment, and insisted on being mown, and not snipped. Then, to stave off as long as possible the horrid wedge-backed thing that was hanging always before my eyes, I purchased pumice-stone, and "flatted" my visage till it looked as though it had been recently scalded. I bought new penknives, for the sake of their first edge, till one day my mother was surprised to find seventeen of those instruments stowed away in my hat-box. In fact, it was not till I had committed matrimony that I was shamed out of my dislike for a razor. By-the-bye, I fancy that, had my newly-made wife heard the key stealthily turn in the lock, and had then, by applying her eye to the keyhole, obtained a fair view of me, pale-faced and haggard—my hand nervously gripping the razor-handle—it's very likely she would have been tempted to knock at the door.

At the happy period above alluded to I was also cured of my prejudice against barbers—not that I had, through my early life, avoided them as I had the principal tool of their craft. I don't know how it was, unless I was guided by the same infatuation that leads people to skate on wafer-ice, and to crawl to the edge of dangerous chasms for the morbid pleasure of imagining what a pretty kettle of fish it would be if the brink were to give way and precipitate them to the bottom; but so it was. As a boy—nay, as a grown-up youth—I could never pass a barber's shop without feeling an itching to peep in. At that time o' day barbers used to extract teeth. There was a celebrated barber-dentist in Wormwood Street, Bishopsgate Street; and many a time, on Wednesday half-holidays, have I strolled to that neighbourhood and gazed on the decayed relics—molar and incisor —till the nerves of my own grinders have vibrated again.

My curiosity concerning barbers' shops, and things thereunto appertaining, has led to my discovering some rather curious facts connected with those individuals who exist by scraping a living from the faces of their fellow-creatures. I've talked with the man whose father it was who opened the first "three-halfpenny" shop in Lambeth Butts. I have had an opportunity of reading the handbill that was issued on that important occasion, and which, I've no doubt, created a considerable panic amongst the shavers of the period. The following is a copy of it:—

"Shaving! Shaving!! Shaving!!! Timothy Weevil begs to announce that, on Sunday, the seventeenth inst., he will, at his hair-dressing and shaving establishment, Lambeth Butts, reduce his price for shaving from twopence to three-halfpence, and for hair-cutting from fourpence to threepence. J. W. warrants to do his work with his usual skill at the reduced prices, and hopes he shall be none the poorer for the reduction."

T. W., junior, confidently informed me that his father *was* no poorer through the adoption of his liberal measure, but that business increased to such an extent that it was one man's work to strop razors. But, alas! such piping times were not to last. Mr. Weevil had set the ball rolling, and in a short time another shaver pitched his tent in the Butts, shaving chins at three-halfpence each, and trusting to the public that *he* "mightn't be any poorer for the reduction."

But Timothy was an enterprising man, and not to be daunted by a little competition; so he caused to be printed, and at the end of his pole published, an announcement, that "On and after Sunday morning next, every customer of his should be presented with a glass of gin or rum."

That was a hit. Every drunkard in the neighbourhood, whom Sunday morning had hitherto found in the aggravating position of having money to buy gin, and no gin to be bought till after church-time, flocked to Weevil's. But the glass was very small, and the barber staunch to his resolution that for *customers* only should it be filled. Many, therefore, were the schemes to procure a double, or even a treble, dose. Never were men so whimsical as those drunken customers of Weevil's. They would just have it off the upper lip—never mind the lower—they thought about cultivating a 'perial. Customer gets his glass, pays his three-halfpence, and sits down a few minutes.

"Hi, mister! I likes a clean chin, arter all. Let's have another scrape."

Another glass, another three-halfpence, and another pause.

"Well, I d'know! S'pose you just tittywates my whiskers a bit!"

And so on; leaving little doubt that the public-houses had only to keep closed all day long for Mr. Weevil to make his fortune, and his customers to go bald as pumpkins.

Weevil, junior, reveals to me these little episodes in his father's life as we sit together in the little parlour behind his shop at Wapping Wall. The reason I am there, and the reason the poor fellow is so obligingly communicative, is that, that same morning, I had had the good fortune to pass his premises just as a broker's man was unscrewing the tricoloured arm from his door-post. I had the pleasure of standing over him while he screwed it on again.

My eyes, wandering from the table whereon still lay the discharged "distraint for rent," encountered the words "Shaving One Halfpenny," painted in big red letters, the full length of his shop-window. I thought I had discovered a solution to the whole business. Here was a man who had ruined himself through working at a rate that could not possibly be remunerative. I told him so.

"Lord bless you, sir," replied he, "shaving for a halfpenny ain't the cause of my misfortune—the halfpenny pays well enough. Why, I know a man who gave *three hundred pounds* for a halfpenny business, in Whitecross Street, St. Luke's, and who don't repent of his bargain either. It ain't the price, nor it ain't the lack of business—it's the *sort* of customers that ruins me."

I was at a loss to know what difference this would make. Was not one chin as good to operate on as another?

"Certainly not," replied he. "You see, sir, this neighbourhood is just made up of coalheavers and whippers, and they are the very worst kind of men to shave. In the first place, taking the throat and the big chin, you have got about three times the ground to go over to what you have on an ordinary face; and, in the second, the grit and coal-dust they carry in their beards never fails to take the edge clean off a razor at one using. I'd 'most as soon go and shave a man sick a-bed as a coal-whipper."

I remarked that shaving a sick man in his bed must be a very distasteful job—one of the worst that ever fell in his way.

"With the exception of shaving a dead man!" said he, shaking his head gravely. "Ah! nobody knows what that is but those who have tried it. The beard seems to have gone dead, too—it loses its crispness, and goes as soft and as tough as whipcord. It falls before the edge of the razor, and you glide over it without cutting a hair. The coldness is the worst, though—it ain't the coldness of ice, nor of anything but what it is. To find *that* creeping into your fingers and up your arms!—ugh!"

The barber took a turn or two across the little parlour, whistling. After half an hour's further conversation with him (in the course of which he munificently offered to cut and curl me gratis, to the end of my days), I took my leave of the face-reaper, understanding that he intended to shift his quarters to a less stony soil.

I was determined to see for myself if it were possible for a man to make his fortune by shaving his fellow-men at a halfpenny each; so, having carefully treasured the address of him whom my friend of Wapping Wall asserted to be the most flourishing barber in London, I set out on Saturday evening—as likely to be the busiest time in the week—and about six o'clock found myself in a dismal little street in Walworth, and ascending the well-worn steps of "Flight's Halfpenny Shaving-shop."

As soon as I put my head inside the door (which was kept on the swing by a strap), I had misgivings as to the truth of the information derived from Wapping Wall. It was such a little place! Evidently it had, at one time, been an ordinary front-parlour. The sitting accommodation consisted of three forms, four chairs, and the three bottom stairs of a flight that led to an upper apartment: certainly not more than twenty persons could possibly have found seats.

The secret, however, was that they were *always* occupied. I sat there for at least an hour (under pretence of waiting for a party), and I can safely say that no one seat was ever empty for the space of half a minute.

Mr. Flight's establishment consisted of himself, two young men, and an apprentice-boy. Only one of the two young men, however, was available for shaving purposes; the other one undertook the hair-cutting, and passed from poll to poll with amazing rapidity. About the centre of the room were placed five chairs, all in a row; and the labour of shaving was divided amongst Mr. Flight and his three helpers in the following very methodical manner.

As soon as one of the five chairs became vacant, and a fresh customer sat down, the young man, leaving for an instant his occupation of stropping, rushed forward, pinned a cloth round the neck of the unshaven one, and immediately returned to his corner. Then the "soap-boy" (who has just finished lathering the last man) takes him in hand.

Armed with a dirty soap-bowl and a big brush, he crosses over to the hob, and plunges the brush into an indescribable brew that simmers there in a saucepan. Then, having dabbed it (the brush) two or three times on the soap, he commences scrubbing away with it at the man's face, much as though it had been dirty wainscot, and he was under orders to renovate the paint. Backwards and forwards, and round and round, darting fiercely at his victim's nostrils, twirling amongst his whiskers, changing the brush deftly from the right hand to the left, working about the man's lips and chin with his fingers, and finishing off by scooping the unnecessary suds from between the man's lips with his thumb-nail—it was certainly a nasty and a most barbarous exhibition.

It seemed to be the boy's special business to keep the individual whom Mr. Flight intended to operate on next "moist" till he was wanted; and, being a sharp boy, he generally managed to keep at least two in reserve—so that Mr. Flight always found a customer ready napkined and lathered to his hand. In nine strokes Mr. Flight finished him. During the time I sat there, I counted at the rate of *thirteen* shaven faces pass out every ten minutes!

THE HOUNDSDITCH JEWELLERY MARKET.

XXII.

THE HOUNDSDITCH JEWELLERY MARKET.

 HAVE reason considerably to modify the opinion I lately expressed concerning the Houndsditch Sunday Fair. A week or two ago, having, as I imagined, explored it thoroughly — having perambulated Moses Square, where the rags and tatters, and secondhand hats and bonnets, and shoes and stockings, were bartered and haggled; and Cutler Street and Petticoat Lane, famous for workmen's tools, musical instruments, and military and marine stores; and Phil's Buildings, where swarm and chaffer among themselves the real "Ole Clo" men and women; and the "Exchange," where, collected from Heaven knows what sources, are constantly exposed for sale silk gowns, satin gowns, costly laces, and shawls of Persia and India, tarnished certainly, but still with a thoroughbred air about them that begot much sympathy for their unfortunate condition—when I had discovered all these things, my impression was that I knew all about the business; and this is what I thought of it:—
That it was, as a business, nasty, and mean, and miserable; that they who embarked in it were to a man or woman Jews; and that its character gave the flattest contradiction to the proverbial cunning of the Jew, likewise to the vaunted value of his organs of vision when directed mammonward; that the Hebrew was, after all, but a low-flying and lumbering, albeit an industrious and copiously perspiring, bird, and content with such fatness as carrion afforded; satisfied to burrow in muck and grow smugly sleek on such scraps and offal as the world and his wife

overlooked, or, knowing the existence of, despised; with no lofty aspiration for the rich stream yielded by fair commerce and enterprise, but meekly eager to churn a livelihood from the City's scum.

Such, however, is no longer my estimate of the Houndsditch Jew, and, as for his market-place, I may say that, having explored and scrutinised it foot by foot, you know of its mysteries very little more than the mariner knows of the mysteries of the sea. Like the said mariner, you may observe the turbulent surface and see all round about you fish pursuing and pursued, with here and there a curiously-snouted monster, whose business, beyond the certainty that it is predatory, cannot be made out. The mariner, unless he be likewise a diver by profession, or becomes, unluckily, one of a wrecked crew, will never know even for a moment what the sea is like at heart. So as to the depths of Houndsditch; unless a man be, as am I, a professional diver, or, just a simple merchantman bound on an eastward land voyage, he be treacherously directed from his proper course by an Israelitish pilot, and finally stranded a sheer hulk on a Whitechapel shore.

Such, I am bound to confess, might I have been for all my diving experience, or, at the least, have dived and found nothing, had I not been carefully directed and instructed by an old cruiser in the intricate Houndsditch waters who now enjoys a pension as a retired police inspector. It was he who set right my presumptuous assertion that I knew all about Rag Fair. He inquired, among other things, "What did you think of the jewellery rooms? Did you look in at Barnet's? Did you have any difficulty in getting admittance at Mendez's? Were you not astonished at the tremendous display of gems and precious metals at Moses Levy's?"

Now, as the reader has been made aware, I had seen vast quantities of jewel-shaped ware, and, to the extent of several tons, of studs and pins, and bangles and bracelets; but the metals of which they were composed were palpably no more precious than brass or copper. As to the ownership of the goods, that might have been claimed by a Levy, or a Mendez, or a Moses, but for certain I could not say. As to the "difficulty of gaining admission," I had not experienced it; on the contrary, Levy, and Mendez, and Moses had each in turn laid violent hands on me with a view of compelling me to inspect the valuables displayed on their boards and benches. All this I explained to my friend, but with no other effect than to convince him that the important feature of the Sunday fair alluded to by him had altogether escaped me. Recent as were my experiences of the inodorous rabble that swarmed at the said fair, I should have been content to have allowed my work to have remained incomplete as it was; but my friend assured me that the *real* jewellery exchanges were highly-respectable places where nobody but rich men—workers in gold, dealers in silver plate, and diamond-merchants—congregated, or, indeed, had business; and he, moreover, drew such graphic and curious pictures of these "back-slum" golcondas that I was fain to take a list of them and promise to go and see.

The list comprised five jewellery marts, all to be found within easy stone's-throw, supposing the speaker to stand in Houndsditch between Bevis Marks and Cutler Street. Two of the five are on the Cutler Street side of the main thoroughfare, and the remaining three so close to the Duke Street orange market that the pungent scent of the refreshing fruit comes in at the open sashes of the crowded show-rooms in a way to be grateful for. Of the Cutler Street emporiums I will say nothing; certainly they were tolerably rich, and it *was* somewhat astonishing and suggestive of the forty thieves and "Open Sesame" to find one tapping "three distinct times" at the battered door of a mangy-looking public-house, so *very* mangy and beetle-browed, with its heavy, overhanging portal and blinking little windows, backed by dingy red curtains—and to find the door gently opened by a ringletted houri, with her bosom in glittering chains, and her ears fettered with masses of gold and cornelian—to find yourself gliding stealthily in with a softness that any one of the celebrated forty might envy, and boldly, and with the aid of a lodger of long standing, crossing the space before the bar, and pushing open a door on which was simply inscribed "Parlour,"—to find yourself crossing the threshold, and the door heavily, though softly, plugging to, and shutting you in—in among a company beady-eyed and hawk-nosed, some with little black beards, some with grey beards resting on their shirt fronts, and all of them chattering like London sparrows —doing, too, as well as talking. On the common-looking tables were common iron teatrays inches deep of silver watches and watch-cases, and naked works that looked as though the cruel Jews had flayed them. Over these trays the beady-eyed ones stooped, and plucked, and poked, and picked, fiercely demanding the price as with a foreknowledge that it would be preposterous, and to discuss it a simple waste of time. At least, you might be led to ascribe such fierceness of bargaining to this cause, were you unaware of the fact that Jews among themselves *never* haggle; they see what comes of it in their transactions with Christians, and carefully eschew "the silly custom." "Ow butch?" asks Mr. Levy, taking up a watch. "Two powd;" and, though he may receive the information with a wriggle as though he had been pricked, if he wants the watch, he merely retires from the way for a moment to screw up his courage, and comes back with the "two powd" in his hand, which is tolerably good evidence that "'bating" is never entertained even to the extent of a penny.

The second Cutler Street jewellery mart was as much like the first as peas in one pod, and, had I seen none other, would have seemed marvellous. But I had yet to see that which put them both in the shade, reducing them to mere pedlar's packs, whereas before they appeared goodly acres of the estate of that Crœsus, Thomas Tiddler. Number one of the Orange Market gold and silver stores was fair enough; there were a few hundred more chains and watches and bracelets than occurred at the other side of Houndsditch, to say nothing of a sprinkling of diamonds, and a measure or so of rubies and emeralds. Number two Orange Market (a shut-up public-house, as was number one) was even more wealthy than the other; but number three!

Number three is situated to the right of the Orange

Market coming from St. Mary Axe. My head is so crammed with Jewish names that I am by no means sure how the proprietor of number three was called. There, however, was his name painted over the doorway of his tavern, and, to the best of my knowledge, it was the same as that of one of the rare old masters in the art of painting. It was about eleven o'clock on the Sunday morning, and the church bells were summoning good folks, and good folks were responding to the summons and wending their way churchward. As to the jewellery mart I was about to enter, it, too, might have been a place of worship, a meeting-house for the Some-of-these-days saints, or at the very least a vestry-room. The tavern itself was, of course, fast closed, but at the side there was a spacious private entrance, the step to the door of which was demurely whitened, while the door itself was so closely ajar that at first sight it seemed shut, and all as quiet and as moral as could be. When you pushed the door, however, it swung easily open, and within you found the hall nicely matted and covered with oilcloth, and at the end, or what seemed to be the end, of the passage was a highly respectable-looking door covered with dark baize. This you likewise pushed open, and found a little bit more passage, with an ordinary sitting-room door in one of the walls of it: of this you turned the handle, and there you were.

Fancy an apartment as long as Fleet Street is broad, and wide in fair proportion, with a line of tables about four feet wide on either side down the whole length of it, with two large windows at one end of it, and at the other end a snug country posting-house liquor-bar. In the roof at the liquor-bar end of the room a broad skylight. Behind the tables and seated on forms, a close row of Jews of every country and complexion, some dark almost as Arabs, others freckled and sickly fair; some so old and shaky that they sat muffled up in cloaks and comforters; others so young and un-Jewish that it seemed a mere temptation to rogues to seat them there as dealers. On the broad tables, on every one of them, and so that they were completely covered, were vessels of gold and of silver, cups and vases, and jugs and goblets, gold chains in great coils; while silver chains in heaps, being of small account, kept in the rear along with silver spoons and other articles in the same inferior metal; bracelets flickering with rare topazes, lockets glaring with ruddy opals, crosses and clasps and necklaces rich with great pearls, and looking chaste as snow; coronets brilliant with clustering emeralds, and earrings ablaze with diamonds. Besides these there were gems unset, piled in the corners of the trays like cherrystones, or stowed in common pillboxes. As to watches of gold and of silver, I am quite certain that had they all been placed in a sack, the strongest porter from the Orange Market outside would have been unable to carry it, even though its contents were the reward of his labour.

The body of the room—capable of holding at least two hundred people—was chokeful. You could not move without endangering your own toes or somebody else's, nor turn your head without the certainty of encountering a great blast of tobacco smoke from somebody's lips, for—and this seemed to me the most curious part of the business—the company, although orderly, was not the most genteel one would wish to meet, and there were seedy-looking and even shabby-looking men amongst it, who smoked cigars almost to a man, so that the place was downright hazy with smoke, and it was a difficult matter to see from one end to the other. And yet there was the mixed company handling the contents of the trays as freely as blackberries, and passing diamonds and pearls to each other, and struggling with costly rings and necklaces through the press that they might examine them at a better light than that afforded near the vendor's stall; and the vendors all the while placid and serene, and evidently in no fear of being robbed. As for the proprietor of the tavern, he lounged over his bar, and chatted to his customers, and served them with brandy and other fiery liquors (the church bells were still ringing); and everybody, even to the seedy man who stood near the door with some sort of pickled vegetable in a tub, and with a row of white saucers in which to serve out pen'orths, seemed so contented, and warm, and comfortable, that the sight was quite affecting.

XXIII.

WITH A SET OF TEASPOONS.

FAR be it from me to give utterance to a single word that may be construed into a justification of drunkenness. To my eyes no sight is more deplorable than that of a gin-wrecked man or woman,—a hideous, blear-eyed wretch, soaked and sodden, the breath of whose body is a pestilence, and the clammy touch of whose palsied hand is a thing to loathe; who cumbers the face of the earth as an unweighted human carcass is sometimes seen cumbering the face of the living ocean—an ugly, shameful drift, tattered and penniless, too vile for shark's food, though the fish be of the rapacious bottle-nosed species, whose lurking-place is behind a pewter-covered bar, and whose maw, as a rule, is not set against offal. If there *is* anything more deplorable, it is the fact that these human beacons, visibly consuming in the liquid fire that fills and torments them, are inefficient to warn off the reckless voyager, who, out of selfishness or despair, or, as has happened many a thousand times, simple, good-natured weakness and a yearning for jolly-good-fellowship, launches on that enchanted sea beneath whose surface, so gay and sparkling, lurks blackness, and death, and such horrible shapes as are never seen but by men whose heads are shaven and whose arms are confined in strait-jackets, lest, in their terrible fright, they should lay murderous hands on themselves to escape therefrom. The honest man who is at the pains to set up buoys and landmarks for the salvation of these reckless ones—nay, who devotes his life to the business of piloting such endangered craft into safe haven, and that without hope or expectation of "salvage," deserves the gratitude of his fellow-men as a hero of high degree, for such he is. Happily, there are many such amongst us; and well would it be for them, as for us all, if their army were strong enough to occupy the field to the exclusion of mistaken meddlers and priggish pretenders, who mistake water on the brain for the irresistible pressure of a "mission," impelling them to run a muck against all vats and beer barrels. Burning with teapot valour, these doughty ones open shop in all quarters of the town, not so much for the purpose of plucking brands from the burning, as of rendering sticks uninflammable by an abundant saturation in a variety of slops spouted from a platform in the shape of speechifying, or purveyed in cups and mugs, to grown sticks, male and female, and to mere twigs of twelve and fourteen, at a price that leaves a decent profit for the purchase of glorification medals.

Pewkers' Hall, in our neighbourhood, is one of these anti-tippling camps. Its founder and secretary, manager and treasurer, is the Rev. Dapple Mookow, a minister of the Alack-a-day Saints persuasion, and the proprietor of the patent movable corrugated-zinc chapel, a little way down the road. Pewkers' Hall is not a building of imposing appearance; indeed, it does not appear at all until you have penetrated an alley diverging from the high street, and which is overhung by a notice-board, inscribed "Pewkers' Hall at the bottom!" Its style of architecture is of the Rebuke-to-Vanity order, and, exteriorly, the hall is not unlike a watchhouse, being plain brick and single-storied, with no other window than a skylight in the roof, and a plain, unpanelled door with a latch, and painted lead-colour, while upon the door and the wall in its immediate vicinity are stuck many printed placards and written notifications relating to the Pewker interest, past, present, or to come. The Pewkers muster strong on Saturday nights (that being the night on which their enemies the drunkards take the field in greatest force); and it was on a recent Saturday night that, happening to walk that way, I turned into the hall to see what was going on.

Enrolled Pewkers—such was my first discovery—were admitted free; but, not being in the enjoyment of that privilege, an entrance-fee of one penny was demanded of me at the door; this slight obstacle overcome, however, I was as free to enter as a Pewker born. The business of the evening had not yet commenced, so I had time to look about me.

The hall was not so large as it seemed from the outside; nevertheless, it was of fair size, being, to the best of my guessing, about fifty feet wide by thirty deep from the street door to the platform, on which was mounted a table and an armchair; and on the table, to my utter astonishment, there was neatly and handily arranged two long pipes, a paper of tobacco, and the sort of wooden hammer that is seen in the hands of the ordinary cheap concert-room chairman. The place was as clean as a soup kitchen. The walls, nay, the very beams overhead, were whitewashed; and the floor, and the tables, and the forms were as meekly clean as soap and scrubbing-brush could make them. Under the tables were earthern spittoons, spotless as dinner plates, and filled with white deal sawdust. In the centre of the room was a gas stove, brilliant as a well-blacked boot, within which primly twinkled a ring of sedate and well-regulated gas-jets. Everywhere the hand of the charwoman —not the ordinary gin-drinking slut, but the abstaining and conscientious charwoman—was visible; and the contrast of Pewkers' Hall to the tavern parlour, with its seductive rubbed mahogany, and its artfully arranged ledges and nooks, its great coal fire, and its delusive snugness and coziness, generally rendered complete.

Pictorial art had been called in for the decoration of the walls. There were George Cruikshank's "Bottle" plates, and his equally effective "Drunkard's Children." Had these been all, it would have been well enough; indeed, Pewker or anti-Pewker, it would have been hard to find more eloquent and appropriate wall-hanging for such a place. But it was not all by a frightful deal.

There were pictures—dozens of them—the subjects of which appeared to be judiciously chosen with a view of affecting at once the mind and the stomach of the beholder. There were anatomical pictures, representing the liver of the drunkard, as well as his various intestinal ducts and canals during the last stage of gin rot. There was an elaborate lilac and crimson drawing of the drunkard's brain as it appeared during an attack of delirium tremens. There were serio-comic pictures of drunkenness—one of a man, brandy-nosed and hideously helpless, with the upper part of his skull sawn off by fiends, while swarms of tiny imps, with horns and tails, clambered about him, rifling him completely. One sturdy devil was perched on the inebriated one's shoulders, and with a sort of coal scoop dug out the drunkard's brain, handing it down in bucketfuls to the clambering imps. Some of the imps, however, were otherwise engaged ; they wriggled in and out of the drunkard's pockets, and stole his money, and his watch, and his spectacles, and his pocket-comb. In the background of the picture stood, amicably posed, the father of lies and deceit (in full uniform and with his tail-tuft arranged as a trident), a publican, and a mad-house-keeper, holding in one extended hand a strait-jacket and in the other several hundredweight of chains and manacles. The brain-bearing imps brought their buckets to the madhouse-keeper; the pickpockets brought their booty to the publican and poured it into his capacious fob; while the devil stood smilingly looking on, calmly confident of the hulk when the wreckers had done their worst with it. There were a dozen other pictures, all of the same school, and containing, along with the representative of drunkenness, at least one horned and tailed devil, and imps, and hell-flames, and toads, and fire-breathing scorpions and poison-snakes. It was quite a relief to turn from them and listen to the homely tinkle of spoons and teacups, and to sniff the grateful aroma of mocha that now came steaming in from the open kitchen-door in the passage by the side of the platform.

While I was examining the pictures the company were coming in, so that when I now looked round, the hall was tolerably full. The majority of those present were sad and meek looking young men, in whom, as was evident at a glance, the faculty for getting drunk was constitutionally wanting—a fact which detracted considerably from their claim to be considered heroes of self-denial in the matter of spirits and malt liquors. There were a few middle-aged men, and the remainder was made up of boys of fourteen or sixteen, who carried their heads defiantly, and whose loins were evidently girded very tight indeed, for a brush with the demon Alcohol, should he dare venture to assail them. A tall woman, with a high-necked frock and the sternest aspect, came round for orders, and presently brought them, fifteen pints, at least, on a big tea-tray, and which she carried with an ease which doubtless acted as a caution to any youthful Pewker disposed to offer her the least atom of impudence. Seeing that coffee was to be had as well as tea, I ordered a cup of it; and, as several gentlemen were smoking, I smoked as well. Just as I had "lit up," and made myself as comfortable as one may on a ten-inch form without a back, in came the chairman.

To my great surprise, it was the Rev. Dapple Mookow himself. It was not surprising that the patron, and secretary, and treasurer should take the chair; but that he should take a public pipe of birdseye as well! This he did, however, jovially acknowledging the plaudits of the auditory by waving the flaming splint with which he ignited his tobacco. The person with the high-necked gown brought him a cup of something—a common cup, blue and brotherly—out of which he sipped, and then faced about and rapped the table for silence.

"Well, and how are we all?" inquired Mr. Mookow, in a motherly tone; "safe and sound, I hope, as when last we met. Eh, is it so? Has any brother to tell of the Devil's tempting him?"

Nobody answered, though, to judge from the visage of a lantern-jawed youth of about fifteen, who sat in the row before mine, the odour of brimstone was in his nostrils, and he strongly suspected Satan of having designs against him. However, as it was a statement of facts and not of suspicions that Mr. Mookow asked for, he merely gasped significantly and held his peace. A general and joyful clapping of hands ensued on the tacit understanding that the old man of sin had tampered with no Pewker since the previous Wednesday. After this Mr. Mookow delivered a longish address on the advantages of "total abstinence" and the frightful results of beer-drinking, which altogether might well have served as text to the blazing pictures on the wall; and I experienced much relief when, after bringing both his fists to the table with a tremendous bang, he consigned the drunkard's soul to everlasting torment, wiped his perspiring brow with his handkerchief, and said, in the blandest of voices—

"And now, after business, let us seek pleasure. Let us show the loathsome drunkard, as we have shown him before, that we can be merry as well as wise, that we can bandy the jest of abstinence, and laugh the temperate laugh, and sing the soul-enlivening song, with as loud a voice and as hearty as he, hiccuppy with strong drink, drivels forth his blasphemous legends in praise of blood-poison—in praise of brain-rot—in praise of a shaven head and a madman's rattling chain! Brothers, we will have a song. What shall it be?"

"Fill up the tea-urn!" "Coffee is my darling!" "The grog-blossomed nose!" These and several other strange and by myself never-before-heard song-titles were bawled out in different parts of the room. "Fill up the tea-urn" was, however, decidedly in the majority; and, teacup in hand, the Rev. Mr. Mookow proceeded to deliver himself of that stirring teetotal ditty, to the tune of "Pour out the Rhine wine":—

> Fill up the tea-urn! let it brim!
> We'll have no stint in measure;
> In the bubbling flood let the congou swim,
> And set it on the hob to draw at leisure.
> For there's nought can cheer the heart that's low
> Like a steaming cup of the good congou.
>
> CHORUS.
> Like a steam-ing cup
> Like a steam-ing cup
> Like a steam-ing cup
> O-o-o-f the good con-gou.

Pour out the cheering nut-brown stream,
  With a hand that's firm and steady!
And an eye that's bright as a glad sunbeam,
  In the cup that's standing milked and sugared ready.
Just try it once, and you'll find it so—
A drink divine is the good congou.

CHORUS.
A drink divine, &c.

Spare not the tea-urn! fill again!
  Nor fear to quaff its brewing.
It brings no pain, like the drunkard's drain,
  Nor rags, nor madness, poverty and ruin.
Then trumpet its fame where'er you go,
And friendship pledge in the good congou.

CHORUS.
And friendship pledge, &c.

This stave, which Mr. Mookow sang very well, was deservedly applauded; and the company "friendship pledged" in the lauded beverage until nothing but grounds remained in every cup, and some little time was spent in replenishing. Order at length restored, Master Shiddlecot (the lantern-jawed one already alluded to) was called on for a song; a call to which he responded with considerable alacrity, and commenced a stave which, from its length and other causes, it is undesirable to give here in its entirety. One verse will serve :—

Our tea! our tea! our wholesome tea;
What a cheering sight is a cup of tea,
  A cup—a cup of tea,
When it's up to the mark and perfectly sound,
And sweetened with sugar that's not over brown'd,
A drop of new milk, and the stir of a spoon,
Completes it—the total abstainer's boon.
Away with your gin, rum, and ale, and give me
The cup that's delightful—a beautiful cup of tea!

"Bravo! Mr. Shiddlecot; what shall we have the pleasure of saying after that very excellent song?" said the chairman.

"Well, sir, I don't know any toasts or sentiments," replied Mr. Shiddlecot. "But if you are agreeable, I'll substitute a conundrum. Why is a drunkard pulling a cat's tail like Mr. Jones's teacup?"

One prolonged giggle at the not unreasonably embarrassed Mr. Jones, and then a dead stillness.

"Come, we give it up, Mr. Shiddlecot," laughed the chairman. "It's one of your posers, I suppose."

"You give it up?" replied Mr. Shiddlecot, glancing proudly triumphant round him. "Then, gentlemen, the reason why a drunkard pulling a cat's tail is like Mr. Jones's teacup is, *because he's tea's in it !*"

Pewkers' Hall was not a handsome edifice, but to be capable of standing, without the slightest tremor, the tremendous explosion of laughter that followed Mr. Shiddlecot's explanation spoke volumes for its great strength. Several riddles followed, but not one of them was fit to hold a candle to that of Mr. Shiddlecot; and after a while Mr. Barker was called on for a stave. This was one of the elderly gentlemen who sat in the front row, and was evidently on terms of intimacy with Mr. Mookow.

"I think I must decline," said Mr. Barker, clearing his voice ready to begin. "I don't know any songs but those I make up myself, and I'm sure you must be tired of hearing them."

"So they must, Barker; so they must," observed a brisk-looking young fellow, who had come in late, and who, judging from his countenance, was not always a Pewker. "That's what I tell them when they call on me."

"Ay, ay; but you won't get out of it, Mr. Jonas," was the universal exclamation, and then followed a rattling of crockery and a cry of "The Fiery Nose! The Fiery Nose!"

"Well, if I must, I must," said Mr. Jonas, modestly; "but at present the call is with Mr. Barker."

And, without further ado, Mr. Barker struck up. His song seemed to have no particular title, and it was adapted to a "nigger" tune popularly known as "Rosa May," and ran as follows:—

> Come, brothers, listen unto me, and a story I'll relate,
> How I in time was rescued from a wretched drunkard's fate.
> I used to swill my nightly fill of ale, and beer, and gin,
> Nor for my wife and family cared I a single pin.

My eyes were bleared, a ragged beard, likewise a drunkard's nose;
My children bare and naked were, because I pawned their clothes;
My wife I bruised, and much ill-used, and, shameful thing to say,
Distrained the bed from under her my tavern score to pay.

But, thanks to Mr. Mookow, now all that is set aside;
Upon my wife and family I now can look with pride.
The reason's plain, I now abstain, and mean to, never fear—
I never more intend to be a slave to gin and beer.

There was a generous amount of applause at this by no means cheerful lay, which had barely subsided when the call for "The Fiery Nose" broke out most vociferously.

"Come, Mr. Jonas," said the chairman, persuasively, "they will have it, you see."

"Well, sir, I will, since you wish it," replied Mr. Jonas. "But it is a painful song for me to sing, it is indeed; not on account of the tune, *that's* easy enough; it's the sentiment that makes it painful."

"Nonsense!" "Tit for Tat!" "Give and Take!" "Serve 'em right!" "Go on, Jonas!" These and similar cries seemed to reassure the teetotal poet, and to the tune of the "Cork Leg," and with voice and action excellent enough to have made his fortune at Canterbury Hall, he commenced "The Fiery Nose":—

A certain man in our town
A tippler was of great renown.
Gin, whiskey, or rum, whichever he saw,
Were welcome to enter his thirsty maw.
    Right toorallooral, &c.

He drank and he drank till, as you may suppose,
He presently sported a fiery nose,
And it grew so hot that it came to this,
If it touched his liquor, it made it "hiss."   Chorus.

At length came a day, so the story is told,
The hot-nosed man caught a terrible cold.
The nose he blew, he'd himself but to blame,
And he blew till it smouldered and burst in a flame.   Chorus.

Though a careful man was this tippling sot,
His house was insured, but his nose was not.
So he rushed to the street, with a gasp and a cough,
And buried his snout in the cool horsetrough.   . Chorus.

N

Though the water began to boil in a minute,
It failed to extinguish the blazing nose in it.
The flame it increased, and grew broader and higher,
Till the trough and the pump were one crackling fire.   Chorus.

Now, finding himself in this terrible plight,
He took to his heels with all his might,
Till he found a distillery yard, when, pat,
He soused head-over-heel in a brimming vat.   Chorus.

Alarmed at sight of the terrible flame,
The distiller himself and his foreman came.
He heard the tippler's story out,
Then winked like a man who knows what he's about.   Chorus.

Said he, "Though I cannot extinguish your nose,
If you'll listen awhile I've a scheme to propose.
I'll give you two hundred a year if you'll stay,
And pass all your time in this self-same way."   Chorus.

The man with the fiery nose agreed.
The distiller his fortune made with speed,
For whenever he wanted a brewing of gin,
He'd a vat fill with water and pop the man in.   Chorus.

An hour in soak was quite enough,
When the liquor became most capital stuff.
How the man with the fiery nose must grin
When he hears the fame of his "sparkling gin!"   Chorus.

The applause was deafening, and an encore unanimously demanded, when, seeing that Mr. Jonas was about to comply, I thought it time to bid the Pewkers good-night.

XXIV.

A JOURNEY TO EPSOM.

THE picture of a solitary individual abroad and astir in Epsom town while it is yet so early that but a slender slip of sunlight twinkles on the bed-room windows on one side of the road, and the pigeons of the place still strut fearlessly upon the pavement, and the policeman has not yet abandoned that solemn, measured tramp which is his night tramp, and very different from the free-and-easy, slack-knee'd step with which he moves through the town when it is up and alive, is likely to suggest thoughts on the probable business of the solitary one—especially as his way tends to the lane which leads to the Downs—of a not particularly flattering sort. Perhaps he is a "tout," or, in other words, a horse spy and a skulker, on his way to the exercise-ground, there to climb a tree or lie flat on his face in the grass, timing the pace of the racers and making note of it. Perhaps he is a hired ruffian with sharp stones in his pocket to be strewn over the ground where Blair Athol takes his morning "breather," in the diabolical hope that one of them may pierce the innocent foot of that sensitive creature and cripple him everlastingly. Perhaps, again—and I think he *does* look a *leetle* too respectable to be either a tout or a horse-lamer; he is more F. than R., as the saying is—some restless wretch of a grocer or pork-butcher, who has pawned his shop and what there is in it, and his wife's earrings and best gown, and his own shirt-studs and silver hunting-watch, that he may "get well on" a horse which, though at long odds, is a "certainty," and of which he has got the "tip," for the small charge of a guinea, from that wideawake tipster, "Weazle," of the *Spouting Life*. Perhaps it *is* "Weazle;" but that is scarcely likely; so remarkable a character must surely be known to the police, whereas the early bird in question passes the representative of the Epsom constabulary without so much as an exchange of nods.

No, the solitary one is neither a "tout," nor a horse-lamer, nor a pork-butcher, nor "Weazle;" he is the reader's very humble servant, the writer, who flatters himself that at this time, five o'clock in the morning of the 25th of May, there is not a happier man in Epsom; and this because he has no sort of business at Epsom at all. He has nothing to sell, no "flys" to let, no appointments to keep, and he doesn't care twopence whether the Derby laurels are carried off by Cambuscan or the rankest outsider. He has already partaken of a cup of coffee and a crust, and his breakfast will be ready at ten o'clock, when he will return to it. Meanwhile, he has plenty of tobacco and some pipelights, and an umbrella in case it should rain, and he is bound for Epsom Downs; and if the reader has a mind we will link arms and leisurely stroll thither together.

Pompeii, on the morning of the day of its devastation, could not have exhibited more serenity than does Epsom town as we enter it from the clock-tower end. Absolutely certain as it is that within six short hours the place, road and pavement, will be overrun by a reckless host, a ravening host, hungry as locusts, and as indomitably bent on devouring every green thing—a parched host, thirsting for drink as the sands of the desert—an uproarious host, fishing for mischief and helter-skelter devilry as though mischief was the essential salt of their lives, and only to be had for the scrambling after once a year at Epsom. Inevitable as is all this, the Epsomites slumber in content; the white blinds at the chamber windows are tranquil as though it were a Sunday morning; and, looking up and down the High-street, the only out-thrust and anxious head appears under a tumbled nightcap at an upper window of the Spread Eagle Tavern, and can belong to no other than a betting-man, whose "book" is made up to the finest points of wind and weather, and who really ought to pull through, considering how handsomely he has backed Providence for sunshine. A little way up a green lane there is the Epsom police-station, and there, in anticipation of a tremendously hard day, two policemen are on duty, one of them in his shirt-sleeves hanging out a blackbird among the flowering creepers that grow about and above the door, and the other with a fragrant pipe at full blast, while with a wisp of bass he secures a refractory hollyhock growing in the pretty garden in front. I should like to see the cells at Epsom station-house. I believe they are made of lattice-work, and painted the cheerfullest green, with a cool thatched roof covered with stonecrop. If I were condemned to hard labour there, I should expect it to consist in shelling green peas or making reed squeakers for the inspector's children. Perhaps, however, I might find myself mistaken. If I were a professional evil-doer on my first visit to Epsom on a Derby Day, and, seeing the tasty little station-house, laughed to think how easy it would be to break out of it if by ill-luck a policeman interrupted me at business at the Grand Stand, I certainly should be very much mistaken; for, knowing the said Grand Stand from the flagstaff to the cellars, I likewise know of a particularly dingy and secure apartment there, in which the police stow brawlers and pickpockets until it is convenient to convey them away in the evening.

Talking of the Grand Stand, as we top that steep and dusty hill, up which many thousands of men, Jack-o'-lantern light of heart, have climbed as buoyantly as though at top were to be found certain rest and luxury that would last, and down which exactly the same number, to a single one, have toiled as wearily as though it were the flintiest steep, chokeful of despair and amazement, and grateful to their jaunty green gauze veils for hiding their troubled faces,—mounting this hill, we come in sight of Mr. Dorling's palace of deal boards, glistening white in the morning sun, and recalling to the mind various images, some profane and gay, and some scriptural.

as well as sepulchral, but withal a well-pitched edifice, and affording capital observation of the racecourse. Everyone is satisfied with the management of the building, including, it is generally understood, the manager; and no wonder, when he is able to accommodate five thousand visitors, and the ready-money system is rigidly enforced.

Satisfactory, however, as are the Grand-Stand arrangements, it seems to me that in one department at least there is room for improvement. I allude to the "betting-ring," which is most unsavourily situated just under the noses of the best class of Grand-Stand visitors. Being commonly engaged in raising mammon, a few whiffs of brimstone of a coarser quality than ordinary might be tolerated in the nostrils of the "upper ten;" but when it comes to sulphur of the Saffron Hill sort, when one is compelled to the reflection that a good percentage of the costermonger clamour heard below is the selfsame that gave tongue on the Field Lane ruins on Saturday last, and that the gentleman in the bran new paletot and glossy hat, from whose mouth the idea of the patent expanding trunk might have taken its origin, and who is so industriously yelping as to the odds he will lay about this, that, and the other, is the same individual who is to be seen any day in the neighbourhood above mentioned, luring numskull butcher-boys and shoemakers' apprentices to stake their half-crowns and shillings, the result is not pleasing to one's dignity or manhood. Is there no room in the cellars for these yellow flies? Or, better still, could they not be accommodated on the roof? If they could, it would be better for themselves—better for everybody. They would no longer offend the organs of sight, and hearing, and smell, in honest men; and they, by being enabled to look out far and wide, would be spared that minute of horrible torture when the racers are lost behind the hill—when they go down like a doubtful swimmer in deep and weedy water, who will presently rise to fling up his arms and drown, or show his confident face and his lusty shoulders, sure tokens of peril past. How will it be? The pulsings of the desperate betting-man's heart took the time of his horse's hoofs—hirrup! hirrup! hirrup!—over the springy turf, when he last saw him; and if that "hirrup" has increased in speed in the same degree with the thumping under the wretch's waistcoat, the gallant horse will "land" the stakes to a certainty. But it is doubtful—so horribly doubtful, that the betting-man's arterial steed will surely gallop itself out of life unless the other makes great haste. Now for it! Now we shall know! No, not yet! Was there ever such a crawling match? For less than a little minute the horses are lost behind the hill, yet there is time enough for the gambler to review all his business with that horse—that magnificent horse—that infernal horse. "Bless him! he's sure to win. Confound him! why did I lay a penny on him?" He thinks of what that cautious fellow, Brown, told him, and curses himself for not taking the advice; and again, in the thousandth part of a second, on what Jones put him up to, and reviles himself as an idiot for thinking for a moment on anything that such a timid donkey as Brown should say. So he shifts his few miserable straws from left to right, and tortures himself with the problem of sink or swim, until——

But, really, to discuss the emotions of the man of "Mammon's acre" is not the purpose of this paper. Who cares whether he sinks or swims? Sink he *must* some day, and as well to-day as to-morrow. He is like a pig which, swimming against the tide, inevitably cuts his throat with his hoofs. It doesn't matter. He didn't fall into the flood—was not pushed in. He took a deliberate "header," trusting to the "Betting-man's Guide," with all the latest dodges and improvements, as a lifebelt. The "Guide" instructed him that the best way to catch flat fish floating blindly with the stream was to take the tide the other way and meet them. And a very profitable game he found it until the "spoony" fry came to know the snout of the hungry pike, and avoided him. Then, in desperation, up came the hoofs for one good, bold dash among the minnows, and his gullet is slit beyond repair. And a good job done. A good job if every pig of the fiendish breed would follow the example of that ancient herd recorded in Sacred Writ, and gratify us with a last view of their heels over the shingle of the seabeach.

Let us turn our backs on the Grand Stand, where the sweepers are busily sweeping and the upholsterers are tacking up extra red baize for the great occasion ; and on the high-railed ring, within which a labourer is hard at work gathering up yesterday's crumpled sandwich-papers and orange-peel; and on the "course," on which a dozen men are busy with shovels and brooms and rammers, smoothing out the dents in the turf made by yesterday's racers, and filling up every hole with almost as much care as a joiner prepares a dining-table for polishing. With these—at least, at present—we have nothing to do. We have climbed the hill, not on business, but for pleasure's sake, and for the gratification of an idle curiosity to know the kind of figure cut by Epsom Downs early in the morning of the great race. It could scarcely be called idle curiosity either, since it grew out of much speculation and laboured puzzling on the singular fact—as proved by observation from the window of our lodging at the London end of the town—that whereas, since Monday morning, at least five thousand individuals had turned into the lane that leads to the hill atop of which the downs begin, not more than two thousand had come back again up to a late hour on Tuesday night. What had become of those other three thousand ? What were they doing up on the bleak downs ? Where did they sleep ? and how ?—for although many had gone up with carts and waggons, and smart caravans with a chimney in the roof and a knocker on the door, in which it was easy enough to lie snug and warm ; hundreds had tramped it afoot, carrying neither bag nor baggage, not so much as a little bundle no bigger than a night-shirt would make. Neither had they any money; for regularly as, limping along on their crooked-heel boots, they came to Bonsor's ham-and-beef shop, with its pillars of brisket and its rounds in mighty hillocks, and a greater number of sausage-rolls than would have filled a cornbin, they invariably halted and indulged in a visionary banquet, picking out the crustiest of the new penny loaves, and helping themselves to fat, and to lean, and to mustard, and taking a bite at the German sausage, and going leisurely in for a ham-knuckle, with pickled cabbage; meanwhile soothing their cruelly-tantalised stomachs under cover of their trouser-pockets; but never on a single occasion had I observed them to enter Bonsor's shop, which I am sure they would have done had they even so much as the price of a sausage-roll about them. Penniless, hungry, and so tired that, even after the first imaginary plateful outside Bonsor's, they might be seen yawning and blinking as they leant against the brass window rail, what on earth could take them to Epsom Downs, and what did they find there that, liking it so very much, they could not leave it? This was part of the riddle it was the purpose of our excursion to solve, but it proved a tougher business than was anticipated. It was a perfect hedgehog of a riddle—the closer you approached it the tighter it curled itself up. There they were, the hungry and penniless ones, crouched against the outer canvas of the booths, huddled dogwise under carts and vans, or lying blankly on the open plain with their faces to the earth, and their caps for a pillow, and their ugly heads of hair blending with the grass and bedewed like it. This, as regards some of them—the lazy ones, or, may be, the midnight arrivals who had manfully achieved the twenty and odd miles from Whitechapel Church to Epsom Clock-tower, but had been dead beaten by the hill, and, spent and pluckless, so soon as they came to a nice soft bit of turf, had there plunged down, in much the same spirit as mad folks plunge from a bridge for a water cure for all their aches and pains.

It seemed so certain that they were lying uncomfortable that it was a great temptation to wake them; but when on looking about one saw what they were like when they *were* awake, the inclination was immediately checked. They were perfect images of neglect, and famine, and dust—especially of dust. Dust was in their hair, their eyes, and their ears; it came in puffs out of the rents and holes in their boots when they walked; it lodged on the ledges the cobbles and patches made in their jackets and trousers; their very skin had the hue of a dusty old felt carpet, and looked as though, if you attempted to beat it, you would be instantly smothered. Yesterday's dust and yesterday's sweat mingled to make their thin hands and faces loathsome, and yesterday's hunger and weariness looked out at their heavy eyes. Some of them, in groups of fours and fives, crouched over a spluttering, smoky fire of gorse and green sticks, were warming their cramped limbs (for, the reader must know, the wind blows chilly at six o'clock on a May morning on Epsom Downs); some meekly skulked close to the big fires the coffee-vendors had by this time kindled under their kettles; and some, the youngest, hung about such of the company as chanced to be engaged in the consumption of victuals, fawning and looking up for a bit like drovers' dogs at a cattle-fair. There was one boy whom I distinctly recollected as gazing in at Bonsor's window yesterday, and now, with about an equal prospect of success, he was Bonsorising a fair-going looking sort of a person with knee-breeches of velveteen, and a cap made of the skin of some bristly animal, and who, squatted on the grass with some cold boiled beef and a loaf, and some beer in a tin bottle, between his outstretched legs, was calmly discussing his breakfast. Presently the beefeater took a bite out of a big crust and then laid it down without the boundary of his legs, and Bonsor, regarding it as a waif, was down upon it instantly. Not so quickly, however, as the beefeater was down upon *him*. He caught Bonsor in the very act, and gave him a rap on the knuckles with the buckhorn handle of his big clasp-knife.

"Hook it, will yer! yer (something) young prig," said he, grinning, with his mouth full of boiled beef; as poor Bonsor gave a howl and a wriggle, and got out of his way. He wriggled close to where I was standing, and, presuming on our slight acquaintance, I ventured to address him—

"Did I not see you yesterday in Epsom town, my man?"

For an instant Bonsor's boy took in my length and

breadth with a glance peculiar to London boys and robins, and then, not feeling fully assured that I was not something in the detective line, replied evasively—

"Well, what on it?"

"Nothing to me," I said; "only you seemed to be looking for something to eat then; and, unless I'm mistaken, that is what you are doing now."

"That is what I *am* doing," replied Bonsor, once more furtively taking my measure while he sucked his sore knuckles. "You don't happen to have a job as would bring a cove in as much as would fetch a bit of grub and a drop of coffee—eh, guvnor?"

"Yes, I have," I replied; "as easy a job as you are likely to find. Answer me three questions, and I will give you a shilling. To begin with, what brought you to Epsom?"

"Chance of picking up a job or so," replied Bonsor, promptly, and with his hands behind him, as though I was questioning him out of the Church Catechism. "That's what brings all us coves down here;" and he gave a comprehensive sweep with his chin, indicating that by "us coves" he meant the sleepers on the grass and the crouchers over the fires.

"In what way?"

"Forty ways," replied Bonsor, with difficulty concealing his contempt for my ignorance; "there's the c'rect card coves—two bob a dozen at the Stand, and a werry tidy pull for coves with a bit of money to lay out; and then there's cigar-lights, and dolls to stick in the hats, and noses and hair, and clean yer boots, and all sorts of amoosing things for gents what wins. Then there's the brushing coves, and them as fetches water, and them as looks arter the empty bottles and the bones. Lor! I can't tell you half on 'em."

"And do they all find it worth their while to tramp all the way from London and back again?"

"Well, don't yer see, it's all speckerlation, and that's the beauty on it," replied Bonsor, wagging his head admiringly. "You never know what's going to turn up one minnit from another. Why, I knows a man who

once had a pound given him for fetching a pail of water.
It's all luck, don't yer know. You might make a crown,
and you mightn't make enough to get a lift home in
a wan."

"Are there many such unlucky ones?"

"I believe yer. Old uns, don't yer know, what's out
of work and too 'spectable like for noses, and hair, and
dolls, and c'rect cards, is no use unless a feller can run;
so they comes out a brushing. Yes; and when they
gets here," continued Bonsor, his extremely dirty face
lighting up at the absurdity of the thing, "when they
gets here they'll see a cove what comes from their parts
in a pleasure-wan, or something of that, and aint got the
cheek to take out their brush arter all, and trot home,
when it's dark, just the same as they come."

And at this Bonsor, conscious that he had given me
my three answers fair and full, and one over, withdrew
his hands from behind him, and twiddled his finger and
thumb expectantly. The next minute he was negotiating
with a coffee man, while I strolled in among the booths
and gipsy-tents, picturing to myself one of the poor, old,
broken-down fellows, "too 'spectable for noses and hair,"
spending the livelong day lurking behind show-vans and
booths, and nut-targets, and wrathfully watching the
van which brought down Jenkins, the ladies' bootmaker,
who lives just over the way where the old fellow lives.
The tablecloth is spread on a board in the van, and the
old fellow, from his miserable hiding, can see the flash
of knives and forks, and the foaming glasses of bottled
beer; and, if he were not such a proud old donkey, he
might hail Jenkins (who is as good a soul as ever lived),
and, in a twinkling, be eating and drinking to his heart's
content. Not he; he hates Jenkins with the deadliest
hatred, and nothing, or so he thinks, would give him
greater pleasure than to see the stuck-up fellow swallow
too large a bit of meat, and choke himself on the spot.
And so he lurks and watches, with a vague intention
of beginning business when Jenkins has gone, till night
approaches, and Jenkins and everyone else goes, and the
foolish old boy goes too, with his respectable old clothes-

brush—the very one with which in better times he has, often and often, proudly flicked the dust from his Sunday clothes—hanging a dead and profitless weight in his pocket, as it has hung ever since his old woman wrapped it in paper for him last night (giving him at the same time her last threepence that he might not want for a half-pint of beer and a bit of 'bacca on the road), he fags homeward in the dust and the deepening dusk, keeping the wall to be out of the way of the lively mob who hold the road; fags along for an hour or more, till it grows quite dark, and the vehicles bowling along past him, less in number, but faster and more uproariously, the drivers being drunk to a man; fags along till he reaches the dark road near to Croydon, by which time it is past midnight, and the inns are closed, and it is full five minutes since he heard the clatter of wheels, and, quite dead beat, he sits down on the grass that skirts the road "just for a rest," and there he sleeps till the sunshine wakes him.

As the Bonsor boy observed, "it's all speckerlation." Speculation fills the Grand Stand and the betting-ring; speculation and the legend of the man who once upon a time got £1 for fetching a pail of water incites decent elderly men, as well as those with whom decency has long ceased to be a consideration, and ruffianly young men, and blackguardly boys, to undertake the lengthy journey. "Speckerlation," then, may be taken as the answer to the riddle respecting the three thousand who went up on to the Downs and did not come down again —that is to say, as far as the brushers, and the water-carriers, and the noses-and-hairs, and the pipelights, and the c'rect cards, went towards making up the total, which was not very considerable. Of the remainder, some were speculators and some were not. Among the former must, I suppose, be classed the various bands of Ethiopian "serenaders," many of whom, divested of their business wool and "long-tail blues," mixed with the crowd or conversed at the coffee-stalls, their nigger masks of yesterday (consisting of ivory-black and beer) looking much the worse for wear and a night's tumbling on straw. And what else than as speculators could you regard the score or so of professional sparrers and glove-boxers who, in the intervals of racing, delight the aristocracy of the Grand Stand with an exhibition of scientific nose-punching and eye-blacking? and who, roused at this early hour, not because they have had sleep enough, but because their drouthy natures were famishing for beer, stroll about with their hands in their trousers pockets, and yawning their great jaws, with countenance about as amiable as that a bull-dog, who had attacked the supposititious calf of a wooden-legged man, might be imagined as wearing.

Then there were the cockshy-men and the Aunt-Sally men, and the men who were not to be mistaken for tailors because they carried a thimble in their pocket, or as persons in the farming interest from the circumstance of their happening to be possessed of two or three peas. And the target-keepers; and the proprietors of pulling, and punching, and weighing machines, and machines at which you will, by-and-by, be invited to "blow," by way of testing the strength of your lungs; and the victuallers, licensed and unlicensed; and the "wheel-of-fortune" keepers, man and woman, attended by their "jollies" (who, as may be explained to the innocent reader, are those wonderfully lucky persons who, coming up quite promiscuously, win and carry away the sets of china and diamond earrings); and the party with the performing dogs; and the gentleman who smashes lumps of granite with his naked fist; and fifty others, speculators all; not forgetting the busy little barber who rushes about among them all, with his belt fuller stuck with sharp-edged weapons than the girdle of an Ojibbeway, crying out, "Now, then! now, then! One at a time! Here's the barber! the barber! the bar-BER!" doing a very good trade at a penny a shave, and being on the best of terms with the fair folks, no one denying him the loan of their fire for his shaving-pot, or making a rumpus when, in the pushing and jostling, he happened to nick a bit out of their chins. And if the reader can imagine the various characters sketched engaged in making preparations for the company who will presently arrive—the booth-keepers sweeping out and hanging up their banners; the gingerbread-nut women arranging their spruce stalls, and darting amongst their great canisters, and joking and laughing amongst themselves with that jollity which the vending of gingerbread seems invariably to confer; and the owners of the rifle-targets adjusting their lengths of tubing, like steamboat funnels; and the cockshy-men squatting about and trimming cockshy-sticks with a spokeshave, or weaving their rush-baskets to hold the earth into which the shy-sticks are stuck; and the niggers, grouped in retired corners, blacking each other's faces, and adjusting their wigs and paper collars before a looking-glass upheld against their monstrous hats; and the brushers and bruisers, and rag and tag generally, aiming aimlessly at that "bob" which is always to be picked up here—and he will have a faithful picture of what Epsom Downs are like early in the morning of the great race.

It is all over—nine hours since by ordinary humdrum time o' day, ages since according to Epsom Downs time, between the start for the "great event" and when the upreared number-board by the judge's chair declared who the victor was. We didn't see the race. We never meant to see it. According to our expressed intention, we came home to breakfast at ten a.m., and remained at home until midnight. It was nothing to us who the winner was, though, as it chanced, we knew as soon almost as anybody in the town, for, at about a quarter past four o'clock, whilst sitting behind the window-curtain, comfortably discussing a delightful little book—the "History of Epsom," by a clergyman—kindly lent us by the landlady, hearing a swift pattering of feet (Epsom town is curiously still from ten till four on a Derby Day), we looked out, and spied the grocer's young man rushing, hatless and breathless, up the street, and when he came to the cheesemonger's young man, who was at his shopdoor to hear the news, he cried with deep emotion, "It's all up, Dick! That blessed Blair Athol has gone and done it!" And so he had: General Peel coming in second, and Scottish Chief third. About the positions of the other horses we need not trouble ourselves.

It's all over. The two hundred thousand who went up the hill have come down again; the judge has pocketed his fifty pounds and gone home, and is by this time—or so we hope, for it is past twelve o'clock—a-bed and calmly asleep, and the thousands whom his judgment made happy or miserable have also gone home, some to bed, and some to celebrate their good luck by getting shockingly tipsy, and some to mourn over their bad luck and pass the remainder of the night wearily figuring and planning how they may find a way out of the bog Blair Athol has flung them into. The turbulent sea that surged over the Downs and reached even to the brow of the great hill has subsided, leaving them blank, save for the booths and vans, which in the distance loom shapelessly and black; save for the lights from torches and lanterns twinkling like glow-worms; and still, save for the snatches of song and laughter coming from the spot where the vans and booths are most thickly clustered; for what has been fun for the sightseers, has been real hard work for those whom we saw so busily "making ready" in the morning, and now that their customers have gone, leaving their money behind 'em, *their* Derby holiday commences, and they arrange comfortable parties, and dance, and sing, and play cards, and eat up what is known as the "overplush" of ham sandwiches and such other food as will not keep handsomely through a warm night. They likewise give a fair share of their patronage to the "overplush" beer, and about two in the morning become rather noisy.

Nobody, however, is ever taken up for being drunk and disorderly on Epsom Downs on the Derby night. There are policemen on the spot, but they are all snugly housed at the Grand Stand in a great room, where there is a jolly fire, and plenty of mattresses, on which the officers recline with their coats and boots off. Just for form's sake, they march out in a body two or three times in the course of the night, but it is only to look in, in a good-humoured way, at the booths where there is most row, and mildly recommend peace and harmony.

The ugliest customers the police have to deal with are the gipsies—those free and blithesome individuals who scorn house-dwelling and prefer to herd in dens no better than dog-kennels. The gipsies, however, are not troublesome on account of their drunken propensities, but from their disposition for plunder. Heaven help the unlucky wretch who, drinking himself past consciousness, lies down in a corner to sleep and is forgotten by the party with whom he came from London! Not only will the gipsies rob and beat him—they will strip him to the skin, and drive him off, pelting him as he runs. The watchmen at the Grand Stand, more than once or twice attracted by the cries of the victim, have found him without a rag shivering at the door, and kindly lent him a sack to cover and comfort him, and enable him to set out on his walk back to London without delay. It is because of these gipsy ruffians that the booth-keepers provide themselves with firearms; and, as the night wanes and the revellers tire, and the twinkling lights grow fewer, there is heard on every side a tremendous banging, caused by the booth-keepers discharging their guns and pistols at their doors to let the gipsies know what they may expect should they venture in after the money-box.

XXV.

THE COSTERS' CARNIVAL.

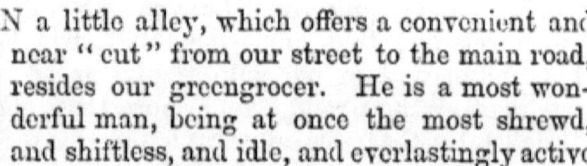N a little alley, which offers a convenient and near "cut" from our street to the main road, resides our greengrocer. He is a most wonderful man, being at once the most shrewd, and shiftless, and idle, and everlastingly active fellow that ever was born. Ours is a new neighbourhood, and we are very glad to patronise Mr. Tibbits and his perambulating store. Blending with the music of the morning muffin-bell you may hear his melodious voice chanting in praise of his cabbages and his plums of "Arline." At midday he may be seen retailing coals, in the afternoon toiling to some carpet-ground with a cart-load of dirty carpeting, and his early evenings are consumed in moving goods or servants' luggage. After that he disappears, and is seen no more that night except by the policeman and such of the public as may happen to be abroad at midnight. Then he is drunk—not helplessly so, inasmuch as he is able to keep his legs by hanging heavily on to the chorus of the last rollicking stave sung at "The Jolly Sandboys"—but very tipsy indeed, beyond question.

This was so last night, the night before, any and every night; yet to-morrow morning, certain as the rising sun, and even before the sun has risen, Mr. Tibbits will be again afoot and at work. It is the invariable habit of this indefatigable one—this cabbage-bawling, carpet-beating, gravel-carting, coal-selling, goods-removing, servants'-box-conveying, "Jolly Sandboy"-boosing person, who never seeks his own door until that of the public-

house is closed against him—it is this man's custom to
work fifteen hours, to waste five, and take no more than
the little remainder for rest, summer and winter, all the
year round. It must be so. Covent Garden is a "solid"
seven miles from Mr. Tibbits's abode, which makes the
double journey fourteen, to say nothing of market stoppages and a load to take home. Mr. Tibbits has but one
holiday a year, and that is at Barnet autumn fair time.

It was only within the last few days that I became
acquainted with the fact that he gave himself this holiday.
On the morning of Tuesday week his voice was unheard
in the street, and we thought, to be sure, that the poor
man was ill. Happening, however, that morning to avail
myself of his short-cut alley, I was agreeably surprised
to perceive a German band before his door, which it was
only natural to suppose would scarcely be allowed if
anything very terrible ailed the poor greengrocer. On
arriving opposite his shop my mind was set quite at ease
as regarded apprehensions as to Mr. Tibbits's state of
health, though I could not quite make out the state of
affairs; for there, arrayed in bran-new corduroys and a
starched and snowy shirt, was our worthy greengrocer
himself, adjusting his blue bird's-eye neckerchief by aid
of a bit of looking-glass stuck against the wall. The
cause of his banishment from the little parlour behind
the shop was evident, a gorgeously-bonneted head being
there visible "putting itself to rights" in the glass over
the mantel-shelf. Having arranged the neckerchief to
his satisfaction, Mr. T. donned a waistcoat of elaborate
design and of the pattern known as "the dog's-paw;"
and, with his thumbs hooked in the armholes thereof,
came to the door, with his hair radiant of bear's-grease
and his face beaming with happiness, to view the
musicians; wagging his head like a loyal subject as the
tow-haired vagabonds squeaked and squealed from their
brazen instruments that magnificent anthem, "God bless
the Prince of Wales," after the performance of which he
appeared much relieved, and producing a half-gallon can
from under the shop-counter, and inviting the instrumentalists to drink, inquired if they knew something "a

little rousier," whereon they stuck up "Annie Laurie," but had scarcely proceeded as far as "Maxwelton braes" when Mr. T. imperiously waved them to silence.

"That's a rare rouser, that is," said he, with mild sarcasm; "ain't you got sense enough to serve your customers with wot's in season? Something in this style, now;" and clearing his throat, Mr. T. favoured the astonished Teutons with the first verse of the ancient stave—

> " Ere older you grow, here's a song you should know,
>   I'd advise you to buy and to larn it,
> T'other day 't happened so, with a friend I did go
>   To see the famed races of Barnet.
>   Sing fol-de-rol fol-de-rol-lay."

It needed not the appearance at this juncture of Mr. Tibbits's cart and horse (the former clean washed and with three Windsor chairs ranged in it, betokening " a party," and the latter with his mane and tail neatly plaited and tied with cherry-coloured ribbon) to explain the mystery. The cat was out. Our greengrocer was going to Barnet Fair. Without doubt this was his holiday of the year. Christmas was nothing to him, for, as I distinctly recollect, he left word the day before " that if extra fruit or anything was wanted, he should be open all day;" on Derby Day he was bawling green-peas and gooseberries; on the Mondays of Whitsun and Easter he was seen at a neighbouring fair with his cart, and up to his elbows in damaged dates, driving a roaring trade. What was there about Barnet Fair that could attract our hard-working greengrocer so powerfully?

I was still puzzling over this problem when I reached the main road (the Holloway Road, which is the direct line to Barnet), and a glance revealed the fact that Tibbits was but one of a thousand bound for the ancient battle-ground whereon, four hundred years ago, the great Earl of Warwick was defeated and slain. The highway was alive with Barnet fair-goers, and to a man they were of the Tibbits sort; though, as a rule, and if appearances might be trusted (and surely on such a day they might), not nearly so well to do. Rattling down the road as it presently did (with three on the cart-seat and the Windsor chairs all occupied—four gentlemen and two ladies in all, the former enjoying at once a "chaw" and a smoke out of their cheroots, and with dahlias decorating the breast button-holes of their velveteen coats), Mr. T.'s equipage outshone by many degrees the generality, which were costermongerish in the extreme. Donkey carts and donkeys were decidedly the majority; handbarrows with elongated handles to attach a quadruped between, and burdened with four and even six hulking men and women, to say nothing of the big stone bottle and the bushel-basketful of victuals. Donkey drays, "half-carts," "shallows," and every other sort of vehicular device peculiar to costermongery, had its representative, drawn by every known shape in equine nature—donkeys fat, and sleek, and prizeworthy, and donkeys spavined, lame, and chapfallen, and looking as though they had been stabled in a damp cellar till mildew had seized on their hides; ponies, fast-trotters, glossy-coated, long-tailed, and frisky, and poor wizened things with that haggard, careworn expression which is the old, ill-used pony's peculiarity; young fiery horses, which were hard to hold in, and splay-legged, Roman-nosed, ancient brutes, which were hard to hold up; "kickers," "roarers," "jibbers;" vixens of fierce blood, and who could do anything but behave themselves, and meek, languid, washed-out horses, with drooping ears, drooping eyes, drooping everything, too deeply settled in melancholy to be stirred by whipcord, and who swung one leg before the other like clockwork horses wound up to their best, and never blinked an eye, let their drivers batter their ribs how they might, and curse and swear in a way calculated to startle them, if anything would. So that, taken as a whole, the road presented a very lively picture; and people said it was many years since there had been such a "Barnet," and generally attributed the improvement to the abolition of turnpikes. Why should not I go to Barnet Fair? True, I had no fast trotter and light-springed cart, nor even a donkey and barrow; but the railway was close at hand, and for an insignificant sum I might, in a very few minutes, be translated quietly at my ease to the coveted spot.

I went, and arrived there about noon. My first impression was my last, and still remains—viz., that Barnet Fair is a disgrace to civilisation. I have witnessed a Warwickshire "mop" fair; I have some recollection of "Bartlemy;" I was at Greenwich when, on account of its increasing abominations, the fair that so long afflicted that Kentish borough was held for the last time; but take all these, and skim them for their scum and precipitate them for their dregs, and even then, unless you throw in a very strong flavouring of the essence of Old Smithfield on a Friday, and a good armful of Colney Hatch and Earlswood sprigs, you will fail to make a brew equal to that of Barnet. It is appalling. Whichever way you turn—to the High Street, where the public-houses are—to the open, where the horse-"dealing" is in progress—to the booths, and tents, and stalls—brutality, drunkenness, or brazen rascality, stare you in the face unwinkingly. Plague-spots thought to be long ago "put down" by the law and obliterated from among the people, here appear bright and vigorous as of old—card-sharpers, dice-sharpers, manipulators of the "little pea," and gentlemen adept at the simple little game known as "prick the garter." Wheels-of-fortune and other gaming-tables obstructed the paths. "Rooge-it-nor, genelmen; a French game, genelmen; just brought over; one can play as well as forty, and forty as well as one. Pop it down, genelmen, on the black or on the red, and, whatever the amount, it will be instantly kivered! Faint heart never won fair lady, so pop it down while the injicator is rewolving! Red wins, and four half-crowns to you, sir; keep horf our gold is all we ask; our silver we don't wally!" Not in a hole-and-corner way this, but bold and loud-mouthed as goods hawked by a licensed hawker.

Disgusting brutality, too, had its representatives in dozens. There were the tents of the pugilists, where, for the small charge of twopence, might be seen the edifying spectacle of one man bruising and battering another;

there was the booth of the showman who amused the
public by lying on his back and allowing three half-
hundredweights to be stacked on the bridge of his nose;
there was the gentleman who put leaden pellets in his
eyes, and drove rows of pins at a blow into a fleshy part
of his leg; and there was a lean and horrible savage (a
"Chicksaw," the showman said he was, "from the island
of High Barbaree") who ate *live rats*. Decidedly, this
was the show of the fair. An iron-wire cage, containing
thirty or forty rats, hung at the door, and beside it stood
the High Barbarian, grinning, and pointing at the rats,
and smacking his blubberous lips significantly. The
sight was more than the people could stand; they rushed
and scrambled up the steps, paying their pennies with
the utmost cheerfulness; and, when the place was full,
the performance was gone through to their entire satisfaction. The High Barbarian really did eat the rats.
He set the cage before him, and, thrusting in his hand,
stirred the animals about till he found one to his liking,
then he ate it as one would eat an apple.

It was among the horses, however, where the chief
business was doing, as may be easily understood when it
is remembered that fully nine-tenths of the thousands
that swarm the town and the fair-ground have in view
the sale, or purchase, or "swop" of a horse, mule, or
donkey. Go to the horse market in Copenhagen Fields
any Friday, and it will be found that the chief difficulty
the market officers encounter in the exercise of their duty
consists in the presence of a score or so of donkey-dealing
ruffians, who set law and order at defiance; a slangy,
low-browed, bull-necked, county-cropped, spindle-legged,
lantern-jawed, big-chinned, long-waisted, tight-breeched
crew, lithe and muscular, carrying a thick ash stick with
a spike at the end of it, and utterly refusing to be "regulated." Let the reader imagine such a crew, multiplied
a hundredfold at the very least, and sprinkle amongst
them a few butchers, a few soldiers, and more than a few
blowsy, flashily-dressed costermonger women, and a
hundred or so decent-looking folk who have come inno-
cently to Barnet to buy a horse; make a mob of these,

and distribute amongst it all the riff-raff and rubbish in the way of horse and donkey flesh to be found within twenty miles of London, and a feeble realisation of the picture presented at the end of the High Street, looking into the space where the horse fair is held, will be the result. Some such scene as this is presented to the eye; but who shall describe the bedlam Babel of sound that arises from the busy, ever-shifting, motley mob? Fifty negotiations towards a sale are taking place at one and the same time, each one accompanied by an amount of yelling, and bellowing, and whip-slashing, and whistling which must have been pleasant to the ears of the "Chicksaw" rat-eater, as reminding him of the habits and customs of his tribe. Such a thing as a "quiet sale" is unknown at Barnet. The big-chinned one, with the battered white hat and the thongless whip, suddenly perceives a timid person of milkmanish mould furtively eyeing a gaunt, wall-eyed quadruped which he (the big-chinned one) has for sale. Instantly he slips the brute's halter from the post, and, vaulting on his back, proceeds to execute several daring feats of horsemanship, not the least of which is dashing amongst the crowd, which is quite unprepared for the manœuvre. A dozen of the horsedealer's friends are on the alert and strenuously exert themselves to bring out the "points" of the animal for the milkman's inspection; they shriek, they make hideous whistlings on their fingers, they clap their hands, they take off their hats and drum frantically on the inside with the butt-ends of their whips; and, when the intended purchaser is supposed to have arrived at a proper appreciation of the animal's valuable qualities, his rider dismounts as abruptly as he mounted, and, leading the panting steed up to the milkman, ejaculates, "Four pun' ten!" Should the milkman buy, you cannot miss the fact. "Hoi, hoi! sold again! sold again!" is roared by the partisans of the wall-eyed one's late owner, who immediately crowd around him to receive the reward of their meritorious exertions.

ON SATURDAY NIGHT.

XXVI.

ON SATURDAY NIGHT.

I.—THE "NAVVY."

LOOKING over the palings that skirted the temporary wooden bridge which crossed the "cutting," and along the cutting as far as it had as yet eaten into the hill, the sight presented was not a little curious and interesting. Within a space of a hundred and twenty yards two hundred and thirty stalwart navvies were high busy. Four hundred and sixty arms, brown, hairy, and muscular, were pulling and hauling, and delving and picking, as though the hill they were assaulting were the domain of the avaricious Thomas Tiddler, and every man was determined on having just a little bit more before Tom came raging at them from round the corner. Here, a dozen shining "picks" attacked a great mass of earth, which had been tumbled entirely from above; there, six daring giants were furiously undermining an overhanging piece of prodigious size, with a backward step, however, and a sharp, upward glance, after every malicious dig, lest the enemy should unexpectedly be down on them. On the sloping bank on each side a hundred spades were bobbing up and down at a tremendous rate, and as many weighty clods perpetually flying through the air in their passage to the "mook" trucks, while now and then came the sharp and sudden cry of "look oop!" followed by the dull crash of an earth mass as big as a labourer's cottage, "crowed" down by the "surface men," whose business it is to second the efforts of the underminers.

Take all this, together with the fantastic costumes of the spaders and pickers—red smocks, blue smocks, white smocks, and no smocks at all, but bare brown arms and chests hairy as the back of a terrier; caps of the woollen "night" sort—green, pink, and yellow, or elaborately barred and spotted with these colours and some others; hairy caps, made of the hide of the cow, the bear, and the badger; tarpaulin and shiny oilskin caps and caps of cloth, worn peak astern invariably—all these various shapes and colours, ever shifting and dodging to and fro, backed by the blue-black clay of the hill, with the engine tearing, and rattling, and whistling, and screaming, and lugging off trucks full laden, or bowling along jauntily over the smooth rails with a seemingly endless tail of "empties" —went to make the curious picture that I saw looking into the railway cutting just as the sober October Saturday afternoon was fading.

Suddenly was heard the clang-clang of a bell, and its effect on the diggers was magical. Was it Tom Tiddler's bell carried and rang by that gentleman himself to warn them of his vengeful coming? For the moment it seemed so, for the host of pickers, and shovellers, and crowbar-wielders at once abruptly—as though they worked by gas power and some one had turned them off at the main—ceased from their labours. They, however, made no attempt to escape. With a deliberation that contrasted strangely with their almost wrathful energy of a minute before, they proceeded to scrape their cloddy boot soles on their shovel blades, tidily scraping the upper leathers clean with a bit of slate. Then they loosened their leather harness—to wit, the straps that preserved the hitch of their trousers above their mighty calves and the broad brass-buckled belt by which their loins were begirt. Then they shook themselves, and with their woollen caps or the tails of their smocks wiped the moisture from their brows, and from the nape of their necks, and from the great bumps in the rear of their ears, where it seemed specially prone to accumulate. By this time the engine, brought to a standstill in their midst, and seeming to regard these preparations for "knocking off" with its great goggle-eyes full of astonishment, arrived at the conviction that its services were no longer required, and, with a prodigious grunt of contempt for such puny and easily-tired things as navvies, scuttled off, while the diggers, with their rush baskets in their hands and their tin cans clinking against their shouldered picks and shovels, strolled away towards a wooden shanty standing in an adjoining field, and the "cutting," just now busy as a beehive, was silent and deserted.

It was from the shanty in the field that the bellringing had arisen. It was Thomas Tiddler's erection. So far from being offended at the big-limbed navvies for coming to pick up gold and silver off his estate at the rate of four shillings and twopence a day, he encouraged them, and had been at the expense of rearing this wooden building, and cutting a hole in one side of it through which each man might receive his share of the gold and silver decently and without unseemly scrambling. The business of disbursing two hundred and thirty separate sums of five-and-twenty shillings, taken at its simplest, would appear to any one uninitiated in Mr. Tiddler's methodical ways a rather formidable undertaking; but taken in connection with the endless complications to which each five-and-twenty shillings is liable—"quarters," and hours, and even half hours lost, picks broke, and new shovels supplied, with fines for this, that, and the other, the task becomes appalling. Under Mr. Tiddler's system, however, all difficulties are smoothed away, and the business of paying is rendered easier by far even than giving each man two sixpences for a shilling. Every man is provided with a tin ticket, which bears a number corresponding with a similar one put against his name in the time and pay books. On Saturday the navvy gives in this ticket inclosed in a little canvas bag, highly branded with the number. In the course of the day, and undisturbed in his little office, the pay clerk makes up the account, and his assistant pops the proper sum into each bag and secures it with its string. Come pay time, the navvy army troops past the pay-hole, and as the clerk calls out the number the bag is deposited on a ledge and is taken up by the owner. The tin ticket also serves another purpose. If his work is satisfactory, the navvy finds the ticket in the bag along with his money; if, however, his services are no longer required, the ticket is retained, and the navvy trudges off for good and all.

I knew all this beforehand, and idle curiosity led me to loiter on the little wooden bridge over which the navvies must one and all pass, with the view of exercising my sagacity towards discovering the ticketless ones, and observing how the calamity affected them; but they came trooping past, every countenance beaming with serenity and that consciousness of power which the possession of wealth invariably confers, till I began to fear that my sagacity was at fault, scarcely daring to hope otherwise. Presently, however, there came two, both unmistakably doomed to the "sack," which they carried between them with much more fortitude than might have been expected.

"I don't fret, never fear," said one, "I knowed what was coming since that heavenly ganger, bless his precious eyes, jacketed me on Thursday."

"Fret! Not much to fret about," replied his companion of the sack. "Why, afflict me with blindness if I hav'nt worked harder in one beatific fortnight in that beatific cutting than I worked in three solid months on the main shore. Come along; I shall be a pot to your pot."

"Where shall we go?"

"Oh! to the old drum, I suppose."

Just then, and as the two sacked ones halted to strike a pipelight against the pailings, three other navvies passed, and, bawling after them, the one who had endured the beatific fortnight exclaimed—

"What cheer, Harry? See yer binneby?"

"Ay, ay, lad. We'll be up at the old drum, I reckon."

Where was the old drum? I was tolerably well acquainted with the signs of the taverns of the locality; but of one known as the "Old Drum" I had not hitherto heard. Clearly it was a place where navvies spent their Saturday evenings, and must be worthy of a visit.

The British navvy is no ordinary individual. He is not a mere dirt-shoveller. He is a skilled workman in his way, and he is paid as good wages as a journeyman watch-maker; he is a model of strength and physical endurance; he works harmoniously with his fellow-men, and is altogether a most cheerful and hearty fellow. How does he employ his leisure? What are his means of recreation and enjoyment? Wherever met he would be recognised; for the bare suggestion that he might disguise himself in a black coat, confine his hairy chest beneath a dandy waistcoat, or encompass his great throat by an all-round collar and a fashionable tie, is too absurd to be entertained for a single instant; yet, whoever saw the navvy at a theatre, a music-hall, or working-man's institute? Perhaps he is superior to the two former frivolities, and has no taste for the calm delights the latter provides. Doubtless the "Old Drum" was the navvies' clubhouse, the institution to which he, eschewing all others, resorted, seeking the society of his brother giants, and passing the evening with them in pleasant and intelligent discourse, or disporting himself in such manly amusements as the establishment provided, thereby keeping his muscles in fine working condition. Musing thus, I quitted the bridge and followed my two Drumward-bound friends, my esteem for the British navvy increasing each moment, and I resolved as I walked that if persuasion, or even the payment of a moderate fee, could gain me admittance to the "Old Drum," I would that evening make myself better acquainted with the navvy and his ways.

Down the lane and into the High Street, past the "Red Cow" and the "Load of Hay;" past even the newly-opened beershop, with its doors wide open and the spick-and-span pots ranged on the counter, and winking most invitingly in the gaslight; past all these, and then a halt at a porkshop, which one of my navvies enters and bargains for a couple of pounds or so of cold boiled leg, while his mate makes a purchase of a four-pound loaf at a neighbouring baker's; and then on again the pair of them, the bread-carrier munching the makeweight piece

as he goes. On, past that skulking, dirty pothouse, the
" Balaclava "——
No, not past the " Balaclava," but into it. Can this
be the " Old Drum ? " Surely not. But yet, as I linger
doubtingly, navvies in twos and threes push their way
into the house with a purposeful air; and presently, as I
get a fair view of the interior, I spy the two who have
"got the sack" quite at home on a barrel, with the
bread and pork between them, and which they are attack-
ing with the calm confidence of men sure of victory. At
the extremity of the bar there is a door, and navvy after
navvy enters at it and does not make his appearance
again; and as I wait and watch, the identical three, with
Harry amongst them—whom one of the pork-eaters had
asked, "What cheer?" on the bridge—turn in deliberately, and make straight for the inner door just mentioned.
It seemed that my speculations as to what sort of institution the " Old Drum " was, were a little wide of the
mark; nevertheless, it undoubtedly *was* the Old Drum
that I had come in search of, and to turn back was not
to be thought of.

The door at the extremity of the bar opened into a
largish room furnished with three great tables and a full
complement of forms. The floor was bare, as were the
yellow-washed walls, as was the ceiling, save for the
coating of gas and tobacco-smoke that begrimed it.
There was a fireplace with no fire in it, though the evening was chilly. The room was capable of containing
fifty or sixty individuals, but at present there were not
more than fifteen assembled. On the tables were fifteen
quart pots, and fifteen foul tobacco pipes sent forth a
blast that made the little ventilator in the corner by the
ceiling spin round with a whir like that of a knife-
grinder's wheel. As my sauntering costume is of humble
sort—consisting, indeed, of an old black wideawake and
a coat that was new in the autumn of '61—my entrance
provoked nothing beyond fifteen momentary stares,
and provided an excuse for fifteen pulls at the beer-pots.

This, however, was not my immediate conviction; for
so dead a silence pervaded the company as I took my

seat as to give me an uncomfortable impression that I
was intruding, and should presently be addressed as I
once was under somewhat similar circumstances. "Well,
do you see anybody here as you wants?" "No." "Do
you see anybody here as looks as though he wanted
you?" "I cannot say that I do." "Wery well, then."
Nothing so unpleasant happened, however, on the present
occasion; and, after the lapse of a minute or so, I
was put quite at my ease by two of the party breaking
into conversation.

"How they things do hum!"

"They do so."

"Wentilator, ain't it?"

"Ah, summat o' that."

Certainly this was not much, but it was very much
better than nothing, as showing that my presence was no
check on their freedom of speech. For the next two
minutes the "wentilator" had it all to itself, when,
happily, the entrance of three other navvies, each
carrying his own quart, provided material for fresh
discourse.

"Hallo, here's Dick! Found your dawg, Dick?"

"Bust him, no!"

"That warn't the one, then, as that chap told you of?"

"No, it worn't. Shove up further."

And the parties addressed having "shoved up further,"
and allowed the new comers a seat on their form, silence
reigned once again, and was only disturbed during the
next few minutes by the puffing of tobacco, the sound of
sighs that followed breath-exhausting draughts of beer,
and the click of the replaced pot on the table. Surely it
cannot go on like this, thought I. It's the way with
these big men; they are hard to move, but, once started,
there is no stopping them. A little more beer will float
them, and then we shall have social, scientific, and
political discussion in any quantity. But the door swung
to and fro, and the company increased to the number of
twenty-five, and at least a dozen pots had been replenish-
ed, and still the ventilator had the best of it—ten to one,
at least. Lord Palmerston's name had not been once

mentioned, "universal suffrage" was not even hinted at, the American war news was equally neglected; and even when Franz Müller was brought to table by the speculative observation of "I wonder if it really was that chap as did it?" no other reply was elicited beyond one of "If as how he did, I hope they'll scrag him;" and then the subject dropped.

More beer. There was no bell in the room, but the company contrived very well to make the landlord alive to their wants by banging the empty pots on the tables, and continuing to bang them till he made his appearance. By the time every man had drank at least three pots the general speech became freer—freer, but not free, inasmuch as it was restricted to a topic with which they were all well acquainted—viz., beer; about betting pots of beer, and winning them, and losing them, and drinking them; about drinking seven pots within the hour, with the story of a sawyer who had won just such wager in such bare time that he staggered down dead with the last pot in his hand, and the dregs trickling from it. It was, as far as I could make out, about these dregs that the dispute arose; the widow claiming the stakes, and the other party taking his stand on the unswallowed driblet to resist the claim. About good beer and bad beer, one gentleman, in a bison skin cap, stoutly maintaining that there was no such thing as "bad" beer; one sort might be better than another, but bad beer there was none—an argument that was rapturously received, and led to universal swigging and further furious banging on the tables with exhausted measures. More beer and increased freedom of speech. Some talk about the goodness of the cabbage and its frightfully high price; an argument as to the number of miles it was from Yarmouth to Norwich; an animated discussion concerning the comparative merits of "toe-plates" and "clinkers;" about boots generally and the use of dubbing; about a kicking case in which a certain navvy had mortally injured a policeman, and was then lying in gaol awaiting his trial; considering a prisoner's deprivation of beer; on the delights of a drayman's life. More beer. Some high words and a trifling pass of fisticuffs between Dick and the person who had misinformed him about his "dawg." Conversation about dogs—about rats—about drains and drain-pipes—about cutty-pipes and " colouring" clays—about soaking one's clay. Tremendous laughter, and more beer.

Clearly, there was no use in staying any longer. It was nearly eleven o'clock, and everybody was perfectly jolly and contented. What they had come to the "Old Drum" to seek they had found, and were now at the heart of it. On the whole, the navvy has disappointed me. Judging him from his manner of spending his Saturday night, I would rather be a little lame tailor, with some brain in my skull, than such a big blockhead.

XXVII.

ON SATURDAY NIGHT.

II.—POOR MOTHER!

Y meeting with poor mother was accidental. It was Saturday night, and I was coming from Highgate. As I came up with her just at the foot of the hill she civilly asked me if I could tell her the time or thereabout. As near as I could guess it, it was half-past eight, and so I told her. "Heart alive of me, you don't say so! I'm much obliged to you, I'm sure!" replied she, and then she mended her pace so resolutely that, had I not mended mine also, she would have been ahead and out of sight in the dark in a very little while. The reason why I mended my pace was this: it had been a dull and threatening evening, and within the last few minutes rain had set in and was falling faster and faster. Though not fashionably attired, the female who had asked what o'clock it was, was decent and respectable looking, and I resolved to offer her a share of my umbrella.

"I don't know how far we may be going the same way, ma'am; but as far as that may be you are very welcome to the shelter of my umbrella, if you like to accept it."

"Thank you kindly, sir," replied she. "I'm going all the way to the Lower Road, worse luck! and if you would have no objection to this little basket, it would be a real favour. I'm neither sugar nor salt, as the saying is. But to tell you the truth, young man, not expecting a fall of anything, when I set out I put on my best bonnet; and if it gets sopped, and the green runs into the straw, I should never forgive myself. Not that finery troubles *me;* only it looks so not to have a decent rag to come out in."

I certainly was not aware of the basket when I made her the offer, but though of the ordinary family marketing sort, it was not full-sized, and the lappets of her shawl nearly covered it. So I assured her that I had not the least objection to the basket, and that it only gave me concern lest it should be fatiguingly heavy.

"There's nothing at all in it, barring the basin for my butter," replied she, pleasantly.

"But you don't mean to say, ma'am, that you come all the way from the Lower Road to Highgate to fetch butter?" I asked.

"Lord love the man! no," replied my free-spoken, little old woman. "It's nothing to carry, and, by bringing it with me, I am able to do my errands at once, for if there is one thing I don't like more than another, it is running in and out like a dog in a fair on Saturday night. Where there's eight of 'em, as is the case with me, sir, and three only able to wash themselves, and they not always willing, and requiring to be looked after with the eyes of a hawk, there's enough to do without running about the streets half the night."

Seeing that I was expected to say something, I remarked "that doubtless a family of eight was a heavy responsibility."

"Eight! Why, there are eleven, and that's speaking only of those alive," replied the chatty old soul, proudly. "I've got a boy and a gal married, and a third that, so she says, has reasons to be in expectation of it. That's the one that I've been to up the hill with her frock and things to-night."

"What, her wedding frock?" I asked.

"Bless the man! no; her starched lilock. Catch *her* being married in a lilock. She's got too much of her sister Ellen about her for that, though it is to be hoped she'll know better how to take care of it if ever she has the same luck. So her father told her the last time she

came out for a holiday with lavender kid gloves on her
hands, above all things. 'You'll bring your noble ninepence to nothing, Mary Ann, if you don't watch it pretty
close,' said he. 'Work away while you're able, as the
little hymn says; you'd better have saved your money
and put something on your back, miss.' But it's like
talking to a post—in at one ear and out at the other.
Not that she's at all a bad girl. Six in family to cook
for, and two in a perambulator between dinner and tea
invariably when it is the least fine, Highgate Hill being
not the smallest of hills to push it up and down, and both
of them so fat that their legs bow under them, is no joke
at seven pounds a year, and her washing and ironing
done at home. It's horse work, that's what I call it.
I made the remark only this night in her kitchen, which
—I will give her her due—is so clean that you might
freely take your dinner off the floor boards, and you can
see yourself in her tins, even to her cullinder. 'Mary
Ann,' said I, 'are you aware that this makes three pair
of boots as good as new, besides the kid and spring sides
that Ellen gave you, in a single quarter?' 'Well, I can't
help it,' said she; 'you shouldn't have got me a place
in such a gravelly part.' 'Well, gravelly or not gravelly,
Mary Ann, your father declares that the next pair shall
be all leather in the uppers, and with tips and sparrow-
bills.' Not that he would be seen doing such a thing, for
a better father and one prouder of his gals never stept."

I don't mean to assert that my little old woman spoke
at this length without pause or interruption; but, as my
share in the conversation was limited almost entirely to
such common-place interjections as "Oh!" "Exactly!"
and "Indeed!" I have not thought it worth while to
record them. Now, however, that an opportunity presented itself, I thought I might venture to say a good
word for the damsel of gravelly ways.

"There's one consideration, however, ma'am; if the
young person of whom you speak is of no assistance to
you, she has ceased to be a hindrance," said I.

"Boots, boots; nothing but boots," continued she,
heedless of my observation, and evidently taking up the

thread of her discourse where she had let it fall slack,
" it's just the bit of victuals, and the rent, and the boots,
and there you are. I'm sure it's a mercy that their father
has a regular seat of work, and is not in and out all his
life, like many others in the tailoring trade. To be sure,
it's piece, and therefore not so brisk sometimes as at
others; but you might set it down all the year round at
a pound, anyhow, which is not so bad in the slop times
we live in."

" But surely a pound a week is not the whole of your
income," said I, " you have other sources of assistance."

" Sources of——"

" Ay ! Amongst the eight at home are there none big
enough to work ? Have you no boys ? "

" Two boys; but only one that sauces," replied poor
mother ; " the other one, Bill, is as civil a lad as you'll
find in a day's walk. He's getting a big boy now—much
too big for four-and-sixpence and just the slop of tea in
the evening, finding his own bread and butter, and walking his legs off with that millinery fly-cage thing chafing
holes in the shoulders of his Sunday jacket, because he
must go respectable, bless your soul! and a clean shirt
three times a week. Believe me, sir, I'd as lief he left
as stayed. Two shillings and ninepence for foreparting
and bits on the heels only last week, and this week
leaking again in a manner that went to your heart
when he came home to see his poor sopped feet. 'Why
you'd better be a coal-boy, Bill,' said I, ' or work up
there at the wood-chopper's, than be such a whitened
sepulchre as you are—genteel, and with fancy caps and
falderals in your basket, and all the while tired as any
dog, and with the heels all ground out of those new
worsted stockings.' 'You let me alone, mother,' is the
answer he makes. ' I ain't a fool, I don't have my tea
in the same room where the machines are working for
nothing. Just you stay till I get an insight; *then* I'll
talk to him.' So he put on his brother's, while I took
his back and told the nasty, cheating fellow what I
thought of him. ' However you could sit there and take
a poor soul's two-and-ninepence,' said I, ' well knowing

that the leather you put was not thicker than brown
paper, and the stitches you might draw out with your
teeth, gets over me.' And there they are, coming to
fifteenpence ever since Thursday; and that idle riff-raff
about the house like a great monkey, and shoeless; and
ours, the most particular of landlords, looking over the
wall and seeing the shelf of the kitchen cupboard in the
act of being sawn up for a rabbit-hutch; and it was
only his presence of mind in calling it a meat-safe, and
pleading dampness of the kitchen shelf as regards victuals
as an excuse for the alteration, that saved a fine row.
Ah! he's a dear boy. He's a blue hen's chick, if ever
a poor soul was troubled with one."

It was somewhat difficult to follow my little old
woman. The "blue hen's chick," and "the riff-raff,"
and "the great monkey and shoeless," were, I presumed,
identical. To make quite sure, however, I made the
remark that it was a great shame, and that he was old
enough to do better.

"Old enough? why, let me see, sir—why, let me see,
that boy was three years old in January as the first Exhibition was opened in May, because I remember making
the remark that if the Exhibition had been opened just
three months to the day earlier, it would have come on Jack's
birthday. Polly is eighteen, and yes—no, there was nobody
between Polly and Jack, which makes him sixteen come
the time. That makes Bill fourteen in August, of course.
And the difference between the brothers! The number
of places that eldest one has had is past all belief. Not
a bad boy in the main, you see, sir, but such a spirit.
I'm sure his last place but two was as comfortable a place
as any boy could wish. That was at the fishmonger's
near the Post Office, as you may perhaps know, sir?
Well, John, he wanted Easter Monday, which, very
naturally, wasn't convenient, and, instead, they set him
cleaning fish, there being a great supper somewhere.
Well, sir, there was nine pounds of fine eels in a tub
standing on the edge of the sink, and what did the rascal
do before he went to his dinner but take up the trap out
of the waste-pipe and tilt the tub on its side, thereby

getting the sack on the spot, besides choking the drainage, and costing us, from first to last, seven-and-twenty shillings."

"That prank cost *him* something as well, I should imagine," said I; "a few sore bones, eh?"

"Lor bless you, no!" replied the confiding old soul; "we daren't touch him, because, you see, my dear sir, he's all for the sea. Why, when that boy was only ten years old, and he lived up here at Crummles's, the confectioner's, and got turned away for some missing sausage-rolls, he never came home, though the rumpus was in the morning. Eight o'clock at night, nine o'clock, still no Jack; and then, come ten, his father went down; and, behold you! there were the shutters up, and the girl going for the beer. So he crossed over to her, and then it came out. 'You can put them on to fry while I am gone,' says he, when he went out; but they might as well have laid raw in the cupboard for all a mouthful of it that was touched that night; and so you would have said had you seen his face when he came back and told me. Ellen and her beau were there at the time, which accounted for the lamb chops for supper, and Sheffield himself, who, though in a large way as a haberdasher, has no more pride about him than you or me, at once got up and put on his great coat, and out they went, hunting high and low to find him till a quarter to one o'clock, when home they came, empty handed. Never shall I forget that night, and how I paced the room thinking of a thousand things, and suicide being the idea uppermost; so that it was only on Sheffield's solemn promise of the drags as soon as daylight that I could be persuaded to lie down. Well, sir; and what was the upshot? Why, at twenty minutes past eight, and just as we had all set down to a wretched breakfast, a knock came at the door that sent all our hearts into our mouths, and, lo and behold you! master Jack. Not downcast and with his eyes swelled out of his head with crying, as you might have expected, but bold as brass, and dressed in a blue guernsey and a blue cloth cap with anchor buttons, which he had sold his good jacket and the boots off his feet to buy. There he stood on the mat, before quite a passage full of us, holding on to the door-knob, and saying it wasn't worth while coming in any further, as he had merely come to bid us good-bye; and it was only when he was begged and entreated into the parlour, and I had got him to swallow a cup of tea and to eat a bit or two of toast, that he up and confessed that he had firmly made up his mind to sail all round the world; that he was a bad boy, and didn't think it likely that he should ever be better; and that he thought the best thing would be to cast himself on some desolate island out Australia way. You laugh, sir! Well, Sheffield, he laughed, till we came to search his pockets and found a jack-knife with a bit of string through the handle, and some filthy black tobacco for chewing, and a bit of Indian ink and a needle, ready to dot the anchor on his arm; and then we found that it was no laughing matter. 'If he's bent on it, let him go,' Sheffield said. But, as I remarked at the time, 'when you come to have them of your own, my good sir, you will alter your tune.' No seafaring boys for me, thank you. Lor bless us, no! I should get the creeps, and so would his father, every time the wind blew. Who he takes after is a puzzle to us, except it is his godfather, that we called up from his boats at Lambeth Stairs and got to stand at his christening at the old church for a shilling. So it is, anyhow; and to this very day he's as strong after the sea as ever. Just put him out in the least, or ask him to clean so much as a window or a knife and fork when it don't suit him, and he flies in a passion, and these are the first words out of his mouth, 'I aint a goin' to stand this. Give me my cap, and I'll go at once and get a ship.' Bless you, you can't think how careful we are obliged to be."

"Well, you'll pardon my saying so," I ventured to remark; "but, from what you have told me of your son John, I think that Mr. Sheffield was quite right when he said, 'If he's bent on going, let him go.' If I were his father, the next time he demanded his cap he should not be kept waiting for it."

"As a stranger, no doubt you would, sir, but when he is known as well as we know him, he is not at all a hard boy to manage. Only give him a good word and he'll turn the mangle like a lamb, or fill your tubs, or help Louisa home with the clean linen, without so much as a wry face. His savagest times are when he doesn't get his victuals to the minute. That's where Mary Ann puts me out so on Saturday night. I feel it my duty to see her once a week, and there goes two or three hours out of the worst night in the whole week. How do I make it out to be the worst night? Oh, my good sir, it is not *me* that makes it the worst; it is the flock I've got to struggle with. 'Life is but a span' I hear sometimes at chapel, on Sunday nights. I don't know what the correct measurement of a span may be, but to my mind it is a week. It is a sinful thing to say; but what's my life but a week? I begin it on Monday morning, and I finish up on Saturday night. It's like the judgment day; there it is at the end of the long lane that's got no turning, blocking it up so that you can't get a peep beyond it. The bit of money you get, counting even Bill's four-and-sixpence, and the trifle of money one can earn at ninepence a dozen, and those chiefly sheets, as I assure you, and large things that wring your arms off, just carries you through the lane, and not an inch to spare—not half an inch—not even so much as an extra half pint of beer, though standing in that cold wash-house till you felt like standing in ice. It looks a lot—it certainly *does* look a lot, when it's put altogether on the table on Saturday night; but it's all laid out, as the saying is, before a farthing is touched; and then there's grumbling and black looks from Master John, who bought a sprigged waistcoat while at the fishmonger's, and which naturally went to make up the deficiency; and there it lays, eating its head off with interest. And there it *must* lay—for to-night, at all events, let him look ever so black; for, believe me or believe me not, sir, by the time I've taken in a bit of something for supper, and settled with the butcher, and got what I want at Gawler's, and fetched Bill's boots, if I've got eighteenpence more than will pay for the baking to-morrow, I shall think myself lucky. Oh! you don't turn down here, sir? Well, good-night, young gentleman, and thank you kindly for my part of the umbrella."

XXVIII.

TWO P.M.—ON BOARD "CITIZEN B."

AS a promoter of brotherly love and kindly regard, and general jolly good-fellowship, there is nothing like water. The poet who penned that sweet and universally accepted line, "One touch of nature makes the whole world kin," no doubt had water in his eye as he wrote. By "nature," he meant the aqueous element. It may be objected that Shakspeare claims the homage of the "whole world" for his panacea, and that at this point the water theory breaks down, inasmuch as regards a large proportion of the world's inhabitants there exists such a horror of the "nature" in question that were they not only "touched" with it, but drenched with it—soused in it—scrubbed with it till they were nearly clean and totally wretched, they would exhibit towards the operators no more good-will than before; probably less, indeed; but the objectors might be met by the suggestion, that the sentiment was penned for Britons—for the inhabitants of the "world" in which the poet lived, and with whose hearts' desires he was so familiar.

Anyhow, if this is not a true rendering of the poet's meaning, it well might be. Blood even is not so potent as water. It may be "thicker," but, as a cement for broken brotherhood, is not for a moment to be compared with simple aqua; for while blood is a stickler for caste and degree, and so prompt to spill (alack for the empty pitcher!) that the common herd may view and judge of its quality, water not more infallibly finds its own level than it levels such of mankind as trust themselves to

THE HALFPENNY STEAMER.

its jurisdiction. It may be proved in a dozen cases, great and small. In the case of the sea, for instance. You have but to touch the hem of its garment, even the faggest hem, such as the beach at Brighton or Hastings, and you are straight translated from your former self as completely as though you had grasped the tail of an electric eel. You discover that it is all a mistake about Britannia ruling the waves; it is the waves that rule Britannia. Your birthright of freedom—of freedom to dress as you please, eat what you please, and go where you please—no longer avails you. Born in the interior, the sea knows you not, but, having entered her dominions, you must do as the rest of the sea subjects. There is no seat for pomp by the side of the sea, and vanity dare not stretch its wings beyond the drawing-room windows of the lodging-houses. No matter the terms for which you enlist in the service of the sea, you must serve beneath her banner faithfully. It is a brown banner, broad and ample, but as plainly brown as a Quaker's coat. Its shadow clothes you. It stirs the air and imparts to it the balminess and fragrance which the cinnamon stick imparts to the bowl of healing cordial, and as you quaff it you are comforted. There is nothing on earth so nice. Every one you meet says so, from their eyes, at least, some being new to it, and twinklingly intoxicated, eager as trouts on a rainy day, and rapturous as early sweethearts; others grown used to it, hummingly contented as honey-bees, and beaming with brown beneficence to the very roots of their hair.

You are all alike, all brownly cheerful and sedately happy; all with warm hearts and none with cold shoulders. "But," says the reader, "it is possible to have too much of the brown banner; there are times—times of dead calm, when it doesn't stir the air in the least, but hangs dull and wooden as its own staff." Dead calm, indeed! Sleep is dead calm; so is snow covering the wheatfield; so is sunset, and a hundred other things, which go to make the ever new to-morrow. Dull! Eve, advised of a worldly sensation from which she was debarred, found the Garden of Eden dull. There came a season, however,

when she would have mightily rejoiced to have got back
again, as you, my friend, will rejoice to get back to the
humdrum brown banner, come the sultry autumn time.

On the sea, even more than by the side of it, is the
influence of the Leveller felt. On land there are grades
of sickness; there is "rich man's" gout and "poor
man's" gout; and often, for want of a guinea, a life is
hampered by a heartload of pain; but sickness born of
the sea is of but one quality—between the man in clouted
boots prostrate in the steerage, to the state cabin in-
habitant burying his unhappy nose in the softness of the
dainty couch cushion, there is at most but the difference
of a twopenny pannikin.

A great ship setting out to sea reckons, say, five hundred
lives aboard, the cabin-boy counting one and the commander one—not one and a quarter; no, nor a sixteenth;
though, come to share the prize-money, he is lumping
weight against any twenty men in the ship. He is great,
and his greatness continues by grace of the quiet sea till
there is an end to the voyage; but should the sea awake,
and, donning its foamy crown, take the command out of
the commander's hands, then blue serge is on a par with
scarlet and gold lace; and no wave of the great sea's
army will be so polite as it sweeps the troubled deck as
to avoid scarlet and gold that it may chase blue serge to
death. Should the wrecked ship go down, than the dead
level to which the cabin-boy, and the commander, and
Pompey the cook will fall, it is impossible to imagine
anything deader.

From the Atlantic to the Thames, from H.M.S.
Vengeance, Commander Ajax, to *Citizen B*, Captain
W. Blinker, and we are aboard the Chelsea boat.
Citizen B starts from London Bridge, and calls at
all the piers up the river. It has called at Temple
Pier and taken up the clerkly young gentleman with
the blue bag and the third volume of the last sensation novel. I wonder who the heroine is? Is it a she
wolf in shape of a countess, according to the prevailing
fashion, or is she a garret-angel—a human sewing-
machine—stitching herself into an early grave at the rate

of threepence-halfpenny a day? If so, he cannot do
better than put aside his stupid book and look about him.
There, in the flesh, sits the heroine whom he so passionately adores in printer's type. True, she has not yet
arrived at that interesting stage when, "by the hectic
roses on her cheek and the light of brighter worlds in her
eye, insidious disease marks her for its own," so graphically described at page 430; but she is none the less
eligible to become his heart's idol on that account. Just
speak to her, and you'll find with what a sweet, bewitching voice she will answer; or, if you are bashful, as is
likely, or cautious—which, being in the "legal" line,
is still more likely—just for a moment cast your eyes
from your book—pretending to read all the time—and
observe with what tenderness she contemplates that
penny bunch of violets in the flower-girl's basket. Think
of the bliss, when you had married her, and made her
happy, and given her, instead of violets to smell, roses
to wear all the year round; think of the pleasure of
having such a pair of eyes to lovingly greet you when
you returned at eve from your musty office in Pump
Court; think of—— But the young fellow thinks of
nothing of the kind. He gets out at Westminster, and
leaves the little needlewoman to cross over to Lambeth
—which completes her penny ride—anxiously debating
within her own mind whether she shall buy the violets
and walk back to London Bridge. Confound that young
fellow's sensation novel! But for that, the genius of
jolly good-fellowship, as represented by the river, might
have induced him to have treated the poor little maid to
a ride all the way to Kew and bought her a bunch of
flowers into the bargain.

But the genius in question has prevailed with every
other soul on board *Citizen B*. The coalheaver is engaged
in friendly discourse with one who but a quarter of an
hour ago was a stranger. The young gentleman with
the puppy-dog hair and the young lady with the blue
parasol are discussing the dimensions of the "platform"
at Cremorne, whither they are bound. Even the man
at the wheel looks as though he was quite ready to set

the laws of his country at defiance, and to "speak" to any one bold enough to begin a conversation. There remains but the foreigner and the happy carpenter. Ignorance of the language of those about him is the sole and simple reason why the French gentleman is companionless; but observe how eloquent are his spectacles!

But the happy carpenter, he, too, is companionless. Is he! He! he! that's all *you* know about it! His wife is down-stairs in the cabin. They are going to Kew. It ain't often he loses half a day, but when he does he likes to enjoy himself. Staying down in that stuffy cabin *isn't* enjoyment. Stay! "What do *you* say, Tomkins? (Tomkins is at *this* end of the boat; his wife is down in the stuffy cabin along with the happy carpenter's wife). Fresh breeze up here, my boy; blow some of the sawdust out of a fellow. Jerooslem, Tomkins! there's a pair of balmorals!"

XXIX.

TEN P.M.—THE DANCING-SALOON.

MAN is essentially a dancing animal. As a savage, saltation is his chief delight. If he be a fierce, head-hunting Dyak, he has his "skull" dance and his "jawbone" dance, as well as many dances of a peaceful sort, including the great days of jigging which distinguish sowing and harvest times. If the savage be a cleft-lipped, ring-nosed Malay, he twiddles his lean shanks to the music of human marrowbones and cleavers; if a cannibal Fan of gorilla land, his wife chants a lively ditty in praise of "long pig" while he polks about the cooking-pot; if a Dahoman, he dances for blood and rum (his Majesty the King leading the ball); while, should he happen to be a greased and ochred Indian of North America—a Pawnee, or an Iroquois, or an Ojibbeway—there is nothing under the sun he will not dance for. He is at it morning, noon, and night. He has a rain dance, and a sunshine dance, and a famine dance, and a feast dance, and a dance for the sun, and for the moon, and a score or so of the stars. He dances when his baby is christened, and, should it live to be a six-foot warrior and die before its father, the old gentleman will foot it sorrowfully round and round the mound under which his offspring lies buried. He detaches the scalp from the head of an enemy and risks reprisal that he may execute a triumphant double-shuffle over the prostrate form of the victim, and he has a special dance on the occasion of his shaking hands all round with a hostile tribe and "burying the hatchet." He has—at least, his brother the Dacota has—a very nasty dance called "the dog-dance," in which boiled dog is hung to a sort of maypole, and snapped at and demolished by mouthfuls by the dancers, men and women, who join hands in a merry-go-round, the dog's-meat pole in the centre. Also, these people have a dance known as the "poor-dance," which is a highly creditable institution. It is for the benefit of the poor, and decrepit, and orphaned of the tribe, and is conducted by the most renowned belles and "swells" in the village. They choose a convenient time, and spend an entire day in roaming from place to place and exhibiting their skill as dancers, and jugglers, and singers to an admiring public, and attended by a couple of porters, one carrying the money-box, and the other ready to burden himself with any "poors-gift" of blanketing, or maize, or tobacco. Even that wretched little pigmy the Australian Bushman occasionally breaks the monotony of his existence, which, as a rule, is given to three occupations—digging up and cooking roots and earthworms, chastising his "gin" with his waddy, and lying on his back smoking tobacco—by engaging in the graceful "carroberry," the soft and delightful "kuri," or the more vigorous and soul-inspiring "palyertatta," in which the performers, in a simple suit of gum-leaves, congregate about the forest bonfire, leaping over it and through it, at the same time brandishing their naked spears and uttering the most appalling yells, while the women sit in a circle a little way off, beating time with their hands, and unanimously raising their voices in imitation of the musical grunt of the red kangaroo. Civilisation is impotent to weed out this relic of barbarism. The King of Dahomey dances, so does the Emperor of the French. Mahtotoppa, the great chief of the Dacotas, danced on the eve of his great victory over the Sacs and Foxes; the Duke of Wellington danced on the eve of Waterloo. At ten p.m. any time this week or next, could the reader see from here to Old Kalabar, he would doubtless discover a select party of Egbos performing saltation at the shrine of a Fetish snake; and if, within the same hour, he took the trouble to walk as far as Bloomsbury, and looked in at "Widdles's Dancing Saloon," he would there find, with some small differences, a repetition of the same performance.

Small differences, indeed! In what particular, pray, does the Old Kalabar heathen orgies resemble Widdles's? What similitude—even the faintest—may be traced between Widdles's patrons and the grease-anointed, face-painted, copper-bangle-wearing Kalabese? Is the likeness of man to the gorilla less positive than the likeness of young Mr. Brussels Prout (with the eyeglass) to a grinning, goggle-eyed native of Kalabar? Is Widdles's M.C. (a shirt-cutter by profession, and not depending for his living on two-and-sixpence per night, be it borne in mind) to be for a moment compared with a shock-headed, ring-nosed savage? Are Mr. Peascod and the master cabinetmaker and his sister barbarians? Is their cousin, the outfitter's daughter from Aldgate, a likely person to bow in worship to a Fetish snake?

Well, she is a very fine woman, and I beg ten times ten thousand pardons if it happens that I am wrong; but truly and sincerely, I *do* believe her to be addicted to fetish worship. There is that in her eyes, in her hair, in her general appearance and ornamentation, which betrays her. Likewise I suspect Peascod—I suspect him chiefly on account of his patent leathers and his teeth; while as for his sister, she has worshipped the serpent till her hair begins to fall off, and it has become necessary to sacrifice the prettiest of pouts and to affect with her lips an expression of severity and determination she has not at all at heart, by way of concealing the fact that her teeth are failing her. Poor little Miss Peascod! The devotion of a lifetime—at least from maidenhood upwards—has in no way softened the nature of the insatiable fetish snake towards her; she has given it all her smiles; she has exhausted the natural bloom of her cheeks in the monster's service; she has suffered headache, heartache, and, for its sake, borne with a cheerful countenance the agony attendant on the possession of three corns (two hard and one soft) palpitating in shoes two sizes too small for her. She has expended the trifle of pin-money her brother allows her for keeping house for him in sashes, and bows, and jewels, and gigumboles, that she might not discredit the monster. This evening she has brought the devouring dragon flowers, and for his delectation she sports an embroidered handkerchief, which it is only merciful to hope she has merely borrowed for the occasion of that magnificent person her Aldgate cousin, and not purchased.

It is merciful to hope that this is the case, because if she *has* bought it she has wasted her money. The cost of her flowers was waste, likewise of her bows and streamers and her elaborate head-dress; likewise—and this is worse than all—are all her past sacrifices to her fetish waste. Her headaches, her heartaches, her rosiness, her pin-money, all, all have gone for nothing! True she has had her "sport for her money," as the saying is, but it is the sport of the angler who catches no fish. Ambition is the name of Miss Peascod's fetish. She was taken to Widdles's when quite a little maid (it was not her brother that escorted her in those times), and there she found a paradise she had hitherto only dreamt of. She found glitter, and sparkle, and music, and an amount of polite attention at the hands of the white-gloved gentlemen assembled that fairly turned her innocent head. Individuals who, judged by their waistcoats and moustaches, might have been barons at the very least, solicited her for "the next set" with a humility which, until she grew a little used to it, was really painful. Clearly she had underrated herself. William was a very nice young man, to be sure, and possibly gentlemen's bootmaking was a decentish trade; but when she thought on William's unfashionable whiskers, and his great hands breaking through the tender stitches of his unwonted white kids, and compared both — his hands and his whiskers—to *some* that were there; to *some*, the owners of which, with fairy lightness (William certainly *was* rather flat-footed), had accompanied her through the mazy dance, and even in one instance at least, and that not the least aristocratic, inquired if that gentleman

(William) was her *brother*, and when this little episode in this first of her Arabian nights crossed her memory, together with the remembrance of the incredulous but eminently gentlemanly stare with which the viscount, or whatever he was, received her blushing answer that he was not her brother but a friend; when, I say, this, among other matters, reappeared to her that night as she sat at her looking-glass putting her curls in paper, there was reflected in it a face with something about it that, could honest William have seen it, would have stabbed his heart more cruelly than his keenest awl could. Her foolish little heart felt itself debased any longer to harbour so mean a lodger as a bootmaker, and from that time she became a fetish worshipper, and so she remains. Since that fatal evening her mind has, of course, been disabused of many of the delusions which then crept into it. Her viscounts have proved to be clerks, and her dukes persons in the tailoring business. Her favourite baron had the felicity of serving her with a yard of pink tarlatan behind a draper's counter in Holborn. But her faith in her fetish is not shaken, and she continues to worship at Widdles's with touching constancy and devotion. Indeed, her infatuation increases with her years; and though she can now find no more agreeable escort than her bachelor brother; though the M.C. has long ceased to bow and scrape, and greet her with a familiar nod; though she occasionally sits for half an hour with no one to speak to her or bring her negus but Mr. Peascod, she finds at Widdles's what she can find nowhere else. It is an oasis in the desert. The glitter and sparkle of music, and flaunting of sashes and rustling of silks, have become essential to her very existence—that is, to her existence as a fetish worshipper. One of these fine nights a brutal giggle, or the rude shock of a very cold shoulder, will break the spell, and she will then discover the heartless wooden idol she has all along been worshipping. I hope when that melancholy time arrives that her brother, the master cabinetmaker, will have found the reward for which he is craving—*his* fetish; and that Mrs. Peascod will afford her a comfortable asylum in which to terminate her everlasting maidenhood; or, her brother failing her, that her outfitting cousin from Aldgate may captivate and marry Mr. Brussels Prout. I should like to see that young gentleman daring to offer any objection to Miss Peascod taking up her abode in his house if Mrs. Prout willed otherwise.

XXX.

REFLECTIONS ON BATTERED BREECHES.— A NEWSPAPER BOY.

HE *is* a "business man," without doubt. While the heads of his customers were as yet pressing their several pillows; while the horrible shrieks of the London and North-Western mail-train whistle was startling the babyhood of day, while the omnibuses, now so prim and bright, still reposed in "the yard," spattered and grimy with yesterday's mire, this small radical was up and doing. He was whistling over Blackfriars Bridge while St. Paul's was chiming four; and before six o'clock he had borne the brunt of four battles in as many newspaper-publishing offices, coming off in each case with flying colours. True, you may find the result of one of his skirmishes recorded in a crimson smudge over the latest American war news; but, don't be alarmed, it was only his nose, and you should have seen the other chap's eye! "Well, and served him right. What call had *he* got to push and shove people about, and call them 'young feller,' because he wore a four-and-nine and had a pencil stuck behind his ear, just as though he was wholesale—'Nine quires, if you please, sir' (just fancy calling the chap behind the counter 'sir'), as stuck up as though he wanted the whole lot for his private reading. 'And, please, sir, rop 'em up in wilit tissue for the genelman, cos he's left his kid gloves at home on the peana,' says I. 'Let me have none of your impertinence, young feller,' says he. 'Well, you don't stand in want of it, havin' a jolly good stock of your own,' says I 'howsomever, p'raps you'll be so perlite as not to scrouge, and to take your hoofs off my toes, or else somethin' might happen to that hat.'" That was the way the row began; in the short space of seven minutes it was all over—the stuck-up one defeated, the quire of *Stars* secured, the wounded nasal organ bathed at the pump, and Battered Breeches is enlivening dosy Fleet Street with "Sally come up the middle" as he makes his way to the office where a supply of "grafts" (B.B.'s playful abbreviation of *Daily Telegraphs*) may be obtained.

And did the publisher of that eminently peaceful newspaper the *Star* permit this pugilistic encounter on his premises? Did he not instantly take measures for the protection of the stuck-up one and the expulsion of Battered Breeches? Did the porter take B.B. by his baggy part and the nape of his neck, and, thrusting him out, warn him never to show his face in Dorset Street again? He did not. The obligations he and his employers are under to B. B. forbade any such unceremonious proceeding. For, be it known, Battered Breeches is one of the chief pillars of the cheap press. Had it not been for B. B. and his numerous friends, that mighty engine the penny paper would have stood still long ago; the requisite "mint sauce" (as that horribly vulgar and slangy B. B. terms money), so necessary for lubricative purposes, would have been wanting; and creaking, and rust, and decay would speedily have ensued. But B. B., like the shrewd fellow he always shows himself, took the matter into his consideration. He was hawking hearthstone at the time at a profit of about sixpence a day, and one morning, just as he was beginning his rounds, he happened to call at a house at the moment when the newspaper boy was delivering a *Times*.

"I wish I had *your* billet, young 'un, and you had mine," said B. B., ruefully contrasting the light bundle under the boy's arm with his own heavy bag. "How much profit might there be on that there lot now?" And the newspaper boy, having leisure and not too much pride to converse with a hearthstone boy, obligingly sat down and made a calculation. "There's one and tuppence on this lot," said he; "that's a quarter profit, don't you see, and a little over."

"Is it a quarter profit on the penny 'uns?" asked B. B.

"It's always a quarter profit," he was answered.

"And can you get as many as you like?"

"The more the merrier."

So the newspaper boy went his way, and for more than an hour B. B. sat in the sun on his hearthstone bag, in the very brownest of studies. Little did the despairing father of the first-born "penny daily," as he that morning contemplated his month-old bantling, starving and pining to death under his anxious eyes, dream that at that very moment good luck was hatching for him. He would not have believed it if he had seen the hatcher; for, truly, B. B., who at that time had neither cap nor boots, was not "a likely-looking bird;" and if he and a gentleman with £500 to lend had simultaneously made their appearance at the office of the *Lightning Conductor*, and each offered his services, there can be little doubt as to which the proprietor would have chosen. Nevertheless, had he accepted the five hundred, and for ever lost humble B. B., he would have done a very foolish thing.

And yet B. B. had but sevenpence in the world. But after an hour's cogitation he rose up a boy with a purpose; and had his life depended on the sale of his hearthstone he could not have hawked it more earnestly. He begged, he implored, with tears in his eyes, as neatly he piled the tempting pen'orth against the area railings, and added another lump, and another, and yet still one more, and cried, "Do, please marm!" in such a way that it was impossible, unless one had a heart ten times harder than he vowed his hearthstone was, to deny him. By evening, although he had dined out of his bag, and afforded himself half a pint of beer at the time, his sevenpence had increased to eighteenpence.

Six o'clock next morning saw him at the office of the *Lightning Conductor*. Eight o'clock saw him at the railway station, astonishing cads and policemen and alarming nervous omnibus-riders by his tremendous activity and the power of his lungs. "Penny daily, sir! penny daily! War with Roosher and horrible murder in Pentonwill! Penny daily, sir! Latest edition!" If he had had long practice as a waiter in an up-stairs dining-room, or any number of months' experience at the Model Prison, he could not have skipped on and off the kerb and up and down the omnibus-steps with greater agility. By half-past eight he had sold his twenty-five "dailys," and bagged ninepence clear. What was the result? Twenty pairs of admiring, envious eyes had observed his success. The crossing-sweep pondered the matter over his fruitless broom; the boys who simply "hung about" held council together. The morning following, when B. B. went for his quire *and a half*, he found to his dismay four other young gentlemen of his own stamp, and on the same errand. Nevertheless, despite his great fear that the market would be glutted and the scheme ruined, he sold out, and the other four adventurers sold out, and the news spread through the town like wildfire (whatever that may be). Day by day the B. B. brigade grew stronger and stronger until it became a thousand strong, and so the penny daily newspaper became a national institution. I wonder how a man would be received if he were to wait on the nabobs of the *Star*, and the *Standard*, and the "*Graft*," and suggest the propriety of a banquet to Battered Breeches!

THE END.

www.ingramcontent.com/pod-product-compliance
Lightning Source LLC
Chambersburg PA
CBHW031343230426
43670CB00006B/424